REGIMES FOR THE OCEAN, OUTER SPACE, AND WEATHER

Seyom Brown, Nina W. Cornell,
Larry L. Fabian, and Edith Brown Weiss

REGIMES FOR THE OCEAN, OUTER SPACE, AND WEATHER

The Brookings Institution
Washington, D.C.

Library of Congress Cataloging in Publication Data:

Main entry under title:
Regimes for the ocean, outer space & weather.

   Includes index.
   1. Marine resources.   2. Satellites, Artificial.
3. Weather.   I. Brown, Seyom.
GC1005.R43   333.9   76-51574
ISBN 0-8157-1156-5
ISBN 0-8157-1155-7 pbk.

9 8 7 6 5 4 3 2 1

THE BROOKINGS INSTITUTION is an independent organization devoted to nonpartisan research, education, and publication in economics, government, foreign policy, and the social sciences generally. Its principal purposes are to aid in the development of sound public policies and to promote public understanding of issues of national importance.

The Institution was founded on December 8, 1927, to merge the activities of the Institute for Government Research, founded in 1916, the Institute of Economics, founded in 1922, and the Robert Brookings Graduate School of Economics and Government, founded in 1924.

The Board of Trustees is responsible for the general administration of the Institution, while the immediate direction of the policies, program, and staff is vested in the President, assisted by an advisory committee of the officers and staff. The by-laws of the Institution state: "It is the function of the Trustees to make possible the conduct of scientific research, and publication, under the most favorable conditions, and to safeguard the independence of the research staff in the pursuit of their studies and in the publication of the results of such studies. It is not a part of their function to determine, control, or influence the conduct of particular investigations or the conclusions reached."

The President bears final responsibility for the decision to publish a manuscript as a Brookings book. In reaching his judgment on the competence, accuracy, and objectivity of each study, the President is advised by the director of the appropriate research program and weighs the views of a panel of expert outside readers who report to him in confidence on the quality of the work. Publication of a work signifies that it is deemed a competent treatment worthy of public consideration but does not imply endorsement of conclusions or recommendations.

The Institution maintains its position of neutrality on issues of public policy in order to safeguard the intellectual freedom of the staff. Hence interpretations or conclusions in Brookings publications should be understood to be solely those of the authors and should not be attributed to the Institution, to its trustees, officers, or other staff members, or to the organizations that support its research.

Foreword

In the last three decades, advancing technology and the growing scarcity of resources have sharpened international competition for control over areas of the globe hitherto considered beyond national jurisdiction. This study analyzes the causes and consequences of that competition in three realms: the ocean, outer space, and the weather and climate. The authors find that, without substantial alteration of the traditional framework for using these international "commons," competition will progressively embitter international relations—especially between the technologically advanced and the technologically lagging countries—and result in waste and degradation of natural resources.

Most countries are responding to the new possibilities for exploiting the ocean and extraterrestrial realms by attempting to extend national sovereignty outward into the sea and upward into the atmosphere and space. The authors' doubts about the suitability of this nationalistic response, and their suggestions for regimes requiring nations to be held accountable to international norms and institutions, are a challenge to prevailing political currents. They criticize the assumptions underlying present policies and argue that seemingly idealistic alternatives may be more consistent with basic natural, technological, and social realities. Their proposals are timely, because the new international regimes now emerging will be strongly influenced by the policy choices that the United States and other countries make over the next five or ten years.

This book is a result of the Technology and International Institutions Project of the Brookings Foreign Policy Studies program. The project, conducted from 1972 to 1976, was supported in part by the National Science Foundation, the National Aeronautics and Space Administration, the Ford Foundation, and the Rockefeller Foundation. Seyom Brown, Nina W. Cornell, Larry L. Fabian, and Edith Brown Weiss were then members of the research staff of the Foreign Policy Studies program, which is directed by Henry Owen.

The authors wish to give special recognition to the research and analysis contributed by Terese Sulikowski, the project's principal research assistant. The work of Jeanette Joseph, Carl Gerber, and Laurel Rabin is also gratefully acknowledged. Typing and administrative burdens were borne by Olive Williams and Georgina Sorzano Hernandez. Deborah Styles edited the manuscript; Florence Robinson prepared the index.

Because the book treats a comprehensive set of issues, the authors consulted with technical experts, public officials, and scholars concerned with the public policy implications of technology. Especially helpful were consultations with Harrison Brown, Robert Bowie, Abram Chayes, Francis T. Christy, Jr., Stephen E. Doyle, Guy F. Erb, Jerry Freibaum, Robert Friedheim, Arnold W. Frutkin, Paul M. Fye, Wreatham E. Gathwright, Ann L. Hollick, William W. Kellog, Robert Lamson, David M. Leive, Thomas Malone, Richard B. Marsten, Edward L. Miles, John Norton Moore, Robert E. Osgood, Sidney Passman, Eugene B. Skolnikoff, Abraham Serkin, Wayne Smith, Robert Stein, Ronald F. Stowe, John Stevenson, Maurice Strong, Lee T. Stull, John Temple Swing, and James Zimmerman.

The views, opinions, and interpretations in this book are solely those of the authors. They should not be ascribed to the National Science Foundation, the National Aeronautics and Space Administration, the Ford Foundation, the Rockefeller Foundation, or to the staff members, officers, or trustees of the Brookings Institution.

BRUCE K. MACLAURY
President

Washington, D.C.
July 1977

Contents

Introduction

As the planet Earth becomes more crowded, there is increasing international concern over the management of the international "commons" —those realms that have remained outside the jurisdiction of any country. These international commons include a number of major river systems, some lakes and inland seas, most of the ocean, Antarctica, the atmosphere beyond the airspace immediately above the land, all of outer space, and the earth's weather and climate.

This study concentrates on three of these realms that are global in scope and that are the object of more and more intense international controversy—the ocean, outer space, and the weather and climate systems.

The expansion of economic and political activity in each of these realms raises basic policy questions. What criteria should determine how the realms are used? How and by whom should the rules for their use be formulated? Who should have authority to implement the rules, and by what processes?

We examine some of the answers to these questions and show how they may affect U.S. foreign policy.

This study is intended to be primarily a layman's introduction to the problems of managing the earth's commonly used resources. These problems have become important to the general public for three reasons:

1. Scientific and technological developments have made it possible to exploit previously inaccessible portions of the earth's common resources.

2. Some of the previously accessible regions and resources of these realms are being exploited more intensively, changing conditions of

abundance to conditions of scarcity, and in some cases severely depleting or despoiling the resources.

3. Governments and special interests are increasingly demanding a say in the use of these realms because of the resources located in them. Who gets what, when, and how in the nonland areas can affect the security, health, economic welfare, and power of ever larger portions of the earth's population.

The general public, if it wishes to influence policy effectively in this important new field, needs to know more about how technological developments will affect the competition for use of the nonland areas and how different regimes are likely to serve broad public interests and various special interests.

We do not intend to tell the policymakers what precise policies to follow or to devise detailed plans for international institutions and policies. Our recommendations are tentative and are meant primarily to stimulate dialogue on the alternatives. We suggest criteria against which to evaluate those alternatives, and we describe the regimes and policies that seem most consistent with our analysis of the nonland resources, the state of international relations, and the interests of the United States.

CHAPTER ONE

Regime Alternatives for the Ocean, Outer Space, and the Weather

The traditional international regimes for the ocean, outer space, and the weather appear poorly suited to the dramatic recent expansion of human capabilities for using and altering the resources of these realms. The existing regimes appear to provide inadequate incentives to stimulate the most efficient uses of the resources in the present, let alone to promote their conservation for the benefit of future generations. The existing regimes also are dangerously weak in international conflict resolution processes at a time when there is an increasing likelihood that the users will get in each other's way.

Characteristics of the Three Realms

There are no effective international processes for allocating resources and resolving conflict among the users of the ocean, outer space, and the weather, largely because the natural characteristics of these realms tend to elude the kinds of local and national regulations applied to commonly used resources on land.

Unsuitability for Division and Appropriation

Unlike the land resources of the earth, many of the most important ocean resources are fluid or moving. The characteristic elements of the weather system and outer space are also mobile and in the main intangible. The farther one moves from the land into any of these realms, the more difficult it becomes to parcel out segments to various parties. There

3

are qualifications to this characteristic, to be sure, but the general condition is nondivisibility.

As the seabed becomes more accessible to human use, it tends to be considered analogous to the land in its solid and stationary features; indeed, it has increasingly become the object of national appropriation, particularly on the continental margins (the undersea areas adjacent to the continents) and even potentially on the deep seabed beyond the margins. But it is difficult to conceive of any human activities on the seabed (except, perhaps, some subsoil activities) that do not affect some of the adjacent fluid ocean resources, which cannot themselves be easily divided and contained.

In outer space, the planets and other celestial bodies could, physically speaking, be occupied or exclusively owned, as are land areas on earth. Outer space, however, is also a medium for communications and travel, a medium in which the earth is continuously revolving. An attempt to give ownership of any part of it to any particular nation might seem absurd. Yet it is quite possible to assign portions of space—say, specified satellite orbits—to particular users. Similarly, bands and frequencies on the electromagnetic spectrum (used for all radio communications) lend themselves to assignment to particular users. By and large, however, outer space lacks a natural basis for being permanently apportioned.

Local weather conditions may appear to belong to a particular area, especially where natural barriers and regional climatological features generate a self-contained local weather system. In fact, however, there is no known way (or prospect of finding a way) to uncouple local weather patterns from the overall weather and climate systems of the earth. A local change will feed into the general system, and a general change will affect local conditions. A moving storm that is induced to drop rain early in its path may tend to have less rain to drop at some point later in its path. An attempt to affect the climate in one continent by changing the flow of rivers or ocean currents could perturb the entire global climatic pattern. Futurologists have conceived of domes over cities to control temperature, precipitation, and other qualities of the air; but even such local air conditioning systems could not be isolated from the weather system as a whole, since the weather outside determines the amount of energy that must be consumed to maintain a comfortable condition inside, and this energy consumption, in turn, gives back heat to the environment outside the dome.

These essential fluid, moving, and/or intangible properties of the non-land areas make it difficult to divide them among jurisdictions or states as land areas and resources are apportioned. The human community's adaptation to these characteristics historically has been to treat the realms as common property, open to free use by all countries.

Open access and free use regimes were universally regarded as both rational and just when it was generally assumed that the usable resources of the nonland areas were vast and abundant. Apart from some coastal navigation and fishing areas, where users might get in each other's way, the high seas seemed abundant enough for everyone's use and, therefore, not in need of any kind of regime to allocate their use. Similarly, an open access and free use regime, analogous to that prevailing on the high seas, seemed only natural for outer space. The weather was thought to be a free good: One could try to adapt to it and anticipate it; one could complain about it; but there was little one could do about it. These assumptions of abundance, however, are now being undermined by scientific and technological developments, which will be described below.

Ubiquity

The ocean, covering 70 percent of the earth's surface, surrounds all the continents. When photographed from space, the earth seems to be a watery planet with large islands. No human societies are totally separated from the ocean, if only because it is an essential link in the weather system. Outer space is part of everyone's environment, even if only visually for most people. And no one really escapes the weather. Ubiquity has created feelings, which are deeply ingrained in the human experience, against exclusive ownership of large parts of these realms. International law has reflected this sentiment in the durable doctrine that these realms are *res nullius,* the property of no one.

Function as Media

Each of these realms serves as a medium for carrying people, materials, and signals among different parts of the planet—for good or for ill. The ocean is still man's most important highway for long-distance commercial and military transport and communications; it is a natural habitat for fish; it is also a major carrier and distributor of unwanted substances—wastes and toxic chemical runoffs from land—among various land areas. Outer space is primarily a medium of communication, and is also a medium for deploying information-gathering stations. The weather carries diseases, industrial wastes, other toxic substances, and various changes in the air quality itself. Weather conditions vitally affect air and ocean transportation.

Scarcity

That these realms are vast and ubiquitous led previous generations to believe that they could, for the most part, be left off the list of resources that might become scarce. With this view, the fact that they could not be divided and taken over raised no major political problem. Recent developments in science and technology, however, have dramatically changed man's uses and perceptions of these realms, severely undercutting the basis for considering them free for all uses and users.

People are more and more aware that the ocean is a central component of the earth's overall life-support system and an ecological system that is itself vulnerable to abuse. The whole ocean must now be regarded as a limited resource, and ways must be devised to allocate its use. The improvements and spread in technologies for exploiting the resources of the sea have made more resources accessible. At the same time, however, they have shown how scarce these resources are—either because the users are getting in one another's way, or because they overexploit some resources until the total supply begins to dwindle (for example, in the case of fishing, species reproduction cannot keep up with the current rate of fishing).

The growing use of outer space for communications and satellites makes increasing demands on two limited resources: the frequency spectrum and the geostationary orbit. Although in gross terms there are enough bands on the frequency spectrum and enough space in the geostationary orbit to accommodate all prospective users, some of the frequencies and some of the orbital slots are preferred by more users (current and prospective) than can occupy them simultaneously. Someone must give way to someone else or alter his preferred uses and equipment to provide room for additional users.

The weather itself is hardly a scarce commodity, but in most parts of the globe the demand for good or suitable weather is almost always greater than the supply. When man could not alter or move the weather, the scarcity of good weather affected the value of various living areas where access to good weather was more or less favorable. The prospect of weather modification technologies, however, dramatically changes the character of the weather as an economic good. If one community can increase its rainfall, this may, in the process, affect the amount of precipitation normally available to other communities. Similarly, the diversion of bad weather may involve dumping it on others who could be injured by it.

The notion of the weather as a free good is also being challenged by the expansion of scientific knowledge about the weather and climate, particularly about the function of weather and climate in the overall ecological balances of the earth. The earth's total supply of good or temperate climate, which is a fundamental requisite of the survival of human life, may itself be reduced by deliberate or inadvertent human activities—from deforestation to different modes of energy production.

Scarcity plus Indivisibility: The Problem of the Commons

Treatment of the nonland realms as common property open to free use by all is an extension of the traditional approach to indivisible and presumably abundant resources on land. River systems, air sheds, and land unsuitable for cultivation all have been treated as commons. But just as many of the land commons can no longer be considered abundant, many of the nonland commons have also become scarce. The causes are basically the same: technological change and population growth.

When the wastelands of agricultural communities began to be valuable (that is, when they became scarce relative to the demands being made upon them), the usual response was to carve them up and give them to individual owners, as in the English enclosure movement. Divisions of this sort tend to be the first alternative considered when a common resource becomes scarce.

The enclosure movement provides us with inappropriate guidance, however, for scarcity problems in commons in which the resources are indivisible. The major examples of indivisible resources on land are fresh water systems and air sheds. Pollution of either air or water indicates that the capacity of that medium to dispose of waste is overused. But since the capacities of water and air to assimilate waste cannot be divided among the individual users, the water systems and air sheds must be managed as a whole by the entire community of users. Many air and water pollution problems, particularly in the western hemisphere, involve part or all of a single country, and are managed by the appropriate local or national communities. The allocation involves rules of access and use set by the government, with civil and sometimes criminal penalties for noncompliance. Such rules are usually more detailed than the laws applying to the use of privately owned resources.

The problem of scarcity is more complex when the resources cross national boundaries. As with air sheds and river systems on land, the overuse of many ocean, outer space, and weather resources cannot be curbed by attempting to divide them up. But there is no international authority similar to a national government that can pass and enforce binding rules upon the users of these resources.

The challenge, therefore, is to devise an effective and internationally acceptable system of management for these nonland realms. A successful system of management must be capable of limiting these realms to as many of the highest priority uses as can be accommodated without harm to the resources themselves. For such a system to be acceptable internationally, it must allow for the participation of concerned members of the international community in the processes that set priorities and limit use.

International recognition of the need to find some system to manage the use of these realms can be seen in the language of United Nations resolutions that the deep seabed is the "common heritage of mankind," and that outer space is the "province of mankind." These phrases do not yet have a universally accepted meaning. To some they are another way of saying that these realms are *res nullius*. Others interpret the UN resolutions as assertions of *res communis*, or common property. But even *res communis* does not carry unambiguous meaning. Who is included in the community—all those now living, or all those now living plus all those still to come? Does the present generation own the resources outright, or only in trust for future generations? The answers to these questions establish (sometimes only implicitly) the philosophical presumptions of the regime alternatives discussed in this book.

Regime Features

Alternative regimes for the nonland realms can be described in three major classifications: user accountability; resource ownership; and criteria for use.

User Accountability

Traditionally, the ocean beyond very narrow offshore bands, usually three miles wide, was open to free use by anyone. Ships were accountable outside territorial waters only to the government that had chartered them. Within territorial waters, the coastal state could exercise exclusive authority, and this authority was usually recognized and respected by foreign ships. Exceptions were certain specially designated international waterways in which the freedoms of the high seas were granted. Similarly, airspace over land and over territorial waters has been subject to the control of the state below; but outer space and the airspace over the oceans beyond territorial waters have been open to free use by anyone—again, with virtually no accountability to any international authority.

As the consequences of unregulated use of the nonland areas have become more widely recognized, international pressures have been building for making any single user accountable to the general community of users. Such increased accountability can be attained by varied approaches.

THROUGH EXTENDED NATIONAL JURISDICTIONS. One approach to regulation—the one that has the most momentum at this writing—is to assign clearly jurisdiction and regulatory authority over commonly used resources to particular national governments; other governments would agree to respect these extended national jurisdictions.

THROUGH STRENGTHENED INTERNATIONAL NORMS. Another approach, not necessarily incompatible with the first, is for national governments to agree to be accountable to strengthened international norms and rules for the use of nonland realms. The application and enforcement of these internally negotiated rules and norms, however, would remain in the hands of national governments. This approach traditionally has been favored by foreign affairs ministries and, indeed, has been the usual response to disputes between countries over commonly used ocean or airspace.

THROUGH STRENGTHENED INTERNATIONAL INSTITUTIONS. Growing dissatisfaction with the current approaches to regulation has prompted proposals to make national governments accountable to international institutions that have the power to enforce strengthened international norms. Varying degrees of authority may be accorded international institutions: They may collect information on compliance with international agreements; they may be empowered to prosecute and penalize offenders; or they may supervise the operation of supranational projects.

Resource Ownership[1]

The traditional notion that the resources of the high seas, outer space, and the atmosphere are owned by no one would not be inconsistent with any of the patterns of accountability sketched above, but it makes it difficult to lodge regulatory authority with anyone, let alone to charge any user rent for the use of scarce resources. The growing recognition of scarcity of the nonland resources and the increasing possibilities for the abuse of the nonland environments have on the one hand increased the impetus for extended national ownership to assure supplies and control of at least adjacent areas, and on the other hand have stimulated discussion of forms of international ownership as a means of assuring responsible national and private use.

NO OWNERSHIP. Until recently, it seemed sensible to keep free of any ownership as much as possible of the nonland realms, because it is so hard to divide them. The resources seemed vast, if not inexhaustible, and there seemed little need to limit their use, except in the territorial seas. On the high seas, once fish had been captured, they would be owned, but before that they would be considered fair game. As we begin to recognize that important nonland resources may be scarce, depletable, or abused, the consensus behind the idea of no ownership has broken down. No consensus has yet emerged, however, to support any other plan. Some countries continue to favor a regime of no ownership. Others, who cannot themselves exploit ocean resources, are seeking ways to obtain rent from or share the benefits with those who can. Still others are attempting to forestall use of the resources until they develop their own exploitation capabilities.

NATIONAL OWNERSHIP. Since the Second World War, there has been a trend toward conferring exclusive national sovereignty, approximating actual ownership, over the resources of the seabed adjacent to coastal states. The national government in effect has title (or, in federal systems,

---

1. The terms "ownership" and "title" in this discussion are used in a political-economic rather than a formal legal sense. Ownership is a concept in domestic law; other terms, such as sovereignty or dominion, are used in international law. The meaning here is the exclusive authority to dispose of, confer rights to, or otherwise affect the conditions of some thing or place—subject, of course, to general community standards.

residual title) to the resources, and corporations or foreign governments wishing to exploit them must obtain leases from the coastal state. Currently, the international debate is not only over the geographic scope of this title, but also over whether exclusive national title should extend to other ocean and nonland resources. The International Telecommunication Union (ITU), for example, is at present considering whether or not to issue virtual ownership rights to portions of the geostationary orbit and the frequency spectrum.

National ownership is attractive because it concentrates responsibility for conservation and effective use of the resources in the only actors on the international stage who have broad enough incentives *and* capabilities to look out for the general public interest and to consider the consequences of their use. National ownership is complicated, however, because fluidity and mobility of the nonland resources make it very difficult to parcel them out or to sustain for a long time any division that might work for a short time.

INTERNATIONAL OWNERSHIP. The indivisibility of these important scarce resources suggests the possibility of vesting entire user communities with their ownership. The pertinent user communities for the resources of the nonland realms are multinational, though they need not always comprise all countries. Thus, the community of countries surrounding a particular ocean basin might appropriately be considered the owner of the resources of the seabed in that basin and of the fish species that do not ordinarily migrate out of the basin. For resources that tend to be globally ubiquitous or mobile, such as aspects of the earth's climate, the appropriate community would be the total international community. Many of the resources we are discussing, however, will in some respects be used by all or most countries, but are likely to be subject to direct and concentrated use by a smaller group of nations in the international community. Where such patterns make it difficult to attribute ownership, it might be possible to vest the entire international community with ultimate ownership, while designating the more intense users as trustees or custodians of the resources on behalf of the total community.

What is the difference between substantial international accountability and international ownership? Under a policy of international ownership, only those uses expressly authorized by community treaties or institutions would be considered legitimate. Under a regime of international accountability, unilateral action, without at least consultation with affected parties, would be considered illegitimate; but the initiative for consultation and cooperative action, as well as the ultimate authority for implementing agreements, would still lie with the separate nation-states.

Meaningful international ownership would require a degree of political and legal integration among nations unprecedented in the history of international relations. This does not mean that it would be impossible to achieve or that it is not a useful goal to work toward; but it does suggest that it is probably not realistic until patterns of substantial international accountability are first built up in a particular field.

Criteria for Use

Regimes for the nonland realms can also be distinguished broadly on the basis of the goals of the dominant users. Users may act for a variety of reasons. For purposes of our analysis, these goals may be grouped under the following four criteria.

MAXIMIZATION OF DIRECT RETURNS TO THE USER. With this objective, the user, whether a private corporation or state enterprise (or a national government considered as a unit), would be operating essentially to increase its own benefits. This policy tends to be championed by those who favor regimes that provide open access and free use; moreover, it is also a behavioral assumption which, in the light of existing political realities, must be taken into account in the design of any regime that is feasible.

MAXIMIZATION OF RETURNS TO THE INTERNATIONAL COMMUNITY. If this is taken as a goal, the user's behavior would be regulated or evaluated in terms of indicators of gross benefits to a region or to the whole of mankind. It would not be simply assumed, as it is among some radical laissez-faire theorists, that a regime allowing individual users to maximize their own returns would, as a matter of course, maximize returns to the international community. The criterion of general community benefit would be feasible in the current international context so long as it only supplemented, and was not presumed to override, national self-interests.

INTERNATIONAL DISTRIBUTION OF RETURNS. This system would have the users acting according to some criteria for distribution that were not necessarily economic in nature—notions of social justice, equity, enlightened internationalism, what have you—to allocate benefits and costs internationally. Such criteria would not be implemented adequately without some deliberate interference with market mechanisms. Developing countries are pushing in many spheres of economic affairs for policies that alter the distribution of resources resulting from existing market forces. These countries will probably agree to new regimes for the nonland areas only if these regimes do alter market outcomes in their favor.

CONSERVATION OF RESOURCES. This objective would make the present users responsible to future generations of users. Their goal would be to minimize damage to the natural environment, even where the potential costs and benefits were intangible and highly uncertain.

Basic Regime Alternatives

While regimes for the ocean, outer space, and the weather can be described by the characteristics outlined above, there are nonetheless a number of basic patterns in which the variables tend to cluster, both in concept and in practice. The patterns can be thought of as alternative types of regimes: open access and free use; national management; or international management.

Open Access and Free Use

This type of regime considers the realm common property, but no one can use it as his own property. No one owns it; no one can be denied entry; no one can collect economic rent for its use; and the only legal constraints on its use are the rules necessary to maintain the open access regime itself. Users have virtually no accountability to the international community, and are accountable to no state other than those in which they hold citizenship. For the most part, they act only to maximize their own direct returns.

For some 300 years now, the concepts of open access and free use have been reflected in state practice and international legal conventions for the ocean. In recent years, these traditional concepts of the law of the sea have been transferred heavily into the evolving law for the use of outer space and the weather and climate. Until recently, the nonland realms have appeared particularly congenial to regimes that allow open access and free use for two reasons: being essentially fluid, moving, and intangible, they have been less susceptible than land areas to being sliced up into multiple political jurisdictions; and their vastness or the presumed abundance of their resources gave little reason to limit their use. Except for areas that could be considered natural borders or extensions of national land areas, no attempts to vest any particular party or country with title or dominion to portions of these realms have proved viable.

As indicated above, however, some resources of the nonland realms that were once plentiful have become scarce and, in some cases, even subject to dangerous depletion or degradation because no substantial regulation existed. The increasing scarcity of these resources has made them more valuable; this, in turn, makes serious conflict among potential exploiters more likely. Meanwhile, changing international political norms and growing world interdependence have made it increasingly difficult for the technologically advanced countries to use these realms at will, without obtaining at least the consent of other countries. The weakening of the premise that there is no important incompatibility among users has begun to undermine confidence in the practicality and legitimacy of open access and free use as the basic regime concept for the nonland realms.

National Management

The most prevalent response thus far to the opening up of the ocean, outer space, and the weather to political and economic competition and ecological damage has been to attempt to increase national responsibility for these realms. National governments are still the best institution for ensuring that users of the nonland areas act in accord with broader public interests, both national and international. It can be argued that, unless nations assert greater authority, no agency possessing real power and economic weight will be responsible for the performance of the increasingly complicated management tasks.

The most conspicuous extensions of national management authority have been occurring in the ocean. The claims of most coastal states to twelve-mile territorial seas are about to be universally recognized— either by a new law of the sea treaty, or by common acquiescence. Many coastal states already claim rights to the resources of the seabed out to 200 miles or to the greatest widths of their continental margins. Many also claim exclusive national fisheries, unilaterally proclaim wide areas for pollution control, and insist on controlling all scientific research activity off their coasts. Hard mineral mining interests are pressuring their governments to license and underwrite commercial exploitation of the deep seabed.

There are practical arguments for these attempts to replace the traditional ocean regime of open access and free use (beyond the narrow three-mile territorial sea) with zones clearly under the control of specific national governments. Developing countries that border the ocean contend this is the only way to protect the resources off their coasts from raiding by more advanced countries or by multinational corporations. Coastal interests cite the need to enforce pollution control, navigation lanes, and traffic separation schemes in congested straits and other crowded international waterways; these situations cannot wait for the sluggish international negotiating process to standardize rules, which would probably be too lax in any event. Mining interests argue that only national governments can provide the security of license and title arrangements that will encourage further progress by the venturesome firms now developing the capability to extract hard minerals from the deep seabed.

The users of outer space are accountable thus far primarily to national space authorities—the International Telecommunication Union and the International Telecommunications Satellite Consortium (INTELSAT) are the principal exceptions. The ITU ostensibly controls frequency spectrum and orbital allocations, but in fact operates as little more than a clearinghouse for arrangements worked out among national telecommunication authorities; it has virtually no power to induce efficient and equitable allocations of these limited resources. INTELSAT has evolved into a true international consortium for transmitting international telephone and television traffic via satellite. But most other current and planned earth-oriented applications of satellites—in such fields as broadcasting, remote sensing, sea and air traffic control—are being developed and managed within national frameworks.

The Outer Space Treaty of 1967 enjoins the participating nations to use space for the common benefit, but under the current regime the obligation to do so is left entirely to those who build and put up the hardware and design the software. The nations that are now active in outer space are themselves interpreting their obligations to the rest of the international society, and they resist any authoritative international direction of their activities.

The nations now operating in space have apparently convincing reasons for preferring to keep decisions about the design, deployment, and management of international space services in their own hands: the field of space applications involves large capital outlays for research and development, and the day-to-day operation of deployed capabilities requires highly trained technical personnel. They argue that the needed investment capital will not be forthcoming from either private sources or public treasuries if performance standards must be lowered to serve the objectives of international participation.

Even in the field of collecting and analyzing weather information, where there has been up to now a rather impressive record of international sharing, the rising pattern of unilateralism has made some countries fearful that the powers capable of operating in space, increasingly able to obtain all the weather information they need from their own satellites, may turn off their automatic transmission of data to the World Weather Watch. When it comes to weather modification, those who have the technology are reluctant to subject their projects to advance international scrutiny, let alone authorization. Here, too, the arguments against multilateralism rest primarily on control over investments and efficiency of operations.

The nationalistic response to the increasing use and value of the nonland realms, however, may turn out to be basically retrogressive. Most nations are becoming more dependent upon the cooperation of others in these realms in order to protect themselves from harm or to implement constructive projects. The fact that mankind has irreversibly become an international society, if not yet a community, is clear at least on the level of material interdependence in the nonland areas. To react to this growing interdependence by attempting to add bricks to the protective walls of national sovereignty might prolong and exacerbate the contradictions between the evolving world of material interdependence and the political world of exclusive sovereignties. If management responsibilities for the nonland areas were assigned to national governments that did not have the technical expertise to administer them adequately, the legitimacy of the national management authorities might be undermined.

International Management

The other basic regime alternative would feature regional and global cooperation, and institutions designed to service not only the interests of their immediate constituents, but also the interests of the whole international community in the nonland realms. At a minimum, attempts would be made to stimulate consultative processes capable of reflecting the involved interests and their current and emerging functional interdependencies. Its fullest elaboration contemplates vesting ultimate ownership of the nonland areas in the whole international community; supranational institutions would have the power to make and enforce rules superior to national policies for the nonland areas; national and multinational authorities with limited membership would be regarded only as custodians, exercising temporary grants of management authority.

International management need not impose a structural unity on the evolving plurality of international arrangements, but it would imply at least substantial international oversight of such arrangements to ensure that the interests of the general international community are served, including the distribution of benefits and the care of global ecologies. Accordingly, international management would bring together highly interdependent functions under umbrella institutions.

Numerous UN resolutions affirm that at least the deep ocean floor and outer space are the common heritage of mankind. This could be taken to mean that they should be used only in ways authorized by the whole community. Additional support for some kind of community regime for these realms is found in the field of political economy.

In domestic economic systems, efficient use of public or collective goods—those which, by nature or by community choice, are precluded from private or special-group ownership—has argued against free-access regimes. Whether the good in question is the community's supply of fresh water, recreational parkland, or essential communications and transportation networks, the hope has proved ill-founded that, in the absence of incentives or sanctions imposed by the community, all users would spontaneously act in their long-term, enlightened self-interests and limit immediate consumption in order to conserve the long-term supply and quality of the resource. Incentives and sanctions run the gamut from charges directly to the user to ownership and management by public corporations. While there remains considerable debate over the substance of the needed limitations on use and the institutions that would enforce them, all modern nation-states have virtually abandoned free-use regimes for handling the resources within their jurisdictions that are not suited for private appropriation.[2]

2. Use of the air has been an exception because of the notion, now rapidly being discredited by the new ecological consciousness, that the air was in no meaningful sense a scarce commodity. Only lately have we become aware that using the air for purposes of waste disposal uses up or degrades air that might be used for respiration.

Domestically, considerations of social justice and equity have tended to reinforce considerations of economic efficiency in the rejection of open-access, free-use regimes for public goods. Even if some users of such goods might take it upon themselves, out of self-interest or community-mindedness, to conserve and care for the resources, social experience suggests that enforced sharing of the burdens of upkeep and protection encourages the users to greater conservation and thus contributes to an overall reduction in the cost of providing the goods. Moreover, such sharing of the burdens strikes most people as just. The other side of the question of domestic social justice relates to the problem of inequitable results: It is generally agreed to be unjust for users who are favored by location or technological capability to act unilaterally, without being held accountable for the consequences to other users—for example, raising the price to others of access to preferred supplies, using up those supplies, or degrading the quality of future supplies.

Internationally, however, such community obligations still operate mostly at the level of aspirations or rhetoric. International management of the nonnational realms presupposes cooperation by the members of the international community (in pursuit of their own best interests) with community norms, interests, and decision processes.

One may conclude that it is more advantageous to act in accord with community interests either because one's own participation in the community yields greater returns (protection or wealth) than could be obtained unilaterally or because one's own support of a community regime is a condition for the participation of others, and *their* subordination to community norms is a more efficient way to influence their behavior than any attempt to influence them unilaterally. (The predominance of such perceptions among members of national societies explains the persistence of relatively cohesive national communities and their institutionalization in the form of nation-states. The emergence of such perceptions among the states of Western Europe is reflected in the evolving, but still fragile, European Community.) On a world scale, such perceptions are still rare, and, in the few fields where they exist, they have given rise only to the loosest forms of supranationalism—as, for example, in the International Atomic Energy Agency, INTELSAT, and some regional fisheries commissions.

CHAPTER TWO

Alternative Regimes for the Ocean

Recent and prospective developments affecting the ocean are severely undercutting the inherited maritime order. The old order was based largely on principles of open access to and free use of the waters, beyond the narrow belts recognized as territorial seas. It is now generally accepted that the open access regime will not (and should not) last out the 1970s. This, indeed, is the premise of the Third United Nations Law of the Sea Conference, which convened in 1973. But the nature of the successor regime is still unclear.

In just a generation the whole ocean has become a field for human activities nearly as varied as those performed on land. Users are getting in one another's way, and disputes over ocean space and material resources are increasing. Meanwhile, the expansion of scientific knowledge about ocean ecologies is undermining the traditional assumption that the ocean is a vast, self-equilibrating system that will rebound to its normal state no matter what is done to it. The more detail is uncovered about the ocean, the more evident it becomes that the current understanding of the multiple ecology systems covering 70 percent of the earth's surface is inadequate. Still, under the prevailing regime, there are few limitations on man's use of the ocean, and he could abuse it in ways that might dangerously unbalance its ecological relationships.

The shape of an ocean regime able to accommodate peacefully its multiple users, preserve its health, make optimal use of its wealth, and yet be regarded as legitimate by most of the world's peoples is currently the subject of international debate.

Basic Technological and Social Forces
Affecting Man's Perspectives on the Ocean

The older view of the ocean, as an abundant natural resource large enough to accommodate all users in an unregulated pursuit of their self-interests, is no longer tenable. New concepts are being fashioned to take account of the revolution in marine technology, the rise of ecological consciousness, the new economics of ocean resource scarcity, rising demands for international income redistribution, the increase in the number of countries with direct interests in the ocean, and efforts to revise ocean law.

The Revolution in Marine Technology

Man's industry now extends from the airspace above the water, throughout the water column, down to and beneath the seabed. Oil, natural gas, and a variety of industrially useful minerals and chemicals have joined food as materials that can be extracted from the ocean.

Aircraft and satellite-carried sensors measure sea level, water temperature, and currents; underwater acoustical instruments and cameras contribute to refined geological surveys; today's oil drilling technology permits seabed penetration to 1,000 meters in waters 6,000 meters deep; and mining of ores rich in copper, nickel, and other valuable metals is projected for depths of 12,000 to 20,000 feet.[1]

Fishing grounds are frequented by long-distance fishermen on giant factory ships equipped with electronic tracking and catching devices, as well as with freezing and processing plants.

Normal intercontinental transportation now takes place above the surface, on the surface, and beneath the surface.

Oil is carried in tankers with capacities of as much as 500,000 tons, and plans for tankers twice that size are now on the drawing boards.

Artificial ports are being constructed tens of miles from shore.

The seabed is increasingly used for storage facilities and for anchorage for a wide variety of military and scientific installations.

Nuclear reactors on the seabed are being planned, and scientists are progressing toward harnessing the energy in the sea's tides and currents.

Meanwhile, the disposal of man-made wastes in the ocean is increasing exponentially.

1. See "Mineral Resources of the Sea," UN Doc. E/4973.

These technological applications are seen by their developers and users as important advances in man's ability to put nature to human purposes. But, as with most technological applications, there are often side effects—external to the purposes of the particular industry, project, device, or activity—that may not be entirely beneficial to humans or the natural environment, or at least to specific human and ecological communities. Until very recently, this "externality" phenomenon was thought to be an exceptional occurrence in the ocean, given the abundance of its resources and its vast imperviousness to man-made disturbances. Current applications of ocean technology are appropriately perceived as revolutionary precisely because of their impact on such assumptions.

The Rise of Ecological Consciousness

The publication of Rachel Carson's book *Silent Spring*, in 1962, sparked the popular realization that major ocean ecologies, like other parts of man's natural habitat, could be critically unbalanced by human abuse. Five years later, the widespread death of aquatic animals and plants from the oil spill caused when the supertanker *Torrey Canyon* ran aground received international publicity; and a full-blown environmentalist movement started in the United States in 1969, with the news of the lethal effects on ocean ecology along the Pacific Coast resulting from a leak in the Union Oil Company's rig in the Santa Barbara Channel.

Over the next few years, numerous books, articles, and television documentaries spread the word that not only accidents, but normal activities—such as the tank washing procedures of oil tankers, thermal heat transfers from power stations, dumping of sewage and industrial wastes into rivers and directly into the sea, the use of pesticides that are carried into the ocean through the atmosphere, seismic explosions, drilling in the seabed, and overfishing—were despoiling the ocean; some commentators said *destroying* it.[2]

Even the more cautious scientists have become concerned. "To people like myself," admits John Knauss, "the greatest worry about ocean pol-

2. See, for example, Colin Moorcraft, *Must the Seas Die?* (Gambit, 1973); and the statement of Jacques Cousteau, in *International Conference on Ocean Pollution,* Hearings before the Senate Subcommittee on Oceans and Atmosphere of the Committee on Commerce (GPO, 1972), pp. 3–17.

lution at this time is the unknown." While few believe there is a serious immediate danger of pollution, "the exponential growth in energy use, natural resource consumption, and man's activities in general suggest that the possibility of oceanwide pollution within the next century is not as radical an idea as one might have thought as little as 25 years ago."[3] As a study sponsored by Resources for the Future observes, "We know all too little of how the sea and its biotic communities impinge on global ecology, but there is every reason to treat this relationship with great respect. Instead we utilize the sea thoughtlessly as the ultimate sink for all sorts of debris and chemicals generated on land and transported by air and water."[4]

The New Economics of Ocean Resource Scarcity

No longer can we sustain the assumption of unlimited ocean resources. The ocean's spatial functions (as a medium of transportation and as a vast disposal sink), its materials (minerals and food), and its environmental functions (as a regulator of the earth's climate and as a source of recreational and aesthetic values) are all the objects of increasingly intense competition—not only among users within each functional category, but also among functions.

If the supply of ocean resources were indeed inexhaustible, as was thought in previous centuries, or if it were at least infinitely elastic, increases in demand would simply cause greater extraction or utilization of a particular resource (sometimes through the development of technologies to reach previously inaccessible supplies). But in most categories of ocean use, the demand for the resource has been rising at a substantially greater rate than the supply, and, indeed, the applications of new technology often serve only to accelerate the depletion of the supply.

Today, the ocean community is slowly coming to grips with the concept that ocean resources are indeed exhaustible. It is now widely accepted that certain resources like the output of reproductive stocks, the throughput capacity of straits and the ability of the ocean to ingest pollution without damage are limited.

3. John A. Knauss, "Ocean Pollution: Status and Prognostication," in John King Gamble, Jr., and Emilio Pontecorvo, eds., *Law of the Sea: The Emerging Regime of the Oceans* (Ballinger, 1974), p. 322.

4. Sterling Brubaker, *To Live on Earth: Man and His Environment in Perspective* (New American Library for Resources for the Future, 1972), p. 148.

Despite the emergence of this view of ocean space, policies continue to treat the oceans as if the supply of resources were infinitely elastic, and as if expectations of future price changes were zero. . . .

In addition, the strong and rapidly increasing interdependence of different uses is further complicating the issue. Stated in simple terms, the supply of ocean resources is increasingly scarce (becoming more inelastic in supply) not only because of each resource's own characteristics but also because the ocean uses are not independent nor are their supply conditions.[5]

In a world where scarcity is a problem, some principle is needed to determine how the scarce goods shall be used. Some argue that only economic efficiency should govern the allocations. A corollary proposition is that the most efficient exploitation of ocean resources will be promoted by a regime that fosters economic competition—both among ocean industries and among ocean- and land-based producers of similar goods. Many adherents to this view also maintain that open access to and free use of ocean resources is the best way to maximize competition (and thus efficiency); accordingly, they feel, the burden of proof should be put on those who would control access to ocean resources, to demonstrate that controls are necessary to increase efficiency. But the extent of interdependencies and externalities in ocean use suggest that, even when the sole criterion is efficiency, substantial controls will be needed. Moreover, economic efficiency is unlikely to be the sole criterion for the choice of an ocean regime.

The New Demands for International Income Redistribution

The existing international distribution of income and wealth has come under increasing attack by many of the less developed countries. Demands for a new international economic order have come to underlie and even dominate the new politics of the ocean. The ongoing Law of the Sea Conference provides the less prosperous countries with a forum and negotiating leverage to press for a larger share of the income generated by both land and ocean resources.

Many developing countries are pressing for allocations of ocean resources and territory determined on grounds other than a country's comparative ability to maximize output. Proposals for creating national fishing zones out to 200 miles, demands for all mining of the seabed to be performed by an international agency and the like, have come forth at

5. Giulio Pontecorvo and Roger Mesznik, "The Wealth of the Oceans and the Law of the Sea: Some Preliminary Observations," *San Diego Law Review,* vol. 11 (May 1974), p. 684.

least partially because of the conviction that countries other than those most technologically capable of exploiting the resources should have a slice of the pie. The technologically advanced countries, on the other hand, are naturally less disturbed by the distributional effects of the present system. Not surprisingly, those who can most easily be first in line tend to like distribution on a first-come, first-served basis.

There is a school of economists that argues that the drive for efficiency will automatically produce widely dispersed benefits, and that there is therefore no need to interfere with the competitive market. Thus,

In the case of the freedom of access to ocean resources, extreme confusion has arisen, particularly over natural resources, from the identification of those who physically exploit a resource with those who obtain the benefits from exploitation. This involves the fallacy that physical ownership conveys all the benefits from exploitation to the producers, which is simply not true. The exploitation of real ocean resources, such as manganese nodules, hydrocarbon deposits, and fisheries, will generate three major types of economic benefit. First, consumers throughout the world will benefit from the greater availability and lower prices of the resources obtained. Second, exploiters may find this a more attractive opportunity than others available, generating higher profits and wages than would otherwise be the case. Third, this new activity may represent a marginal addition to the world's tax base.[6]

Such an approach, however, raises several problems: In the first place, since reduction in the cost of consuming a good would allocate benefits in proportion to the quantity consumed, the initial distribution of income that allowed for certain quantities to be consumed by certain buyers will tend to be repeated in any benefits gained from a reduction in cost. Or, put another way, only if the initial distribution of income is equitable will the distribution of new benefits (via cost reduction) be equitable.

A second problem with the argument that efficiency produces equity is that exploitation by the most efficient producers may not always have the expected impact upon the price and availability of goods. Where the industry is small—perhaps even a cartel (as might occur with the exploitation of manganese nodules)—price and availability may not change to the advantage of consumers.

6. Robert D. Tollison and Thomas D. Willett, "Institutional Mechanisms for Dealing with International Externalities: A Public Choice Perspective," in Ryan C. Amacher and Richard J. Sweeney, eds., *The Law of the Sea: U.S. Interests and Alternatives* (American Enterprise Institute for Public Policy Research, 1976), p. 93.

Finally, if only a few rich countries are capable of engaging in certain types of ocean exploitation, only those countries will reap the benefits of production and taxation. If, in the absence of any ocean production in a particular industry, future productive activity (and with it some production and tax benefits) becomes widely dispersed around the globe, the addition of this new source of production may well exacerbate income inequities even as efficiency increases.

Whatever the theoretical validity of the various equity-efficiency arguments, however, the demands for special allocations and decision-making processes that give weight to distributional criteria are affecting basic regime choices.

The New Politics of the Ocean

Basic regime choices are also being affected by the diminution of the power of the major maritime states to impose their will on others. Any durable and legitimate ocean order will have to be substantially responsive to the preferences of many countries with diverse interests. This changed political basis for the evolving law of the sea is the product of these interrelated developments: the increase in the number of independent countries with direct material interests in how the ocean is used; inhibitions on the use of military force, especially by the great powers; and the international coalitions that have formed around particular ocean issues.

The doubling of the number of nation-states between the end of the Second World War and the 1970s has had considerable impact on international bargaining over rights and obligations in the ocean. Before the recent period of decolonization, virtually all populations outside the Americas and the landlocked countries of East Central Europe were under the jurisdiction of one of the important maritime nations. Today, some 130 independent countries border the ocean. Twenty-five of these coastal states abut straits that are important for international shipping. All of the coastal states have fishing industries, and ninety-eight have substantial continental margins with mineral wealth. Not to be left out are the thirty landlocked countries, each of which consumes commodities shipped across the sea and food and minerals extracted from it. Some landlocked and some coastal states produce commodities competitive with those now (or potentially) produced in the ocean; they may thus want a voice in the production or marketing of the ocean-based commodities. Finally, most countries now perceive that their welfare is highly dependent upon general environmental conditions that are affected, in ways not yet fully comprehended, by the condition of the sea.[7]

Inhibitions on use of military force or blatant economic coercion by the great powers have been growing in recent years. In part, the reluctance of the powers to use force is a product of their competition for influence over countries that would be alienated by crude attempts at coercion. And in part, such inhibitions have resulted from their awareness of the tremendous material costs of trying to sustain imperial relationships in the face of virulent contemporary nationalism. In addition, the great powers fear that unilateral military interventions might provoke counterinterventions and uncontrollable escalations of conflict. In this context, Peru could seize the boats of U.S. tuna fishermen who violated Peru's self-proclaimed 200-mile fishing zone, with no fear of retaliation from the U.S. Navy, and Iceland could force concessions from the United Kingdom in their Cod War of the early 1970s.

The pattern of coalitions that has been forming around contemporary ocean issues further limits the abilities and inclinations of the major maritime powers to impose their preferences on other countries. Nature itself has had the heaviest hand in aligning countries in ocean politics. It makes a considerable difference to a country's position on the issue of the breadth of territorial seas, for example, if a country borders on the ocean or is landlocked, if its coastline is long or short, if its continental shelf is rich or barren, broad or narrow. Technology's impact on a country's geological and biological inheritance is an increasingly weighty determinant, sometimes transforming friendly states into adversaries by extending their reach into one another's coastal waters. Ideology is less important than geography and technology in determining a country's position in ocean politics; this has made it difficult for the superpowers to mobilize support for their own position on most controversial ocean issues among the nations that are nominally in their camp.

A Third World coalition of sorts has been active in the Law of the Sea Conference and shows surprising cohesion across a range of issues, considering the differences in material interests among the various de-

7. For a categorization of countries on the basis of their material interests in the ocean, see Lewis M. Alexander, "Indices of National Interests in the Oceans," *Ocean Development and International Law Journal,* vol. 1 (Spring 1973), pp. 21–49.

veloping countries, especially among the coastal as opposed to the land-locked states. But this broad coalition appears to have been held to-gether more by its animus toward the affluent maritime powers than by any solid consensus on specific issues. During the conference, China has assumed the role of spokesman for the group of nations favoring extreme antimaritime positions (exclusive coastal state jurisdiction out to 200 miles; stringent limitations on scientific exploration), and for substantial redistribution of income and political power (direct control by an international agency over the operations and revenues of mining in the deep sea; majority rule in ocean agencies).

There is less basis for organizing a countercoalition by the maritime countries. The group of states supporting pervasive national control in wide offshore zones, for example, comprises not only most of the coastal states of the Third World, but also some members of the North Atlantic Treaty Organization (Canada, Norway, Iceland), plus Spain, Australia, and New Zealand. The United States, the USSR, France, and Japan tend to agree on preserving as much unrestricted maritime mobility as possible. Although the USSR and Japan are rivals over the fishing areas in the waters between them, they are both long-distance fishing powers, and therefore strongly oppose exclusive coastal-state fishing zones. The United States has been more ambivalent on the subject of fishing zones, being responsive to the disparate needs of its fishing interests in New England and its long-distance tuna fishermen on the West Coast.

The ambivalence of the United States on fishing issues typifies the phenomenon of crosscutting coalitions, which has emerged as the hall-mark of the new international politics.[8] Not only are blocks of countries pressured in different directions by the varying national interests of their members in different aspects of ocean use, but national governments themselves are pressured to seek different goals by various domestic constituencies, some of whom are allies with their counterparts in other countries on particular ocean issues. The more industrialized and complex a society, the more likely it is to be subject to such multifarious pressures. This condition tends to discourage the advanced maritime countries from escalating particular conflicts on questions of ocean use to matters of high national interest.

8. See Seyom Brown, "The Changing Essence of Power," *Foreign Affairs*, vol. 51 (January 1973), pp. 286–99; and Seyom Brown and Larry L. Fabian, "Diplomats at Sea," *Foreign Affairs*, vol. 52 (January 1974), pp. 301–21.

The Law of the Sea Conference

Finally, the basic regime choices are being affected profoundly—but by no means irrevocably—by the negotiations in the Conference on the Law of the Sea (1973). The General Assembly gave the conference a mandate to deal with the establishment of an equitable international regime for the deep seabed and other outstanding issues, such as the breadth of territorial seas and national zones of resource management, navigation through straits and other major international waterways, the control of ocean pollution, and the prerogatives of ocean scientists. The conference has been characterized by intense disagreement among the various interests described above. Forecasts of the outcome of the conference range all the way from a complete breakdown of the meetings, to a number of separate treaties on special issues, to a comprehensive treaty draft, full of holes and vague principles to be filled in and elaborated.

While much of the outcome remains uncertain, it is clear that a long-term process of negotiating basic ocean regime issues has been set in motion, whether the present conference ends in success or failure. Moreover, a consensus does appear to be forming on some issues. Although these do not provide a sufficient body of rules to govern the use of the ocean, they do set some of the parameters within which the outstanding regime choices are likely to take place.

As of this writing the following propositions appear likely to be endorsed by a majority of the more than 140 countries in the Law of the Sea Conference—a majority including most of the maritime countries, developing countries with seacoasts, and landlocked countries.[9]

Territorial seas will be established up to twelve miles from shore; within these boundaries, coastal countries will exercise nearly complete sovereignty, subject to internationally agreed rules of navigation.

In straits that are narrower than twenty-four miles (i.e., overlapped by territorial seas of the littoral countries), foreign ships will be granted

9. Office of Law of the Sea Negotiations, U.S. Department of State, Third United Nations Conference on the Law of the Sea, "Informal Single Negotiating Text and Text on Settlement of Disputes," A/Conf. 62/WP.8/Pts. I, II, and III, May 7, 1975; see also statement of John Norton Moore in *Law of the Sea*, Hearings before the Subcommittee on Oceans and International Environment of the Senate Foreign Relations Committee, 94:1 (GPO, 1975), pp. 5–15.

virtually unimpeded rights of transit within, on, and over internationally agreed lanes.

Coastal states will have economic zones that extend beyond the 12-mile territorial seas out to 200 miles. Each coastal state will exercise sovereignty over the natural resources of its economic zone—namely, the minerals of the seabed (petroleum and hard minerals) and the living resources (fish and other animal and plant life), except for species that normally migrate out of the jurisdiction. Substantial international prerogatives will be retained in the zone for international navigation and communications.

The area beyond the 200-mile limit will continue to be regarded as essentially international, but countries may be accorded some degree of jurisdiction over mining sites on the seabed.

Thus far, the emerging consensus fails to encompass some of the central points of contention, such as: Which kinds of interests, coastal or navigational, shall be accorded priority when they come into conflict in straits, territorial seas, and economic zones? How far toward shore do international community prerogatives reach for conserving living resources and preventing ocean pollution? What rules and institutions should govern the exploitation of the minerals of the deep sea?

Most important, the conference's deliberations have not yet developed a consensus on the basic regime concept that should apply ultimately, or residually, to cover situations not explicitly included in international agreements on jurisdiction or rules of use. Where the international community has not spoken, should it be assumed that a regime of open access and free use still prevails? Should the field be open for national appropriation? Or should the international community and its institutions retain presumptive authority?

The Major Regime Alternatives

The alternative ways of organizing the human uses of the ocean can be grouped in three regime concepts: open access and free use, national management, and international management. Each regime alternative has its vociferous proponents and opponents, for each has substantial practical consequences for different groups with important interests in the ocean.

Open Access and Free Use

The international legal principle that most of the ocean should be accessible to all, and that no one should be charged a fee for its use was premised on the assumption that the ocean resources (ocean space as well as materials) were abundant and that they were unsuitable for division or ownership. The water itself, covering nearly three-fourths of the globe, was hardly scarce, and its fluidity would make a mockery of assignments of title. Harvestable fish, also mobile, were thought to be abundant, if not inexhaustible, and subject to the apparently sensible rule that capture confers ownership.

The seminal statement of this doctrine was provided by the seventeenth-century Dutch jurist, Hugo Grotius, whose conceptions still dominate international discourse about the law of the sea. The sea can be the property of no one, maintained Grotius, because its natural characteristics make it incapable of being seized or divided. God must have intended it for common use, because all require its use for navigation and fish. Moreover, he contended, with its inexhaustible supply of waters and food, there can be no morally justifiable grounds for any state to deny its use to any other state.[10]

Actually, Grotius published his *Mare Liberum* (Freedom of the Seas) nearly thirty years after Queen Elizabeth I asserted and enforced the principle of open access and free use against Spain and Portugal. The two Iberian countries, acting under the authority of a Papal Bull that divided the Atlantic Ocean between them, had been attempting to interfere with British and Dutch trade with the East Indies. Elizabeth frontally challenged their authority with a major buildup of British naval power, and pronounced in 1580 that "the use of the Sea and air is common to all; neither can any title to the ocean belong to any people or private man, forasmuch as neither nature nor regard of the public use permitteth any possession thereof."[11]

Although freedom of access and movement on the high seas was consistent with their naval and shipping interests, the British found the Elizabethan-Grotian conception inadequate protection against continental invasions of their coastal fishing beds. An Englishman, John

10. Hugo Grotius, *The Freedom of the Seas*, trans. Ralph Van Deman Magoffin (London: Oxford University Press, 1916).

11. Quoted in Frans De Pauw, *Grotius and the Law of the Sea*, trans. P. J. Arthern (Brussels: University of Brussels, 1965), p. 10.

Selden, led the doctrinal counterattack against Grotius, arguing in his treatise *Mare Clausum* that the right of dominion gave nations the right to exclude others from claimed portions of the sea, to prevent fishing, navigating and landing, and the taking of gems within territorial waters. Tolls and other restrictions of access could be imposed. The ocean's resources *were* exhaustible, argued Selden; its space *could* be divided; its uses could be effectively controlled. Grotius was compelled, by state practice more than by conceding Selden's arguments, to modify his doctrine to the point that it allowed every country to exercise sovereignty over its coastal waters. The real problem, he admitted, was to determine how far such coastal prerogatives should extend. But this real problem, given the lack of incentive to extend territorial jurisdiction far from shore, turned out in fact to be a relatively minor issue among the powerful states until the technological revolution of the mid-twentieth century transformed man's uses of the ocean.

Despite the difficulties of maintaining open access to the ocean and free use of its resources as ocean uses proliferate, this principle continues to be propounded as the most valid basis for a general regime by some interests—notably military users, shippers, long-distance fishermen, and oceanographers. These interests have been satisfied with the tradition of relatively unimpeded access to the ocean, and are generally opposed to attempts to restrict their movements or put constraints on the type of vessels or equipment they deploy.

National Management

Although various maritime interests continue to endorse freedom of the seas, the actual regime that has evolved since the Second World War is more accurately characterized as a regime of creeping national jurisdiction. Unilateral national extensions of areas of oil exploitation, beginning with the Truman Proclamation of 1945,[12] were followed by similar unilateral claims to broad national fishing zones. The Law of the Sea conferences of 1958 and 1960 attempted to redefine the limits of national jurisdictions to bring international law into some correspondence with unilateral practice. But the conferences failed to agree on precise territorial sea limits, leaving a legal vacuum for further unilateral

12. Proclamation 2667: Policy of the United States With Respect to the Natural Resources of the Subsoil and Sea Bed of the Continental Shelf, September 28, 1945, in *Public Papers of the Presidents of the United States: Harry S. Truman, 1945* (GPO, 1961), pp. 352–53.

claims. Instead of a real settlement of the controversy over rights to the continental shelf, the conferences endorsed a masterpiece of permissiveness—a convention according coastal states sovereignty over the seabed and subsoil "to a depth of 200 meters or beyond that limit where the depth of the superadjacent waters admits of the exploitation of the natural resources of the said areas."[13]

By the time the Third Law of the Sea Conference convened in 1973, maritime law was a shambles. Only twenty-five countries still adhered to the three-mile territorial sea limit; four nations claimed four-mile limits; eleven claimed six miles; one claimed ten miles; fifty-four claimed twelve miles; one claimed fifteen miles; one claimed eighteen; three claimed thirty; one claimed fifty; one claimed one hundred thirty miles; and ten claimed two hundred miles.[14] Assertions of exclusive national fishing zones were almost as varied, although few coastal states claimed less than twelve miles. Many states claimed special-purpose zones of differing widths, some for pollution control, others for conservation, still others for general economic or security purposes.

Why not let what has been happening in fact become the new regime in law? Why not make the test of jurisdictional legality whether other countries will respect a unilateral claim? Indeed, it can be argued that such a "positivistic" approach to the law of the sea is fully consistent with the way the interstate system works.

Some economists contend that clear assignment to particular nations of jurisdictional areas of the seabed would cause a more stable investment climate which, in turn, would promote efficient development of ocean resources, reducing their prices to consumers. Many coastal states feel that they could more effectively prevent overfishing, pollution, and general ecological abuse if they were given unambiguous authority over all activities in extended territorial waters.

Some would go so far as to have international law endorse national ownership of all resources in extended coastal zones. Their chief argument is that assigning legal title to national governments would remove two major sources of irresponsibility in regard to care of the resources—namely, the instability of ownership of the resources and, therefore, the lack of sufficient assurance of future gains from present conservation and care; and the inability to insist (under the mantle of international law)

13. Convention on the Continental Shelf, Art. 1, 15 U.S.T. 471, T.I.A.S. 5578.

14. Alexander, "Indices of National Interests in the Oceans," pp. 43–46.

that others who penetrate the domain adhere to the local standards of use.

International Management

The case for substantial international management of the ocean derives from the premise that many ocean resources have become *scarce*, yet remain essentially *indivisible*. The national management approach is a response to the growing scarcity of the resources, but appears to bypass their persisting indivisibility. Advocates of international management fault national management of the ocean on the grounds that it lacks the means to assure that interdependent uses, some of which would be under different national jurisdictions, would be adequately coordinated with one another. National authorities, they argue, would have spans of control too narrow to allocate the relevant external costs.

To reflect adequately the far-flung, often global, interdependencies of ocean users, broadly based negotiating and decisionmaking forums would be required to implement the international management concept. Moreover, the periodic readjustment of jurisdictional boundaries, the renegotiation of exploitation and fishing quotas—all of which is inevitable as expanding technologies affect the use of the ocean—point to the importance of permanent multinational institutions.

A regime of international management would feature processes and institutions to assure that ocean users would be accountable to those whom they substantially and directly affect; and that ocean users who significantly affect the condition of the ocean itself would be answerable for their actions to the international community. Processes would be needed to relate the various ocean uses to one another and to effect exchanges among them.

International management should be seen more as a process than as a particular institutional configuration. It could evolve incrementally, and eclectically, where it is attractive to core groups of countries because they wish to avoid conflict or because it is more economical to work together. Some of the institutions could be regional, some would be global; some uses could continue to be managed on a predominantly national basis; for other uses there might be little if any international regulation, and the traditional pattern of open access and free use might persist.

Underlying these processes and institutions would be a basic agreement, perhaps tacit, by the members of the international community

that the ocean belongs to all human beings in common. Therefore, no
segment of the human community, be it a corporation or nation-state,
has ocean rights other than those conferred on it by the international
community. This would not rule out, before universal collective arrangements are set up, temporary management of parts of the ocean by
particular regional or national authorities, who would act as custodians
for the human community and remain accountable to it.

The following chapters will examine the advantages and disadvantages of these regime alternatives for managing ocean uses of various
kinds and for managing the interactions of uses. The concluding chapter
on the ocean will return to the issue of an overall concept for ocean management and trace the institutional and U.S. policy implications of our
recommended concept.

CHAPTER THREE

The Management of Navigation

The prevailing ocean regime is largely an inherited complex of rules formulated by the maritime states. These rules have been influenced somewhat by fishing and other coastal interests; but for the most part the law of the sea has been a maritime order designed by and for merchant marine and naval interests, who use the ocean as a bridge between the land masses. Merchant and naval interests traditionally have been granted virtually unimpeded movement across this multidirectional bridge.

A number of developments are challenging the traditional maritime order, however. Increases in the number of ships and changes in ship size, speed, and maneuverability have congested many navigational routes, particularly narrow seas and straits and approaches to busy harbors. The same areas are being used increasingly for oceanography, mining, and military deployments, all of which impede navigation. Finally, coastal and environmental interests have been more and more concerned by the enlarged risk of collisions posed by the increasing traffic and installations, and the possibilities of major damage to ocean ecologies that result from those collisions.

These developments, singly and in combination, raise two basic regime issues. First, to what extent should the navigational interests be entrusted with self-regulation? Second, what should be the division of regulatory authority between individual coastal states and the international community? Cutting across these issues is the problem of naval prerogatives in the ocean. No navigational regime will endure if it severely restricts the naval mobility of the powerful countries, particularly the United States and the USSR.

Merchant Shipping Developments and Problems

The world's merchant shipping has increased dramatically since the early 1960s. World ocean commerce doubled to 268 million tons between 1961 and 1972, and the current rate is estimated to double in eight years.[1] Increases in commercial tonnage chiefly reflect increases in the size of ships. The new, larger ships pose greater hazards, not only to ocean fleets and their personnel, but also to important ecological systems and land interests.

The increased trip length imposed upon merchant shipping by the closing of the Suez Canal in 1967 gave shipbuilders incentives to implement economies of scale. Shipbuilders and shipping companies have found that shipping costs do not rise in proportion to the size of the vessel. Not only does the use of one ship instead of two or three save on port charges, pilot fees, and general administration; an increase of about 25 percent in a ship's dimensions is estimated to provide about a 95 percent increase in load capacity. The machinery costs are also less if additions are made to the size of ships rather than to the number of ships in a fleet, and there are associated savings in shipboard personnel. Finally, because the big ships glide easily through the water, once in motion they require less propulsive power. The discovery of these economies of scale shows up in the phenomenal recent increases in the dimensions of tankers used to transport oil and natural gas. By 1974, more than one-quarter of the 5,000 tankers afloat were supertankers of 200,000 tons or more, and some "ultra" supers, of half a million tons or more, were under construction. As a point of comparison, at the close of the Second World War, the maximum size was 18,000 tons.[2]

Additional economies were achieved by departing from traditional shipbuilding practices. Previously, it was normal to outfit merchant ships with at least two boilers in case one failed. Many great tankers today have only one boiler. The boiler is the ship's lifeblood—powering the

1. Charles C. Bates and Paul Yost, "Where Trends the Flow of Merchant Ships," in John K. Gamble, Jr., and Giulio Pontecorvo, eds., *Law of the Sea: The Emerging Regime of the Oceans* (Ballinger, 1974), pp. 249–84.

2. Noël Mostert, "Supertankers—I," *The New Yorker*, May 13, 1974, pp. 45–100; and "Supertankers—II," *The New Yorker*, May 20, 1974, pp. 46–99. The tonnage referred to is calculated in deadweight tons, i.e., the weight of cargo, fuel, stores, and ballast that a ship can carry before riding lower in the water than is safe.

propulsion system and the lights, radar, and other essential navigation equipment. Similarly, to save on construction costs and reduce the selling price, nearly all of the very large tankers have been built with single propeller systems.

Some critics charge that savings on the boiler and propeller systems have been purchased at the cost of safety, and at risk to the ocean environment: Not only do multiple systems serve as backups in case of malfunction, but they also could serve as a means of altering the ship's normal thrust in case of emergencies. With a single boiler system, for example, a supertanker of 250,000 tons traveling at 16 knots now takes more than 3 nautical miles and 21 minutes to stop, and there is a strong sideslip in the stopping maneuver.[3]

There is also concern over the pollution hazard created by the normal operation of tankers. These ships carry oil cargoes only in one direction, and must make the return voyage empty. In order to move safely on the return trip, they must take on water as ballast, and for virtually all tankers, the only place to store such ballast is in the empty cargo tanks. Thus, petroleum that remains on the sides of the tanks after a cargo has been discharged mixes with ballast water on the return voyage. When ballast is dumped, as it is several times on a voyage in response to changing weather and sea conditions, the oil from the tanks is washed into the ocean.

The new concern over normal tanker operations has been stimulated in part by several large oil spills from tanker accidents. One was the 1967 wreck of the *Torrey Canyon*, a supertanker that ran aground and broke up off the coast of the United Kingdom, spilling 30,000 tons of oil, which severely damaged plant and animal life. Another large spill occurred in waters off Cape Cod, when a tanker carrying refined oil lost its cargo.

The studies prompted by such spills indicate that refined petroleum products are likely to be even more damaging to ocean life than is crude petroleum. Crude oil spills may cause partial, but temporary, devastation of a local ecology, but refined petroleum products may produce total and enduring devastation, apparently because many such products are not naturally occurring substances, and thus may not be degraded. The dumping of waste lubrication oils and other petroleum products that are mixed up in the bilge of ships—a practice common to all ships,

3. See Mostert, "Supertankers—I," p. 51.

not just tankers—may be putting many such synthetic substances into the oceans.[4]

Prevailing Responses to the New Hazards

The growing recognition that the ocean environment can be harmed if subjected to unregulated use has stimulated popular pressures in many countries to tighten controls on shipping. These pressures are manifested in efforts to strengthen the existing international maritime regulatory system; in more stringent controls by coastal states on navigation through their waters; and in efforts to commit all states and shippers to new restraints on ocean pollution through the Law of the Sea Conference.

Working through IMCO

The centerpiece of the international maritime regulatory system is the Inter-governmental Maritime Consultative Organization (IMCO). The smallest of the UN specialized agencies (in 1974, its annual budget was $2.4 million, and its staff numbered sixty-five), IMCO's convention went into effect in 1958. Its mandate is to promote standards of safety, efficiency, and fair competition within the maritime industry and to facilitate international cooperation in technical and operational matters.[5] Before the *Torrey Canyon* disaster of 1967, IMCO's functions in the field of oil pollution were largely to act as a depository of intergovernmental conventions and a collector and disseminator of technical information about oil pollution. But the growing public concern since *Torrey Canyon* about tanker pollution has prompted a flurry of IMCO initiatives to tighten existing oil cargo and navigational conventions.[6]

IMCO has recommended new navigational rules of the road—particularly navigational lanes, traffic separation schemes, and improvements in shore-to-ship communications. Under specific consideration are mandatory ship separation lanes in heavily trafficked international

---

4. For more detail on the effect of oil on the oceans see *Background Papers for a Workshop on Inputs, Fates, and Effects of Petroleum in the Marine Environment*, Ocean Affairs Board (National Academy of Sciences, 1973); and Donald F. Boesch, Carl H. Hershner, and Jerome H. Milgram, *Oil Spills and the Marine Environment* (Ballinger, 1974).

5. Samuel A. Lawrence, *International Sea Transport: The Years Ahead* (D.C. Heath, 1972), p. 35.

6. Robert A. Shinn, *The International Politics of Marine Pollution Control* (Praeger, 1974), p. 111.

waterways; mandatory nationally imposed sea lanes in coastal waters; radar monitoring and improved traffic control systems in congested pilotage waters; requirements for better and continuous ship-to-harbor radio contact; requirements for using English as a universal maritime language; planning of route information; and stiffer license and training requirements for ships' officers.[7]

With respect to the normal dumping of oil wastes from ships, current IMCO regulations prohibit the discharge of oil generally within 50 miles of land, or within 100 miles of special pollution-prone areas. But the apprehension of violators is usually left to the country of the ship's registry. IMCO has also negotiated a convention that would require separate ballast tanks on new oil tankers (those for which the building contract is dated after December 31, 1975) of more than 70,000 tons.[8] The treaty has not yet come into force, however, because the required number of countries has not yet ratified it. Some critics feel the treaty is too lenient. Many shipyards have a backlog of contracts that permit deficient ships to be started after 1975 while technically complying with the convention. Moreover, the 70,000-ton threshold is an escape clause for smaller oil tankers.

A major issue is whether the various risks should be dealt with primarily through ship operating rules, such as traffic separation, or whether there should also be mandatory changes in ship design. Shippers do not like the latter alternative, because changes in ship design are likely to increase the cost of ships, countering the savings in transport costs already achieved by the modifications of the last decade.

There is some understandable suspicion by environmentalists that these actions by IMCO are mainly defensive holding operations on the part of the oil companies and shippers against the new determination of coastal interests to limit freedom of navigation.[9] This suspicion is reflected in a concern that IMCO's structure and decision processes, at least up to now, constitute little more than *self*-regulation by the shipping interests.

Eighty-nine countries belong to IMCO, but its main work has been performed by its Council and its Maritime Safety Committee, both of which have been dominated by the shipping interests. The IMCO found-

7. Inter-governmental Maritime Consultative Organization, *The Activities of the Inter-Governmental Maritime Consultative Organization in Relation to Shipping and Related Maritime Matters* (London, 1974).

8. Ibid.

9. Mostert, "Supertankers—II," pp. 74–75, 86–95, 98–99.

ing convention stipulates that the Council shall consist of eighteen members, of which six are to be from states "with the largest interests in providing international shipping services," six are to be from states "with the largest interest in international seaborne trade," and six are to be from states "which have special interests in maritime transport or navigation." The sixteen-member Maritime Safety Committee is similarly weighted.[10]

Amendments to the IMCO founding convention that would alter the present weighted membership of the Council and Maritime Safety Committee were voted in 1974. When the amendments are ratified, the Council will be expanded to twenty-four, with the additional six members coming from "states which have special interests in maritime transport or navigation, and whose election . . . will ensure the representation of all major geographic areas of the world." This will make a total of twelve states in this category on the Council. The Maritime Safety Committee is to be opened to all members of IMCO.

Nonshipping interests may have a greater opportunity to influence IMCO decisions because of a 1973 reform in the organization, which established the Marine Environmental Protection Committee (MEPC). All IMCO members are invited to participate in the MEPC, and this committee is authorized to formulate amendments to the IMCO convention and submit proposals directly to states for their approval.

These organizational changes do represent some weakening of the traditional dominance of the shippers. It remains to be seen, however, whether governments will attempt to use IMCO to further substantially their antipollution interests or will continue to rely on it principally to serve their navigational interests.

In any event, IMCO, as reflected in its title and explicitly stipulated in its founding convention, is still essentially a consultative and advisory body, designed to help states arrive at standards. It has no powers as a direct decisionmaker, and cannot levy sanctions on parties that break any intergovernmental agreements it may sponsor.

Coastal State Controls on Navigation

In the absence of more effective international controls, some states whose interests in the ocean are not primarily defined by the shipping

10. Robert M. Hallman, *Towards an Environmentally Sound Law of the Seas*, A Report of the International Institute for Environment and Development (1974), p. 48n.

industry have themselves taken new initiatives to control the activities of ships off their coasts. Thus in 1970, Canada, one of the most internationalist of states, felt compelled for pollution control purposes to extend its jurisdiction over commercial shipping out to 100 miles from its coastline. It established safety control zones, within which ships would have to comply with technical requirements relating to hull structure, navigational aids, qualifications of personnel, and time and route of passage. Ships not meeting these requirements would not be permitted to enter the safety control zones.

In proclaiming Canada's extended jurisdiction, government spokesmen cited the disasters of the *Torrey Canyon* off the coast of the United Kingdom and the tanker *Arrow* in Chedabucto Bay, Mexico. They rejected all the traditional principles of absolute freedom of navigation that might prevent coastal states from action necessary to protect their environment. States should not be expected to await the gradual development of multilateral approaches, argued the Canadians:

Maritime law is evolving, but more slowly than we would wish in Canada. For centuries emphasis has been placed on the right of shipping to the use of the world's sea lanes without any regard to the effect that this might have on adjacent coastal states. While this may have been practical before, now, when millions of barrels of oil are afloat in tankers on the high seas on any given day the threat of pollution is real, and the interests of coastal states, as opposed to nations that have large commercial fleets, must be recognized. A state, and particularly those offering flags of convenience, cannot expect in the world community to continue these activities without regard to the interests of other nations.

At the World Shipping Conference in Brussels . . . it was obvious that these states [with large commercial fleets] continue to expect to have absolute priorities for their particular requirements. It became clear to the government of Canada that unilateral action would have to be taken at this time if Canada was to protect its own urgent interest.[11]

The new regulatory authority over navigation asserted by the states bordering the Strait of Malacca is also a sign of the times. The Strait of

11. Jean Chrétien, "Address to the House of Commons on the Second Reading of the Arctic Waters Pollution Prevention Bill," April 16, 1970 (Ottawa: Queen's Printer for Canada, 1971), p. 5939. See also "Summary of Canadian Note to the United States Government," tabled in the House of Commons, April 17, 1970, by the Secretary of State for External Affairs (Canadian Embassy, April 21, 1970; processed); and Allan Gotlieb and Charles Dalfen, "National Jurisdiction and International Responsibility: New Canadian Approaches to International Law," *American Journal of International Law*, vol. 67 (April 1973), pp. 229–58.

Malacca, on the shortest route between the Indian and Pacific oceans, handles about 100 ships a day—making it the busiest strait in the world, after the Strait of Dover. In view of Indonesia's standing declaration that all the straits within its vast archipelago are internal waters and also the fact that the only other route capable of handling large ships between the Indian and Pacific oceans is around Australia, maritime shippers are not at all happy with the assertion of unilateral authority over the Strait of Malacca by the Southeast Asian riparian states. The Japanese are particularly concerned, since 90 percent of their oil comes from the Persian Gulf in tankers via the Southeast Asian passages.[12]

But it is precisely Japan's tanker traffic and its threat to coastal interests that has provided Malaysia, Indonesia, and Singapore with their strongest justifications for local authority over navigation through Malacca. In 1967, shortly after the *Torrey Canyon* episode near England, the 151,288-ton Japanese tanker, *Tokyo Maru*, scraped its bottom in the Strait of Malacca, arousing fears of a major catastrophe. In June 1971, two tankers of 210,000 tons each scraped bottom just south of Singapore. And in January 1975, the *Showa Maru* went aground at the southeastern end of the Strait of Malacca, spilling 4,500 tons of oil. In the meantime, Japan had joined the three riparian states in a series of surveys that pointed to the need for deepening parts of the strait and for special traffic separation schemes. Japan had indicated willingness to cooperate and to provide technical and financial help for these improvements. Nonetheless, in November 1971, the three riparian states declared that navigation in the Strait of Malacca and Singapore was "the responsibility of the states concerned," and agreed to establish a tripartite body, excluding Japan, to coordinate safety measures. Indonesia and Malaysia also stated (with Singapore only "noting" their statement) that "the two straits were not international straits although they fully recognized their use for international shipping in accordance with the principle of innocent passage."[13]

Efforts to Revise the Law of the Sea

The declarations by Indonesia, Malaysia, and Singapore about the Strait of Malacca and the positions of those nations and of others border-

12. Richard A. Miller, "Indonesia's Archipelago Doctrine and Japan's Jugular," *United States Naval Institute Proceedings*, vol. 98 (October 1972), pp. 27–33.

13. George G. Thomson, "The Malacca Straits: Who Has the Last Word?" *Pacific Community*, vol. 13 (July 1972), p. 684.

ing straits in the bargaining surrounding the current Law of the Sea Conference indicate that the established principle of innocent passage is being reshaped to thrust the burden of demonstrating innocence on the shippers rather than—as it used to be—putting the burden of demonstrating guilt on the state adjoining the strait.[14] Moreover, the concept of innocence, which traditionally meant intending no *military* harm, is being redefined to include acts not likely to harm local ecologies, geological formations, or artificial coastal installations. Accordingly, the 1973 draft articles on the territorial seas and straits offered by Greece, Cyprus, Indonesia, Malaysia, Morocco, the Philippines, Spain, and Yemen (and supported by China) stipulated that the coastal state may regulate passage in its territorial waters of nuclear powered ships or ships carrying nuclear weapons, ships carrying nuclear substances or any other material that may endanger the coastal state or seriously pollute the marine environment, and ships engaged in research on the marine environment.[15]

As it became evident that the impending Law of the Sea Conference would in all likelihood extend territorial sea limits to twelve miles, thus encompassing many key straits, such a redefinition of the principle of innocent passage appeared threatening to the navigational interests of many states. The United States, the USSR, and other maritime powers insisted upon retaining free or unimpeded transit along international navigational routes, especially through straits. At the start of the Law of the Sea Conference, U.S. spokesmen said that free transit was so vital a national interest as to be nonnegotiable.

As of this writing, however, there does appear to be some prospect that a maritime/coastal-state agreement on navigation, clearly weighted in favor of the coastal states, will emerge from the Law of the Sea Conference negotiations.

The general agreement would involve a right of virtually unimpeded

14. Under the 1958 Convention on the Territorial Sea and the Contiguous Zone, passage is defined as innocent "so long as it is not prejudicial to the peace, good order or security of the coastal state"; but it also stipulates that "there shall be no suspension of the innocent passage of foreign ships through straits which are used for international navigation between one part of the high seas and another part of the high seas or the territorial sea of a foreign state." Articles 14, 15, and 16, 15 U.S.T. 1606.

15. "Cyprus, Greece, Indonesia, Malaysia, Morocco, Philippines, Spain, and Yemen: Draft Articles on Navigation Through the Territorial Sea Including Straits Used for International Navigation," UN Doc. A/AC.138/SC.II/ L. 18 (March 27, 1973), p. 6.

transit through straits, a right of only "innocent passage" through the rest of the territorial waters of coastal states, and general freedom for all countries to navigate, overfly, and lay submarine cables in the economic zones of coastal states between twelve and two hundred miles out to sea.

Innocent passage would be defined strictly, excluding passage through territorial waters if accompanied by any exercise or practice with weapons of any kind; the launching or taking on board of any aircraft; the launching or taking on board of any military device; the taking on board or putting overboard of any commodity, currency, or person in contravention of the customs, fiscal, immigration, or sanitary regulations of the coastal state; any act of willful pollution; research or survey activities; any act interfering with the communication systems of the coastal state; any act interfering with facilities or installations of the coastal state; and, finally, any other activity not directly bearing on the passage itself.[16]

In addition, the coastal state would have the authority to make laws and regulations in its territorial sea concerning the safety of navigation and the regulation of marine traffic, including the designation of shipping lanes and the establishment of traffic separation schemes; the protection of navigational facilities or installations, including those for exploiting marine resources; the protection of cables and pipelines; the conservation of living resources; the protection of the environment of the coastal state; oceanographic research; and the usual coastal zone administrative functions of customs, sanitation, immigration, and the like.[17]

By contrast, the limitations on interference by a coastal state with navigation through the territorial sea would be rather few. The coastal states would refrain from imposing requirements on foreign ships that would deny or prejudice innocent passage; they would not discriminate against the ships of any state, or against ships carrying cargoes to or from any state; they would levy no charges upon foreign ships for passage through territorial waters; and they would publicize any dangers to navigation within the territorial sea.[18]

16. U.S. State Department, Office of Law of the Sea Negotiations, Third United Nations Conference on the Law of the Sea, "Informal Single Negotiating Text and Text on Settlement of Disputes," UN Doc. A/CONF. 62/WP.8/ Pts. I, II, and III (May 7, 1975), pp. 8–9.

17. Ibid., pp. 9–10.

18. Ibid., p. 11.

In the economic zones beyond twelve miles, navigational rules would, for the most part, be formulated by the international community (presumably through IMCO). In the waters immediately surrounding artificial islands or installations constructed by the coastal state, however, the coastal state would have authority to set navigational procedures.[19]

If the above provisions do indeed emerge as a central part of the package produced by the current Law of the Sea Conference, it will represent not much more than a legal codification of the prerogatives already being asserted unilaterally by most coastal states. Some coastal states want to go further, and assert sovereignty over navigation in the 200-mile zone as complete as is now being legitimated for the 12-mile territorial sea—in effect, establishing a 200-mile territorial sea. Thus, to the extent that the Law of the Sea Conference is able to give international legitimacy to any international navigational prerogatives in the zone between 12 and 200 miles offshore, it will at least have forestalled the more extreme nationalistic grabs that could otherwise become the norm.

Even though they are not always directed specifically at military users, the growing challenges to the traditional ocean regime of open access and free use hit the navies of the world right where they live: in their habits of unrestricted naval transit, particularly through straits; and in their expectation that their home governments will back their deployment of military capabilities anywhere on, beneath, or above the ocean, except within the narrow territorial jurisdictions of objecting states.

A major concern of military planners has been that the twelve-mile width for territorial seas (about to receive universal recognition), in bringing under national control more than 100 straits that were previously considered international waterways, would subject missile-carrying submarines to the regulations of innocent passage. This would require them to go through these straits on the surface. When a missile-carrying submarine surfaces, it compromises the most important aspect of its invulnerability—namely, its ability to keep its location concealed from the enemy.[20]

19. Ibid., p. 20.

20. It is unlikely, however, that either superpower would ever funnel more than a small proportion of its strategic submarines through straits at any one time. Moreover, the deployment of submarine-based missiles with ranges in excess of 4,000 miles substantially reduces the need to rely on straits passage to perform the naval strategic missions.

A regime that incorporated the principle of innocent passage through straits might also substantially affect the ability of the various maritime powers to deploy military forces to certain theaters. There are a number of straits that are strategic in this sense: the Straits of Gibraltar, Bab el Mandeb, Malacca, Korea, and Bering; the Dardanelles/Bosporus; and the exits from the Baltic Sea. Regulations requiring ships and aircraft to demonstrate their harmlessness to the states on either side of a strait before being certified for transit could well be used by a state controlling a strait to inhibit and seriously delay the deployment of military forces and supplies.

In addition, military planners are concerned that a new law of the sea treaty not inhibit their ability to engage in surveillance from the ocean. The two superpowers reportedly have been proceeding to install sonar listening devices on the continental shelves of foreign countries and on mid-ocean rises mainly for the purpose of detecting each other's submarines.[21]

It was in part to protect their respective rights to conduct military surveillance from the seabed that the two superpowers, in negotiating the 1971 treaty demilitarizing the seabed, limited the coverage of that agreement to nuclear weapons and other weapons of mass destruction.[22]

The U.S. Navy has been willing to trade away other U.S. ocean interests in the Law of the Sea negotiations for new guarantees of its traditional freedoms of the high seas. The Department of Defense championed the U.S. comprehensive draft treaty of 1970. It conceded broadening of territorial seas from three to twelve miles and turning over the minerals on the deep seabed to international management—in return for assured rights of free transit in straits and in the air above straits, and for noninterference with military deployments beyond the twelve-mile limit.[23] Military apprehension about a restrictive straits regime

21. Robert E. Osgood, "U.S. Security Interests in Ocean Law," *Ocean Development and International Law: The Journal of Marine Affairs*, vol. 2 (Spring 1974), pp. 20–21. From the point of view of the U.S. military planners, according to Osgood, the crucial monitoring areas are the Greenland-Iceland-United Kingdom gap, the Arctic Ocean, the North Pacific Ocean, and the Caribbean Sea.

22. *Seabed Arms Control Treaty*, Hearing before the Senate Foreign Relations Committee, 92:2 (GPO, 1972).

23. For the Defense Department's role in the formulation of the U.S. draft treaty, see Ann L. Hollick, "Seabeds Make Strange Politics," *Foreign Policy*, no. 9 (Winter 1972–73), pp. 148–70.

has apparently been partly responsible for the U.S. government's willingness to accommodate to coastal states' insistence on national economic zones out to 200 miles.

Toward Strengthened International Management of Navigation

The current assertions of control by coastal states over navigation are a reflection of the weakness of existing international agencies, mainly operating through IMCO, in holding shipping interests accountable to the wide array of other interests they affect. Countries involved in transoceanic commerce, however, are unlikely to be satisfied by the decentralized navigational regime that appears to be emerging; if a variety of specifications set by coastal states is imposed on ship designs and operations, the cost of goods transported in ships is likely to rise. Nor are some of the coastal states that are motivated by environmental considerations likely to secure adequate protection for themselves through navigational controls that are unilaterally formulated and enforced; in many cases, accidents or deliberate oil spills within other jurisdictions where standards are lax can affect the ocean ecologies of the more environmentally responsible states.

Thus, strengthened international management of navigation is a basic long-term need of both the maritime interests (including the transporters and producers and consumers of ocean-carried goods) and the coastal environmental interests. Indeed, this is the chief argument advanced by Canada in justifying its assertion of coastal control as an interim policy during the negotiations on an international regime for navigation. Developing coastal states, to be sure, suspect any international regime proposed by the maritime powers to be a device to preserve their control over ocean affairs; some of the less endowed countries that do have large shipping fleets, such as Liberia, are not at all enthusiastic about internationally imposed standards that would reduce their competitive advantages. These pressures against strengthened international management might be overcome by a regime that gave coastal states a greater voice in the decisionmaking processes than has been characteristic of IMCO.

Such strengthened international management of navigation could be accomplished through two routes: making IMCO more relevant by giving all interests affected by ocean shipping an appropriate voice in the organization's councils, plus increasing IMCO's authority to make and implement navigational policy; and giving a comprehensive ocean institution substantial review authority over IMCO's functions. We regard both of these routes as desirable for making ocean navigation more efficient, resolving international conflict, and protecting the ocean environment. It would be best if both proceeded simultaneously. Either one, however, could be undertaken independently of the other.

Making IMCO More Relevant

The 1974 reforms in IMCO's organizational structure could be amplified in two respects. First, the Council's membership could be made to reflect more accurately the variety of interests affected by navigation. The impending expansion of the Council from eighteen to twenty-four members, with twelve members to be states with special (nonshipping) interests in maritime transport or navigation, could be explicitly interpreted by the Council to require that at least six of the twelve be states whose primary interests in navigation are as coastal states. Second, the Council could be made responsive to policy guidance emanating from IMCO's Maritime Safety Committee (which includes all IMCO members), by an explicit rule that no decisions by the Council be inconsistent with resolutions of the Maritime Safety Committee.

IMCO's authority over policies for navigational safety and ecological protection could be strengthened by according it the power to license ships. An international treaty might be negotiated to establish the rule that only ships that were licensed internationally could legally use the ocean, and that license fees should be assessed on the basis of ship tonnage, size, and type of cargo. IMCO would be assigned the licensing responsibility, and perhaps some rights to inspect ships. But on-the-spot enforcement of the international regulations, including detailed inspection, would probably have to remain a responsibility of the coastal states, as would the actual collection of license fees. If a ship were found not to conform with international specifications for ship design or norms of navigational safety, IMCO might increase its licensing fees for the offending ships or, in extreme cases, deny its license.

Oversight of IMCO by a Comprehensive Ocean Authority

Even if IMCO's decisionmaking processes are reformed to give greater weight to nonnavigational interests, the fact that its primary mandate is in navigation probably means that de facto domination of the organization by ocean transportation interests will continue. One way to assure that nonnavigational interests are adequately taken into account by IMCO might be to broaden the functions of the institution as well as its formal basis of representation. But broadening its functions to assure accountability to nonnavigational interests might dilute IMCO's special expertise and competence over ship design and navigation problems. IMCO's specialized competence could be preserved by retaining the functional specificity of its mandate, but subjecting IMCO policy and operations to oversight and broad guidance by a multifunctional ocean institution mandated to reconcile functional conflicts of interest in the ocean.

CHAPTER FOUR

The Management of Fisheries

In nearly every part of the globe today, some fish stocks are either already overfished or are threatened with depletion. In response to this threat, some countries have established regional fishery commissions and have entered into agreements to abide by certain rules for stock conservation. But so far, these multilateral arrangements are only minor variants of the basic international regime of open access and freedom to fish and of the norm that capture establishes property rights. In other regions, the prevailing response to emerging fish scarcities has been unilateral extension of national fishing jurisdictions. The Law of the Sea Conference is likely to endorse wide coastal fishing zones. The extension of national control, however, fails to come to grips with the transnational mobility of some stocks and the interdependence of species.[1] An analysis of the sources of and possible remedies to the growing problem of overfishing demonstrates the ineffectiveness of both the national and multinational approaches, and points toward more extensive and intensive international management.

The Problem of Overfishing

Exploitation of ocean fish on a sizable scale, once primarily an activity of the northern hemisphere, has spread to virtually all coastal areas. Those unable to catch their customary amount increasingly find themselves competing not only with neighbors, but also with fishermen from

1. All organisms that are closely related and biologically similar form a species. Those fish of a given species that live in a given area constitute a stock, and most fish species are divided into many stocks.

distant countries with advanced technology. While fishing technologies vary all over the world, the most modern techniques harvest with such thoroughness that they are able to seriously deplete a stock in just two years.[2]

For various species of fish, the level of fishing in many areas of the world is now close to or in excess of the level that permits roughly equal yields from one year to the next. The stocks of some species are being seriously depleted in one or both of two ways: Fishing is at such intensity that spawning populations are being depleted below the numbers required to produce a steady level of juvenile fish; or the average size of the fish in the stock is reduced to the point at which the same number of harvested fish begins to result in lower tonnages. Despite evidence of continuing depletion surpassing the level of maximum sustainable yield, the existing incentives for fishermen encourage them to harvest as much as they can today, regardless of the effect on future stocks.

Causes

The demands for fish and fish products have been rising more than the supply, with the result that the value of a fixed harvest has been growing. The higher value, reflected in higher prices, has in turn stimulated an expansion of fishing. Under the prevailing regime, the fish are the property of no one until they are caught; thus, there are no incentives to conserve stocks or to invest in the improvement of stocks. Indeed, the dominant incentives are to catch as much as one can while the catching is good.

Fish species have different values and the most valued stocks will be overfished before less valued stocks have been fully exploited. Rising demand for a highly valued species means rising prices. Rising prices make the return on smaller catches enough to cover the costs of catching them, despite the effects of depletion. The most highly valued species are subject to the greatest increases in demand. The rise in prices and average returns continues to attract fishermen to those stocks despite increased depletion. The result is to induce fishermen to enter an already crowded fishery instead of seeking an unused but edible species. In some cases, the fact that different groups value different species can

2. J. A. Gulland, "Distant-Water Fisheries and Their Relation to Development and Management," paper given at the United Nations FAO Technical Conference on Fishery Management and Development, Technical Session IV, Vancouver (February 13–23, 1973), p. 6.

help spread the fishing pressure more widely; but where stocks are intermingled, as are cod and haddock in the northwest Atlantic, conflict over fishing grounds can be exacerbated.

The problem of depletion is compounded wherever there is no limit to entry into fisheries. In this condition, newcomers will be attracted to a given area when they see others doing well. Each new entrant is likely to increase the total yield available from the stock, but the amount by which the yield increases is smaller with each new entrant, up to the point of maximum sustainable yield. After that, each new entrant may actually lower the total yield in tons, because the stock becomes depleted.

At the same time that each new entrant to a fishery affects the total available yield, he also adds to the total cost of catching the fish. The first entrant to fish a stock finds the resource abundant, and does not have to look very hard to find enough fish to fill his boat. With more and more fishermen harvesting the stock, each of them has to look harder to find all the fish needed to fill his boat. As long as the cost of filling the boat is less than the value of the fish caught, more boats will be attracted to the stock. The nature of fishing costs often is such that the number of fishermen exceeds the number that would catch the maximum sustainable yield before the value of fish caught equals the cost of catching them.[3]

Technology: The Solution That Is Part of the Problem

With no ability to reserve a share of a fish stock for the time he wants to catch it, each fisherman is pushed into purchase of equipment that enables him to catch his load as quickly as possible. This leads to an overinvestment in equipment: Fishermen are increasingly able to catch the year's yield of a stock in only a few days or a few weeks. Then they must either sit idle for the rest of the year or move on to other stocks. If the fisheries were divided up before the fish were caught, fewer men and less equipment could be used for each fishery and the fishing spread out over more of the year.

The incentives that have led to overinvestment in equipment have also encouraged the development of new technologies for fishing. As with all modern technologies, however, the new techniques are not uni-

3. For more detail on how open access depletes fish stocks, see Francis T. Christy, Jr., and Anthony Scott, *The Common Wealth in Ocean Fisheries* (Johns Hopkins Press for Resources for the Future, 1965), pp. 80–86, 233–34.

formly distributed. Some fish are harvested by techniques that rely on the fish coming to the harvesting devices, such as lobster and crab pots, fixed nets in shallow waters, and baited long lines. Most fish, however, are caught by man going to the resources. Once found, they are usually caught by nets; a few carnivorous species are caught with baited hooks.

Despite the similarity of fishing technology implied by the preceding statements, however, there is a wide diversity in effectiveness of harvesting by different groups because of differences in three major characteristics: mobility of the fishermen, ability to catch a variety of species, and efficiency of harvesting. These differences are attributable to differences in boats, net materials, the energy source used for lifting the nets out of the water, and aids available for locating the fish initially.

The boats used in fishing, which of course determine the geographical mobility of the fishermen, vary from small, hand-paddled canoes, with a severely limited range, to fleets of sophisticated seagoing vessels with a virtually unlimited range. These fleets include trawlers that seek and catch the fish, floating factories that process the fish caught by the trawlers, and tenders that supply both the trawlers and the factories. Between these two extremes are various sizes of powered fishing vessels that can range varying distances from shore.

While the artisan canoe fisheries and the fleets represent opposites in terms of geographic mobility, both tend to have flexibility in the species they can catch, although they achieve their flexibility in different ways. Many of the artisan fisheries are found in the tropics, where fish species live interspersed. Fish of many species that are relatively immobile are caught and sold on the same day; thus, the fishermen do not need specialized storage or processing facilities on their boats. The large fleets fish mostly for nontropical species, which are not interspersed, but the factory ships have so many different processing techniques that they can use almost any species they can find.[4] The powered fishing vessels

4. The ability of such factory fleets to process almost every species caught has led to the development of pulse fishing. Using this technique, a fleet moves into an area and goes after all the fish, rather than specific species. Once the area is swept clean of fish, the fleet moves on, allowing the area to be recolonized by surrounding species. The idea is similar to forms of agriculture that use no fertilizers but work a plot of ground for two or three years and then move on, allowing natural vegetation to move in and restore the fertility of the soil (this technique is called fallowing). The problems with pulse fishing are similar to the problems with fallowing: as demand for agricultural land increased, the period of fallowing was shortened, and eventually it became too short to refertilize the soil. The danger is that pulse fleets will return too

that fit between these two extremes, however, tend to be limited to a very few species. Even the sophisticated tuna boats that can and do circumnavigate the globe are equipped to catch and store only a few species of tuna and related fish.

Differences in the efficiency with which fish can be harvested relate more to the nature of the equipment on board the ships than to the type of ship involved. Nets made from nylon (or other synthetic materials) that are removed from the water by a power block can hold many more fish than can nets of natural fiber, which must be hauled in by hand. The advent of nylon nets and power blocks enabled tuna fishermen to use nets instead of baited hooks to capture schools of large tuna. The switch enables fishermen to take all members of the school that are too big to swim through the mesh. With baited hooks, the fishermen could not determine what size fish or how much of a given school would be caught. The efficiency with which a fishing vessel can harvest a stock is enhanced by its ability to use advanced methods for finding and delineating schools of fish. These advanced methods consist of onboard sonar and spotter aircraft. Experiments are under way on the use of satellite data to locate fish.

The use of factory ships to serve a fleet of trawlers also increases the efficiency of the harvest. This is because catches of other than the desired species do not always have to be thrown back, but can be turned into fishmeal if the species caught is suitable. Trawlers not serviced by a factory ship tend to throw back such fish in order to save storage space for the species they want.[5]

Alternative Approaches to a Solution

If overfishing is to end, there will have to be a change from the present underlying principle that nobody owns the fish until they are caught. There probably will also have to be some international allocation of the benefits from fishing.

---

quickly to areas that have been exhausted of fish or that the exhausted areas will become too large for easy recolonization.

5. The number of such unwanted catches is high. U.S. trawlers throw back up to 70 percent of the fish they catch, according to George C. Wilson, "A Wasted Ocean of Food," *Washington Post*, June 30, 1974. Such fish usually die, as the pressure changes are lethal to them.

Ownership Determined by Stocks or Species

For ownership to mean anything, an owner must be able to control access to all of the resource in question. In the case of fish, this means controlling each stock for its entire life cycle and throughout its geographical range. Unfortunately for simple management schemes, fish stocks are not sedentary, separate items that are easily distributed among separate owners. Assigning ownership of entire stocks to separate owners runs into problems, because stocks are interdependent.

Another superficially attractive solution is to give certain nations title to particular species in a demarcated part of the ocean. But this too ignores the realities of fish ecologies. While fish of different species may live at different depths, all species are affected by the health of other species. Like land-based ecologies, the species in ocean ecologies are connected by serving as a food supply for another species, either directly or indirectly. Thus the division among separate owners by species is unlikely to give the owner real control over the health of the stock.

Extended National Fisheries

It is hardly surprising that many countries, particularly those not too well equipped to play an influential role in international decisionmaking processes, are reacting to the scarcity of fisheries by pressing for international recognition of their claims to national control or ownership of fisheries, or portions of fisheries, off their coasts. Because many fisheries are the objects of competition between neighboring states or between mobile fishermen and more stationary fishermen, many of the allocations will have to be internationally negotiated. Recognition of this is reflected in the effort to have national jurisdiction over extensive fisheries granted by the Law of the Sea Conference and by the negotiations accompanying the U.S. declaration of a 200-mile national fishing zone.

One proposal for national fisheries, represented by the draft articles submitted by Canada, India, Kenya, Madagascar, Senegal, and Sri Lanka to the Law of the Sea Conference, gives the coastal states exclusive fishing rights in zones that are coterminous with the zones in which they have rights to the resources of the seabed (presumably out to 200 miles from shore). Each coastal state would have special responsibilities for maintaining the productivity of the living resources within its economic zone, and would have preferential rights to those resources. Beyond their zones the coastal states could regulate the living resources

that have limited migratory characteristics but are ecologically interdependent with the resources in the zone. Highly migratory species
would be regulated by multinational authorities established specifically
for such purposes.[6]

Proposals such as these would allocate the rights to fish before capture on the basis of proximity. This would change the current distribution of fish resources, which has been based on the ability to harvest.
Some of the nations that favor this approach have already acted unilaterally to effect the change—for example, Peru, Ecuador, Chile, Brazil,
Argentina, Iceland, the United States, and the USSR.

Allocation of rights on the basis of proximity is opposed by those who
claim historic rights to certain fish stocks. During the long period of
freedom of the seas for fishing, fleets have gone far from their own
shores. The states that own these fleets feel that their past activities
establish their rights to the stocks they have fished. The USSR, despite
its own assertion of a 200-mile zone, particularly opposes any allocation
system that does not preserve in some way the system of allocation based
on past captures. Many other countries find themselves in the same
position. The Japanese have fishing fleets all over the globe; Poles and
East Germans fish in the North Sea; Portuguese fish in the Northwest
Atlantic; Spaniards fish off the coast of West Africa. The Philippines,
Ghana, Nigeria, Thailand, and others have been developing fleets with
the expectation of being able to go relatively far afield for stocks. South
Korea's fleet was initially developed with UN assistance.

An attempt to compromise between these two groups is represented
by a proposal from Australia and New Zealand. It vests in the coastal
states responsibility for and control over species that inhabit nutrient-
bearing areas adjacent to the coast. Their draft articles also vest in the
coastal states an obligation to ensure that fishing does not exceed maximum sustainable yields and to ensure that whatever restrictions they
impose on fishing do not interfere with maximum utilization of stocks
within sound conservation limits.[7] The problem with such a formulation
is that there is no mechanism for determining what constitutes maximum utilization of stocks within sound conservation limits.

6. "Draft Articles on Fisheries," UN Doc. A/AC.138/SC.II/L.38 and
Corr. 1, July 16, 1973. For a similar, but even more exclusive proposal, see
"Draft Articles on Fisheries in National and International Zones in Ocean
Space," 28 REP. III, 107 (1973; processed).

7. "Australia and New Zealand: Principles for a Fisheries Regime," 27
REP. 183–87 (1972; processed).

Most of the current proposals for expanded national jurisdiction treat the allocation of fishing rights as though it were an allocation of ownership. As noted earlier, such an approach is unlikely to give nations enough direct control over use of the fish to prevent continued overfishing. Rights to fish would be granted on the basis of propinquity, but for most stocks several nations would be granting rights to the total take, with no mechanism to ensure that the sum of rights granted would not exceed the maximum sustainable yield.

Another problem would be the lack of any way to settle differences over which species were the most important, for example, predator species or their prey. Claimants to the parts of a single marine ecological system could decide that issue differently, with the result that all might lose. In addition, such a conflict could help to spawn new technologies that might worsen ecological problems.[8]

An approach that gave control of fisheries to the states might also promote work on fish farming. Fishing today may be approaching the level of the ocean's natural productivity, estimated variously between 80 million and 2,000 million metric tons.[9] Just as the development of land farming increased the potential of land to produce food, so might fish farming. Such activity would involve altering natural ecological systems so that productivity would be concentrated in desired species, while undesired species and predators would be kept to a minimum or removed from the area farmed. Such ecological simplification could create the same kinds of international problems as air fences or techniques to attract fish.

8. Any allocation system that gives rights to stocks before they are actually harvested would be likely to promote research on harvesting techniques that are stationary, and on techniques that work by attracting the fish to the harvesting area, rather than by attracting the fishermen to the fisheries, as is common today. Work has been done on techniques to attract fish, particularly the use of lights and electricity. Some shrimp boats now use electricity to attract shrimp out of their burrows in the bottom. Without international regulation, application of such techniques by some nations might seriously disturb the complex food webs of the ocean. Proposed developments such as air or electrical fences, designed to end traditional fish migrations, would limit the food supply of the affected species' predators. Tony Loftas, *The Last Resource* (Regnery, 1970), p. 29; and Jon L. Jacobson, "Future Fisheries—Related Technologies and the Third Law of the Sea Conference" (1973; processed).

9. A. Suda, "Development of Fisheries for Non-Conventional Species," paper given at the United Nations FAO Technical Conference on Fishery Management and Development, Technical Session III, Vancouver (February 13–23, 1973), p. 2.

The major argument against establishing national fisheries is that fish do not obey national boundaries. Some fish move parallel to the shoreline, but cover long distances, crossing any seaward extension of land boundaries. Other fish swim perpendicular to shorelines, some going far beyond the 200 miles now advocated by many countries as the range of their fishing jurisdiction. In some areas, the fish swim in large circles, as for example the herring in the North Sea, which spend part of their life cycle off the coast of Holland, part of it off the coast of England, and part near Scandinavia. One very important determinant of the swimming patterns of fish seems to be the patterns of ocean currents. These currents hardly ever correspond with seaward extensions of terrestrial boundaries. All over the globe, many exploitable stocks do not remain wholly within the territorial waters of a single country during their life cycles. Some of the most prolific and heavily fished regions of the world—the Georges Bank in the northwest Atlantic, the Humboldt Current in the east central Pacific, the Yellow Sea, and others—involve stocks that swim through the waters of several countries.

Regional Fisheries Commissions

Most regions already have some form of regional fishing agency. These agencies were established largely to develop fisheries in regions where fish were underutilized. Unfortunately, with only a few exceptions, they have been unsuccessful in preventing depletion or pressures to overfish. Fundamentally, the reason for their lack of success is their failure to allocate fishery rights prior to actual catches. If fishing grounds or particular stocks are not closed off, even if the signatory countries obey all the necessary guidelines for preserving a stock, other nations, such as the USSR and Japan, with their world-ranging fleets, can come in to harvest where the signatories abstained.

Regional fisheries commissions, like most other international institutions, have not yet been granted either the authority or the resources to do as much as might be done. Their budgets are small, ranging from $8,000 to $754,000, and do not allow much room for effective research, regulation, or enforcement. With few exceptions, the commissions meet only once a year. This prevents timely action and assumes a static environment, which is, of course, contrary to the needs of changing fishery situations.[10]

10. Albert W. Koers, *International Regulation of Marine Fisheries: A Study of Regional Fisheries Organizations* (London: Fishing News [Books] Ltd., 1973), pp. 149, 165.

Most fisheries commissions can only make recommendations, which are not binding on member states. There are six commissions, mostly in the Atlantic Ocean, and their recommendations become binding on all member countries who do not object to them within a specified period. In the few commissions that are authorized by their charters to make binding rules, decisions require a unanimous vote, and the membership is very small—e.g., the North Pacific Fur Seal Commission (four members); the Mixed Commission for Black Sea Fisheries (three members); the International Pacific Salmon Fisheries Commission (two members); and the Soviet-Japanese Fishing Commission (two members).

Where supposedly binding rules have been agreed to, enforcement is usually by the state under whose flag the fishing boats operate. Several of the commissions with limited membership, however, have gone so far as to authorize officials of any member country to search and seize offending vessels on the high seas.

The international commissions are not even given adequate authority to collect basic data on the status or potential of stocks. Only the Inter-American Tropical Tuna Commission, the International Pacific Halibut Commission, and the International Pacific Salmon Fisheries Commission employ staff for research (Canada and the United States are the only members of the last two commissions). All others rely on data from the participating member states.

The picture can be summed up in the words of the *Report on Regulatory Fishery Bodies* of the Food and Agriculture Organization of the United Nations (FAO), presented in 1972 to the UN Committee on the Peaceful Use of the Seabed and the Ocean Floor Beyond the Limits of National Jurisdiction: "Regulatory fishery bodies do not possess supranational powers and the conservation measures they formulate and adopt are not directly binding on individual fishermen without legislative action being taken to this effect by member countries. In fact, these measures are seldom binding on member countries themselves."[11]

Strengthened International Management

Some combination of national fisheries and regional commissions is likely to be the international community's dominant response to the overfishing, economic waste, and international conflict associated with

11. "UN FAO Department of Fisheries Report on Regulatory Fishery Bodies," FAO Fisheries Circular 138, FID/c/138 (Rome, 1972; processed), pp. 12–13. For details on the various regional commissions, see also FAO Fisheries Circular 139, FID/c/139 (Rome, 1972; processed).

the regime that allows open access to the resources of the oceans. But this compromise cannot significantly ease those problems, unless it is informed by a concept of shared responsibility, which can be elaborated in a set of basic principles, institutional imperatives, and policy guidelines for internationally managing the ocean's living resources.

BASIC PRINCIPLES. Because the living resources of the ocean are shared, any group with management authority or exploitation rights over a portion of these resources should be considered a trustee of the only real owners, the international community. This means that any limited-member community cannot claim absolute ownership rights to any of the ocean's living resources that happen to lie within its jurisdiction. This principle should apply whether it is deemed that the fish resources are owned by the entire world, or whether ownership is divided among the large regional groups around the major oceans.

Delegation of management authority (which subsumes authority to allocate exploitation areas and harvesting quotas) to particular communities should be based on the communities' technical and political competence to implement conservation measures. Moreover, the appropriate scope of management authority should be defined by the unique ecological characteristics of the species encompassed.

INSTITUTIONAL IMPERATIVES. The controlling guidelines for implementing the above principles should be established by a Global Fisheries Commission, an institution with universal membership. One of the most important responsibilities of this commission would be to appoint a nonpolitical, scientific board to determine levels of maximum sustainable yield for specific stocks or species. The Global Fisheries Commission should absorb those services of the FAO that deal with fish. Where necessary, it should empanel continuing and ad hoc groups of experts to determine any other conservation requirements for various species (including those whose management is delegated to local and regional commissions).

National and regional fishing commissions should have direct authority over conservation and over the allocation of fishing quotas. The Global Fisheries Commission should have the authority to delegate management authority to particular countries or to groups of countries that want to share management functions in regional or functional commissions. Such bodies would also be primarily responsible for resolving disputes and determining the facts of any case in litigation. Within the controlling guidelines established by the Global Fisheries Commission, the local or functional commissions should have the authority to set their own rules and regulations. The Global Fisheries Commission would have direct management and allocation authority for such highly migratory species as tuna and whales, as well as for fish in internationalized areas such as the Antarctic.

POLICY GUIDELINES. All states should commit themselves to abide by certain specific processes for the allocation of exploitation rights and for the settlement of disputes. A treaty should also provide for countries to abide by limits on maximum sustainable yield, as determined by a non-political, scientific institution. In addition to establishing the institutional pattern and committing nations to certain procedures, the treaty would establish which countries belong in which regions, if regional ownership were decided upon. This determination need not require a country to belong to only one region. If historic use far from a country's shores is considered a legitimate claim upon a stock, a nation with historic rights could be considered part of the region involved.

The regional bodies should allocate to nations a *percentage* of the scientifically determined, maximum sustainable yield. This would help reduce political pressure on the determination of maximum sustainable yields—in most cases no state could unilaterally improve its take by a change in the yield limit. The allocations should be infrequently rene-gotiated (like a long-term lease). The recipients of such allocations should be free to sublease their exploitation rights or to reserve them solely for their own nationals, even if this means that some stocks would be underexploited. Subleasing of exploitation rights would not alter membership and voting rights in either the regional or global commissions.

The need for enforcement measures might be lessened by instituting a mandatory insurance fund, to which each state must contribute in order to receive a quota. If a vessel violated the regulations, once the violation was proved, the insurance would compensate nonviolating states. The flag state of the offending vessel would have to reimburse the fund for the money paid out. If the offending state declined to re-imburse the fund, its allocation would be rescinded.

In sum, because of the wide interdependencies among the ocean's living resources, attempts to conserve fish by strengthening national management within demarcated coastal zones will be inadequate. We therefore recommend strengthening existing regional fishing commissions and establishing new ones to make binding allocations of stocks among the countries of a region. Allocations should be made in the form of an explicit percentage of the maximum sustainable yield of that stock, a level that would be determined by a nonpolitical, scientific board attached to a global fisheries commission. The global commission would manage directly highly migratory species such as whales and tuna, and the living resources of Antarctica.

CHAPTER FIVE

Offshore Oil and Gas Exploitation

The exploration for and exploitation of oil and gas at progressively greater depths and distances offshore has been an important catalyst to the revision of the traditional open access law of the sea. Thus far, revisions have been mainly in the form of unilateral extensions of national jurisdiction by coastal states over all petroleum resources in their adjacent continental shelves. As more and more countries have asserted such jurisdiction, however, the inadequacy of the unilateral approach has become evident, for many potential hydrocarbon deposits lie in areas claimed by several states. Several local confrontations have already occurred over some of these deposits. The problem is compounded by the fact that the proliferation of petroleum installations is often in coastal areas that are at the same time experiencing a rapid expansion of other uses. Attempts to resolve this problem reflect the contemporary debate over the future international economic order. Proposed solutions range from schemes to share internationally some of the revenues from offshore petroleum production to international rules and procedures for protecting the security of investments in capital equipment.

The United States began the process of unilaterally grabbing control of offshore petroleum resources in 1945, when President Truman proclaimed "that natural resources of the sub-soil and sea-bed of the continental shelf beneath the high seas but contiguous to the coasts of the U.S." were henceforth "subject to the jurisdiction and control" of the U.S. government.[1] By 1958, on the eve of the First United Nations Law

1. "Proclamation Concerning United States Jurisdiction over Natural Resources in Coastal Areas and the High Seas," *Department of State Bulletin*, vol. 13 (September 30, 1945), pp. 484–87.

of the Sea Conference, twenty countries had made similar unilateral claims to jurisdiction over their adjacent continental shelves. The 1958 Conference did little but endorse such unilateralism, according coastal states sovereignty over the seabed and subsoil out to the limits of their capabilities to exploit the natural resources of the continental shelf.[2]

Because technological capabilities for deep-sea drilling were still rather limited in the late 1950s, the open-ended writ for coastal state jurisdiction contained in the Continental Shelf Convention occasioned little international controversy. But continual technological refinements in the field of mineral extraction, combined with the growing worldwide demand for petroleum, have made all countries vitally interested in who controls which hydrocarbon resources of the seabed, and what international rules are to constrain their exploitation.

Extent and Distribution of Hydrocarbon Resources

The sea floor is still very much a geologic frontier, and little is known about its history or dynamics; but enough has already been discovered and surmised about its hydrocarbon deposits to make it the scene of the "black gold rush of the 1970s." Lewis G. Weeks estimates that there are 2.3 trillion barrels of petroleum ultimately extractable from beneath the sea.[3] Estimates of future oil production show offshore sources providing 30 to 40 percent of the world's supply by 1980, and up to 50 percent by the year 2000.

Almost every coastal state has adjacent offshore areas that may contain substantial amounts of undersea petroleum. The continental margins, because of their thick layers of sediments, and small ocean basins are the primary sources.[4]

Serious search for oil in the North Sea began in 1964, but the first

2. Convention on the Continental Shelf, Art. 1, 15 U.S.T. 471, T.I.A.S. 5578.

3. *Ocean Industry,* vol. 9 (April 1974), p. 212.

4. The following sketch of offshore hydrocarbon potential is based largely on John P. Albers, "Offshore Petroleum: Its Geography and Technology," in John King Gamble, Jr., and Giulio Pontecorvo, eds., *Law of the Sea: The Emerging Regime of the Oceans* (Ballinger, 1973), pp. 293–310; and *Long Range Forecast of Activities in the Marine Environment With Implications for Planning Coast Guard Search and Rescue Operations* (Washington: National Planning Association for the U.S. Coast Guard, February 1971), pt. 3, chap. 8.

major oil discoveries were made in 1970. Within the next three years, five giant oil fields were discovered. Estimates of the North Sea oil potential now range from 40 billion to 150 billion barrels—more than twice the reserves of Kuwait.

Deposits of very large size also may surround the North American continent, from the Gulf of Alaska and the Canadian Arctic waters to the Atlantic continental margin.

Geophysical maps indicate that the Caribbean Sea and the Gulf of Mexico contain vast, unexploited oil deposits. Sites in water up to 2,000 feet in depth have already been licensed off Trinidad-Tobago. Lake Maracaibo has Venezuela's richest oil fields, and new deposits have recently been discovered in the Gulf of Venezuela. There are also large deposits on the South American continental shelf, off the coasts of southern Brazil, Argentina, and southern Chile.

Large sedimentary basins are located along the West African continental margins, and there is much exploratory activity off the coast of Nigeria.

The Mediterranean Sea is thought to have considerable oil, and the pace of exploration is now accelerating. Oil was discovered in the Aegean Sea in 1973, and immediately became a source of contention between Greece and Turkey.

Australia, which until a few years ago imported all its oil, is in the process of becoming self-sufficient as a result of offshore production. The northwest Australian shelf also has large natural gas deposits.

Much exploratory activity is now under way on most of the continental shelf areas of the Far East. The seabed between Taiwan and Japan is thought to house one of the richest oil reservoirs in the world. Hydrocarbon deposits in the South China Sea were apparently part of the reason China grabbed the Paracel Islands from South Vietnam in January 1974. Indonesia's margins, especially on the extensive Sunda shelf, appear to have a large potential of both oil and gas.

The USSR has been actively exploring the shelves in the Baltic Sea and in the Arctic waters of the Barents and Kara seas. The latter area is alleged to contain about half of the USSR's total potential offshore gas reserve.

Finally, even the farther reaches of the seabed, beyond what is conventionally thought to be the continental margin, may be saturated with hydrocarbons. Ocean scientists are now exploring signs of significant deposits on the deep ocean floor where the continents may once have extended.

Problems of Jurisdiction and Allocation

The geographic and geologic features of hydrocarbon deposits in the seabed have affected the pattern of competition for access to them, and have given rise to special allocation problems. Most of the exploitable hydrocarbon resources are on continental margins, but there is substantial disagreement among the coastal states on the objective criteria for dividing the margins. There is also disagreement over how to allocate petroleum pools that may traverse national jurisdictions. A number of current conflicts reflect these inherent difficulties.

The conflicting interests of Greece and Turkey over the oil in the area of the Aegean Sea between them has led to confrontations in which both countries have put their armed forces on alert. The Turks have been challenging Greek assertions of sole rights to this portion of the shelf. Typically, the Turks will sail a survey vessel into the area accompanied by a naval escort, whereupon the Greeks will institute military alerts along the Aegean Sea and their border with Turkey in Thrace, and the Turks will reciprocate with a military alert of their own.[5]

Similar jurisdictional conflicts are brewing in Asian waters. China insists that the continental shelf is a natural extension of the continent (meaning China), and has accordingly challenged as an infringement of Chinese sovereignty the Japanese-Korean agreement to develop jointly the oil between Kyushu Island and the southern tip of the Korean Peninsula. Both China and Japan object to Taiwan's unilateral drilling concessions to oil companies in the area of the Senkaku Islands between Taiwan and Okinawa. China's military *fait accompli* in taking over the Paracel Islands in 1974 was a warning to countries immediately bordering the South China Sea—North Vietnam, South Vietnam, Malaysia, the Philippines, Taiwan—that they would need to clear it with China before attempting to exploit the resources of the seabed in this area.[6]

5. See, for example, "Turkey, Greece Alert Forces in Dispute Over Aegean Oil," *Washington Post*, May 31, 1974.

6. Fox Butterfield, "Now for Far East Oil Disputes," *New York Times*, February 17, 1974; Thomas R. Ragland, "A Harbinger: The Senkaku Islands," *San Diego Law Review*, vol. 10 (May 1973), pp. 664–91; *Ocean Industry*, vol. 9 (April 1974), p. 182; *Oil and Asian Rivals: Sino-Soviet Conflict; Japan and the Oil Crisis*, Hearings before the Subcommittee on Asian and Pacific Affairs of the House Foreign Affairs Committee, 93:1 and 2 (GPO, 1974), pp. 1–98.

The countries bordering the North Sea have thus far avoided such intense jurisdictional conflicts, having apportioned most of the shelf among them in the mid-1960s before they had reason to suspect how rich it was in hydrocarbon resources. Even so, the Federal Republic of Germany objected to the method used to delimit the boundaries— drawing a median line between countries equidistant from points along their coastlines—because of the Federal Republic's concave coastline. The North Sea boundary line between the German, Dutch, and Danish zones was determined by the World Court in 1969, and in subsequent bilateral negotiations essentially in favor of the Federal Republic.[7] Further north, however, some potentially contentious jurisdictional determinations remain unsettled. The decisions of the 1960s left open the question of how far seaward to extend jurisdictions of the United Kingdom, Iceland, the Greenland territories of Denmark, and Norway— a question whose answers are also of major interest to the USSR.[8]

Even if the issue of jurisdiction over contested portions of the continental margins were resolved, some potential for dispute would still exist because of the geologic nature of oil deposits. Oil and gas form in pools, which are completely enclosed and under pressure. When a well is drilled into such a pool at any point, the previous level of pressure is reduced elsewhere in the pool. This in turn increases the extraction costs to others who wish to tap the same pool. Thus, Norway has had to develop its portion of the Ecofisk pool in the North Sea at a faster rate than it may have wished, because England was moving ahead in its part of the pool.

Conflicts with Other Ocean Uses

The increasing offshore exploitation of oil and gas is coming into conflict with other uses of the same ocean space. For the next decade, most offshore oil is likely to be extracted from areas close to shore,

7. Jon McLin, *Resources and Authority in the North-East Atlantic: Part I, The Evolving Politics and Law of the Sea in Northern Europe,* American University Field Staff, West Europe Series, vol. 8, no. 5 (1973), p. 6.

8. Overlapping Norwegian and Soviet claims to the continental shelf under the Barents Sea involve issues of strategic importance to both countries: rights to the hydrocarbon resources and transit privileges for the Soviet fleet based in Murmansk. See Christopher S. Wren, "Moscow and Oslo Open Arctic Talks," *New York Times,* November 26, 1974.

where the most fish live, where commercial shipping converges, and where the sea up to now has offered the greatest recreational and aesthetic enjoyments. The intensification of offshore oil production impinges on these other uses by compounding the risks of pollution and adding to the congestion of shipping lanes.

Oil pollution can occur at any stage in the production of oil once a well has been drilled into an oil pool. Both exploratory and production wells are susceptible to blowouts if the pressure containing the oil has not been correctly estimated. This kind of accident can release large quantities of oil into the ocean in a short period. Despite the publicity with which such episodes are greeted, they may not be responsible for the largest amounts of oil that offshore production puts into the ocean, for such blowouts usually can be stopped before substantial ecological damage occurs.

Transportation of oil from the production wells to the shore for refinement appears to pose the more serious hazard for spills. The two forms of transit, pipelines and barges, each involve special risks. Pipelines, however, are likely to be less polluting than barges. Pipelines are either buried in the sediments of the sea floor or laid on top of it, where they may severely conflict with bottom-dragging operations or large fishing nets. In addition to reducing the effectiveness of these operations, their interference can sometimes cause pipelines to break, spilling their contents.

When barge transportation is used, oil is first accumulated and stored at the platforms or in large tanks on the sea floor. The barges are then loaded at sea, with risk of spillage particularly due to human error. The barges then must be emptied at the shore with similar risks. The barges also can pollute the ocean during the blasting and cleaning operations they must perform, which are similar to the cleaning procedures of oil tankers.

Conflict between the use of ocean space for oil extraction and for shipping can also occur at various stages in the extraction process. Seismic surveys, which are typically the first step in exploring for new deposits, themselves create little if any interference with shipping, beyond the fact that seismic survey vessels may add marginally to congested navigation lanes. Exploratory drilling of the kind that requires stationing a vessel over a potential source area for a considerable time can interfere with normal shipping patterns, and special provisions may be required to avoid accidents. During extraction, drilling platforms of relatively permanent construction are installed on the sea floor, a single platform often servicing more than fifty wells. In a given hydrocarbon field there may be numerous multiple drilling systems of this sort that can indeed pose navigational hazards to tankers, freighters, and fishing boats. The dangers of oil spills from collisions or blowouts are substantial.

Landing extracted oil by barge, in addition to the intrinsic risks and spills described above, can add a particularly large burden to the navigational use of a coastal area, as, for example, in the Georges Bank area of the Atlantic coast.

The equipment thus used in the exploitation of offshore petroleum increases the difficulties of maintaining safe navigational patterns, even in relatively calm ocean areas like the Persian Gulf. In the stormy waters of the North Sea—the site of one-tenth of all accidents in the ocean and half of all shipping collisions—the dangers are compounded. Accommodating the multiple users of the North Sea poses problems enough apart from petroleum exploitation. Rich in fish, and therefore dense with fishing boats from all of Europe, the North Sea is also the water highway between the major ports of Europe and a critical navigational route for navies. Tourism and recreational industries further contribute to its congestion. Add to all of this the need to protect the one hundred or more major petroleum installations expected to be in place by 1980, and the scope of the management problem becomes evident.[9]

Distributional Issues

Ocean hydrocarbons, like all ocean resources, have become one element of many in the global disputes over how the world's resources and income should be divided up among nations. In the debate on ocean hydrocarbon exploitation, the issue of distribution comes to the fore in discussions of security of investments and of revenue sharing.

Most developing coastal states insist upon complete sovereignty over the terms under which they will allow companies to come in and exploit the resources. Because of the importance of nationalist ideologies in the politics of the developing countries, no government can hope to stay in power if it can be branded as a tool of the multinational oil corporations.

9. Tony Loftas, "The Threat to Europe's Oil Fields," *New Scientist*, vol. 63 (August 29, 1974), pp. 516–19.

The international oil companies, for their part, want some restraints on nationalization of investments and on changes in the rules of the game after companies have begun operations. If there is no security of investment, oil companies are likely to stay out of waters held by the most volatile countries, lowering the total amount extracted and raising the price. How these disagreements are settled can affect the quantity and price of oil in future years.

The new importance of issues of international distribution is also reflected in proposals that the oil exploiters share some of their revenues with the rest of the international community. The 1970 U.S. draft treaty proposed revenue sharing in the "trusteeship zones," which that draft had offered as alternative zones of national economic sovereignty. The United States said it was willing to share some unspecified portion of its oil and gas revenues in exchange for other objectives it hoped to gain in renegotiating the Law of the Sea. Many of the countries that would have to contribute revenues under the U.S. plan, however, are themselves part of the nationalistic coalition of developing nations that is attempting to extend the sovereignty of coastal states over their continental margins, and they are balking at any international claim over the resources.

Requirements of Effective Management

Effective management of the exploitation of offshore oil and gas will require arrangements that permit the resources to be exploited efficiently, with minimal potential for dangerous international conflict, and with due consideration for the rights of other users and the condition of the sea itself. The achievement of these desiderata appears to require some international restrictions upon the national management of the hydrocarbon deposits.

The first requirement is for international agreement on the criteria for allocating jurisdictional rights on the continental margins. As of this writing, this problem is being debated at the Law of the Sea Conference. There is still considerable contention over how to deal with irregularly shaped coastlines, the status of margin areas surrounding natural and artificial islands, the difference between trenches through margins and at the edges of margins, and the like. There is no way objectively to derive solutions to these issues from first principles, so their resolution must await the give and take of the bargaining process in the continuing negotiations.

The international adjustments that are required to implement agreements allocating oil pools point to the need for strengthened international machinery for resolving disputes. We do not believe that the disputes will be so frequent in this field, however, as to require a special institution for their resolution. Rather, such disputes as may arise should be funneled through the machinery for resolving disputes of existing international institutions. Our preference would be that issues of oil allocation between countries be handled by a comprehensive ocean authority.

Transregional or global forums and institutions may be the best place to resolve disputes between the hydrocarbon exploiters and other users and to allocate the externalities, especially the costs of pollution. International navigation standards and traffic patterns are likely to be formulated by a global institution like IMCO, as are the minimal antipollution standards. Similarly, management of international fisheries is likely to be the responsibility of regional commissions whose jurisdictions are not congruent with regions of hydrocarbon exploitation, and of global authorities for highly migratory species. The reconciliation of the diverse needs of the hydrocarbon exploiters with these other interests, therefore, will frequently need to be accomplished in forums that represent them all. This is the principal rationale for the comprehensive ocean authority proposed in chapter 8.

One possible approach to the controversies over sharing revenues from hydrocarbon exploitations is that the notion of geographical equity could be combined with the notion of income distribution equity to determine the amount of revenue a particular coastal state would share with the international authority. Rates paid to the international community would increase positively with exploitation activities farther from shore, but these would be moderated by a country's ability to pay, as determined by some index of economic development such as per capita gross national product (GNP).[10]

If revenue sharing is adopted, the idea of increasing revenues, or economic rent, paid to the international community and decreasing the amount paid to national authorities, as oil drilling is undertaken farther

10. Kanenas (a pseudonym), "Wide Limits and 'Equitable' Distribution of Seabed Resources," *Ocean Development and International Law Journal,* vol. 1 (Summer 1973), p. 148.

from shore, strikes us as sound. But if tax rates increase also with GNP, those most capable of exploiting important new ocean-based sources of petroleum may be deterred, and the most inefficient producers encouraged to drill, thereby further increasing the price. It would be better, we believe, to rely on formulas for redistributing revenues to achieve equity of income distribution.

CHAPTER SIX

Hard Mineral Exploitation of the Deep Seabed

The existence of small nodules of metal on the ocean floor has been known since the 1870s, when the British ship *Challenger* dredged them up from the deep seabed of the Pacific Ocean. Composed mainly of manganese, with varying amounts of other minerals, the nodules remained primarily objects of scientific curiosity until after the Second World War, when new techniques of undersea photography revealed vast concentrations of them, with densities of as much as 100,000 tons per square mile. The possibility that many of the deposits might contain commercially marketable quantities of minerals for which there was growing industrial demand stimulated exploratory work and scientific analysis in the late 1950s and early 1960s.

The Ocean Floor Becomes Part of International Politics

In the mid-1960s, statesmen began to consider the economic and political implications of the potential wealth on the ocean floor. President Lyndon Johnson asserted in 1966: "under no circumstances . . . must we ever allow the prospects of rich harvests and mineral wealth to create a new form of colonial competition among the maritime nations. We must be careful to avoid a race to grab and hold the lands under the high seas. We must ensure that the deep seas and the ocean bottoms are, and remain, the legacy of all human beings."[1] Johnson's

1. "Remarks at the Commissioning of the Research Ship *Oceanographer*," July 13, 1966, in *Public Papers of the Presidents of the United States: Lyndon B. Johnson, 1966*, vol. 2 (GPO, 1967), p. 724.

statement reflected the concern of U.S. corporations planning to become active in this field that preferred locations not be appropriated by others, and that a regime of open access be maintained, pending agreed rules for exploitation.

In 1967, the terms of the growing international dialogue shifted as the Maltese Ambassador to the United Nations, Dr. Arvid Pardo, called for a treaty to assure that the resources of the deep seabed, being mankind's "common heritage," would be exploited by the international community for its own benefit.[2] Heretofore, the notion of international common property in ocean resources was used to justify open access to such property and its free use by all members of the international community. Pardo turned the concept around, insisting that the international community's common ownership of the resources of the deep seabed meant that the international community, acting through international institutions, should govern the exploitation of the resources and reap the rewards, and that any exploitation of the deep seabed not authorized by the international community was illegitimate.

Most developing countries enthusiastically endorsed the Pardo interpretation, stimulated in the main by inflated expectations of vast mineral wealth on the ocean floor waiting to be exploited. Although initially opposed by those countries that were developing technological capabilities for deep-sea mining (primarily the United States, the USSR, France, the United Kingdom, and Japan), a majority of UN members espoused so enthusiastically the concept of an international authority for the deep seabed that the United States and other maritime powers soon calculated that if they made some concessions on this issue they might be able to secure concessions from the UN majority on navigation rights. Such a calculation evidently underlay the 1970–71 proposals of the administration of Richard Nixon for an international authority to govern the seabed. It also explains why the major champion within the United States government for such an international regime was the Department of Defense.[3] Similarly, the maritime powers' perceived need (and opportunity) to court the developing-country majority on this issue explains the nearly unanimous vote in the General Assembly on December 17, 1970, in favor of the Declaration of Principles Governing the Sea-Bed and the Ocean Floor, and the Subsoil Thereof, beyond the

2. UN Doc. A/C.1/PV 15/5, November 1, 1967; UN Doc. A/C.1/PV 15/6, November 1, 1967, pp. 1–3.

3. See Ann L. Hollick, "Seabeds Make Strange Politics," *Foreign Policy,* no. 9 (Winter 1972–73), pp. 148–70.

Limits of National Jurisdiction. This vague but revolutionary declaration affirmed:

The [area] beyond the limits of national jurisdiction [whose spatial boundaries remained undefined], as well as the resources of the area, are the common heritage of mankind.

The area shall not be subject to appropriation by any means by States or persons, natural or juridical, and no State shall claim or exercise sovereignty or sovereign rights over any part thereof. . . .

All activities regarding the exploration and exploitation of the resources of the area and other related activities shall be governed by the international regime to be established. . . .

The exploration of the area and the exploitation of its resources shall be carried out for the benefit of mankind as a whole, irrespective of the geographical location of States, whether land-locked or coastal, and taking into particular consideration the interests and needs of the developing countries. . . .

On the basis of the principles of this Declaration, an international regime applying to the area and its resources and including appropriate international machinery to give effect to its provisions shall be established by an international treaty of a universal character, generally agreed upon. The regime shall, *inter alia*, provide for the orderly and safe development and rational management of the area and its resources and for expanding opportunities in the use thereof, and ensure the equitable sharing by States in the benefits derived therefrom, taking into particular consideration the interests and needs of the developing countries, whether land-locked or coastal.[4]

Revolutionary as the declaration was, its rather platitudinous formulations left unresolved a number of highly contentious issues. What would be the powers of the international authority with respect to the actual exploration and exploitation activities (registration, licensing, setting of standards, allocation of mining areas, direct management of mining operations)? By what criteria would the international authority determine what was for "the benefit of mankind as a whole" and how a compromise was to be reached between the general benefit and "the interests and needs of the developing countries" (a phrase that is also capable of numerous conflicting interpretations)? How should the decisionmaking processes of the international machinery be structured—control by universal plenary bodies in which all nations would have voting equality; special councils dominated by the technologically advanced countries; decentralization of control to regional bodies or corporate consortia; requirements for unanimous decisions, which would assure vetoes, or provisions for majority rule, which would facilitate supranational decisions?

At this writing, answers to these questions are being sought through

4. UN General Assembly Res. 2749 (XXV), December 17, 1970.

the give and take of the international negotiating process centered on the Law of the Sea Conference. Yet the economic and political implications of alternative regimes are significantly predetermined by the nature of the mineral resources on the ocean floor and the basic technical and economic factors constraining their exploitation. Before attempting to evaluate alternative regimes, a further elaboration of the characteristics of the manganese nodules and of the developing nodule-mining industry is in order.

Characteristics and Exploitability of the Manganese Nodules

Manganese nodules are small, potato-sized objects continuously being formed in the sediment processes of the oceans, and located on the deep ocean bed. Although they are a renewable resource (over the long term) and are found in numerous parts of the major oceans, they are still a scarce resource from a commercial perspective, for their chemical composition and density vary from place to place. Commercially, their most important elements are nickel, copper, cobalt; their other elements with commercial value are aluminum, iron, zinc, molybdenum, and vanadium. Nodules with the highest percentages of nickel and copper (approximately 2 percent each) are found in parts of the Pacific Ocean. In addition to varying metallurgically, manganese nodules also vary in the density with which they are found on the ocean floor. Unlike land-based ores, manganese nodule deposits lie in a single layer on the surface of the ocean floor, and have virtually no depth. The density can vary widely, with average densities ranging from 0.5 to 3.0 pounds (wet) per square foot. An average density of two pounds of wet nodules per square foot is held to be necessary for successful mining. Most companies known to be prospecting for the nodules are concentrating their searchers in a relatively narrow band of the Pacific lying roughly within the area bounded by 17° south, 17° north, 180° west, and the west coasts of the American continents. Even within this area, however, the density and conditions of the sea floor vary widely.[5]

5. Statement of Leigh S. Ratiner, *Mineral Resources of the Deep Seabed*, Hearings before the Subcommittee on Minerals, Materials, and Fuels of the Senate Committee on Interior and Insular Affairs, 93:1, pt. 1 (GPO, 1973), p. 27; F. L. LaQue, "Prospects for and from Deep Ocean Mining," *Law of the*

The technology available for exploitation further limits the number of sites that may be economically viable. There are believed to be three methods of mining, each under development by a different commercial organization. One is a pneumatic lift system, developed and tested by Deep Sea Ventures, Incorporated, which is a subsidiary of Tenneco. This type of mining rig would have to be custom-built for each actual mining site chosen, because actual elements of its design depend upon such characteristics of the mining site as depth, water velocity, and the like. The second is a continuous-line bucket system, invented by Yoshio Masuda of Japan. The third system, developed by Hughes Tool, is believed to be a hydraulic lift system, and could be an outgrowth of oil drilling technology, a Hughes specialty.[6]

All of these technologies require a relatively unimpeded ocean floor on which to operate. It must not be strewn with boulders, nor can it be broken up by rifts and valleys. The sediment layer must not be too soft to support the mining equipment. In addition, the area of the ocean under which the mine is found must not have too rough surface conditions of weather and waves, or the ships doing the mining will not be able to hold sufficiently to their courses.[7]

The total number of commercially viable sites is likely to be limited, and some of them will be more valuable than others. The number of "best" sites is almost certain to be less than the number of potential miners, when it is considered that a single mine on such a site would have to cover about 8,880 square miles to yield enough nodules over a forty-year life. (This large size is required because nodules, as noted above, have essentially no thickness, only surface area.)[8]

In sum, despite the ubiquity of manganese as a geological phenom-

---

Sea and Peaceful Uses of the Seabeds, Hearings before the Subcommittee on International Organization and Movements of the House Committee on Foreign Affairs, 92:2 (GPO, 1972), p. 67. See also written statement by T. S. Ary, in Mineral Resources of the Deep Seabed, pt. 1, p. 185.

6. For a time it was believed that the Hughes Tool Company was developing a hydraulic lift technology for mining the nodules. It is now unclear whether Hughes has or will enter this industry. See "CIA Salvage Ship Brought Up Part of Soviet Sub Lost in 1968," New York Times, March 19, 1975.

7. J. E. Flipse, M. A. Dubs, and R. J. Greenwald, "Pre-Production Manganese Nodule Mining Activities and Requirements," in Mineral Resources of the Deep Seabed, Hearings, pt. 1, pp. 625–81.

8. Ary, in Mineral Resources of the Deep Seabed, Hearings, pt. 1, p. 186.

enon, commercially valuable deposits will be rare. It is likely that there will be a scarcity of the best mine sites.

The Nodule Industry

The mining of manganese nodules appears unlikely to be an openly competitive industry. While there are currently more than twenty-five firms expressing an interest in mining, only a few are actually likely to mine. The number of mines will probably be even less, as some companies are likely to form consortia or joint ventures for this endeavor.[9] The major reason for such a contraction in numbers is the high capital cost of a mining venture.

The high capital costs depend in part upon the form of processing to be employed. There seem to be at least two alternatives: the sulfate-roast method and the hydrogen chloride method. The first method apparently results in slightly lower percentages of metal recovery than the second, but has been in commercial use for nickel recovery from ores mined on land. This is apparently the process Kennecott will use. The sulfate-roast method of processing yields copper, cobalt, and nickel, along with much smaller quantities of several other minerals. Apparently it can also yield manganese oxide, but it is unclear whether the manganese will be utilized. In general, the sulfate-roast method is referred to as a three-metal recovery system. The hydrogen chloride method, referred to as a four-metal recovery system, was developed by Deep Sea Ventures and has been used successfully at a pilot plant. It reportedly yields 98 percent recovery of minerals, and yields manganese as a pure metal. Moreover, according to testimony submitted in June 1972, this method can yield marketable quantities of zinc, molybdenum, and vanadium.[10]

Estimates have varied in the past, but there seems to be an emerging consensus on capital costs and size of operation: $250 million to $400

9. For a partial listing of the companies, including some that are already members of consortia, see Arnold J. Rothstein and Raymond Kaufman, "The Approaching Maturity of Deep Ocean Mining—The Pace Quickens," in ibid., pp. 202–04, 215.

10. Statement by N. W. Freeman, in *Development of Hard Mineral Resources of the Deep Seabed*, Hearings before the Subcommittee on Minerals, Materials, and Fuels of the Senate Committee on Interior and Insular Affairs, 92:2 (GPO, 1972), p. 74.

million for mining operations yielding either 1 million or 3 million tons of nodules.[11] The larger tonnage is for an operation that does not recover manganese. Such an operation apparently requires several ocean installations for each processing plant.

Estimates released recently by representatives of the companies involved in nodule mining indicate that operating costs per ton are declining over the range of tonnages under consideration.[12] For output of 1 million tons of nodules, Rothstein and Kaufman show operating costs ranging from $55 to $73 per ton. For output of 3 million tons per year, they estimate operating costs to be between $35 and $54 per ton. The estimate of a Kennecott spokesman was between $21 and $30 per ton for a venture mining 3 million tons of nodules per year.[13]

Revenue and Market Impact

Although the capital cost is high, the estimated rate of return on the investments also appears to be high. The revenue estimates depend primarily upon assumptions about world demand for manganese, cobalt, nickel, and copper, and how prices would be affected by the new ocean-based supplies.

Manganese

Most manganese in use today is used either as ore or as ferromanganese, and almost all is used in the production of steel. A small amount of pure manganese metal (electrolytic manganese) is produced and used; in 1970, consumption of manganese metal amounted to about 2 percent by weight of all manganese consumed. The processes for extracting manganese from nodules will yield manganese either as metal or as manganese oxide. Manganese would be a substitute for manganese ore in steel production. Manganese metal would result from the four-metal mining system, manganese oxide from the three-metal system. It is unclear whether the production of manganese oxide is economical,

11. Statement by Ratiner in *Mineral Resources of the Deep Seabed*, Hearings, pt. 1, p. 45.

12. Rothstein and Kaufman in ibid., p. 217.

13. Statement by Marne A. Dubs, in *Marine Industries: Problems and Opportunities*, Proceedings of the Ninth Annual Conference of the Marine Technology Society (Washington: MTS, 1973), p. 259.

however, and most discussions of the revenue potential of a recovery system that processes 3 million tons per year do not include it.

The manganese metal output from one nodule mining operation capable of producing 1 million tons a year would be ten times the U.S. consumption of manganese metal in 1970. Clearly, the price would fall from the 1970 level. According to Wayne Smith, manganese metal can successfully substitute in some steel production for high-carbon ferromanganese and yield a slightly better steel.[14] The substitution is not likely to be pound for pound, that is, one pound of pure metal replacing one pound of ferromanganese. Because the total manganese content of the steel would not be changed, the substitution is likely to be one pound of pure metal for one pound of contained manganese in ferromanganese. As ferromanganese averages about 75 percent manganese, the substitution would be roughly one pound of pure metal for one and one-third pounds of ferromanganese. On this basis, the output from a million tons of nodules would amount to 21 percent of the U.S. consumption of high-carbon ferromanganese in 1970. The implication is that the price of manganese metal relative to that of ferromanganese would fall, perhaps to a level reflecting merely the differences in manganese content. Moreover, the price of high-carbon ferromanganese might fall slightly because of the greatly expanded supply of it and manganese metal.

Cobalt

The price of cobalt would be almost certain to fall once commercial mining of nodules began. This price decline, like that of manganese metal, would reflect the changed supply relationship. The cobalt extracted from one million tons of nodules would be 33 percent of U.S. consumption of cobalt. Cobalt is a close substitute for nickel in some steel production. What restrains its use is its price, which has been as much as double that of nickel in the past. The total cobalt production from a mining operation producing one million tons a year would equal roughly 1.4 percent of U.S. consumption of nickel in 1970 and 1.3 percent of U.S. consumption of nickel and cobalt combined in 1970. The impact of such increases in the supply of cobalt is thus likely to remove the price difference between nickel and cobalt, but it is not likely to have any impact upon the price level of nickel. What happens to that level depends only on the impact of the nickel content of the nodules.

14. Wayne Smith, "Economic Considerations of Deep Sea Mineral Resources" (Woods Hole Oceanographic Institution, 1972; processed).

Nickel

The impact of nodule mining on nickel prices depends upon two things: the number of mining operations, and the response of the existing nickel suppliers. A mining operation yielding one million tons a year would yield roughly 8 percent of the U.S. consumption of nickel in 1970. It would yield roughly 2 percent of world production in 1970. With proper planning and cooperation, the number of mining operations by 1980 and beyond could be kept to the number able to fulfill increases in demand since 1970 without changing prices. This would mean mining only 4 million to 6 million tons of nodules by 1980.[15] Such a situation, however, also depends upon the expansion plans of the existing nickel industry and its price response to new entrants in the field. The nickel industry is an oligopoly dominated by the International Nickel Company (INCO), and the price is set by that firm. Assuming that INCO does not respond to new entrants by lowering the price and that only a few mining operations are established (a realistic assumption, in view of the high capital cost), then the price of nickel probably will not fall.

Copper

The copper in the manganese nodules would constitute only a minor part of world copper supply. A mining operation that produced one million tons of nodules a year would yield only 0.6 percent of U.S. consumption in 1970, and only 0.1 percent of world production in 1970. Thus, it would be unlikely that the price of copper would change as a result of nodule mining.

Other Minerals

Deep Sea Ventures has testified that it would also retrieve small quantities of vanadium, molybdenum, and zinc from the nodules with its processing techniques.[16] These are probably the same minerals that are produced as by-products with the three-metal recovery system. No figures have been given on the concentrations of these minerals in the deposits Deep Sea Ventures has explored. John Mero, however, gives a

15. "Possible Impact of Sea-Bed Mineral Production in the Area Beyond National Jurisdiction on World Markets, With Special Reference to the Problems of Developing Countries: A Preliminary Assessment," UN Doc. A/AC. 128/36 (May 28, 1971), pp. 50–58.
16. Statement by Dubs, *Marine Industries*.

variety of mineral compositions for nodules dredged up in scientific voyages.[17] The maximum concentrations of these three minerals for nodules found in the Pacific Ocean were 0.11 percent vanadium, 0.08 percent zinc, and 0.15 percent molybdenum. These figures would translate into 2.2 pounds of vanadium, 1.6 pounds of zinc, and 2.9 pounds of molybdenum for each ton of nodules mined. From one million tons of nodules, the impact of all three metals on the respective metal markets is likely to be imperceptible. Only in the case of vanadium is the probable quantity a significant proportion of U.S. consumption or production; but it would amount to only 6.7 percent of total world production in 1970.

The past levels of prices for the minerals that are the expected products of a nodule mining industry seem to indicate that with present technology and costs nodule mining will be profitable only if the industry remains small enough not to cause the world price of nickel to change significantly.[18]

Conflicting Economic Interests

The two groups most concerned about the terms under which mining will occur are the technologically advanced countries with prospective capabilities to mine the nodules and less developed countries that export minerals. They disagree primarily over whether the criteria for use of the nodules should be private economic gain or international distribution. In economic terms, the issue is who should get the economic rent from mining the nodules.

The technologically advanced group that wants to be able to mine the nodules is made up of public and private companies from five industrial countries: the United States (with three interested companies, and perhaps a lead in the necessary technology), Japan, West Germany, France, and the USSR.

The U.S. companies would like to become active suppliers of the metals, particularly nickel; at present, insignificant proportions of the

17. John Mero, *The Mineral Resources of the Sea* (Elsevier, 1965), pp. 179–221.

18. For a discussion of this point, see Nina W. Cornell, "Manganese Nodule Mining and Economic Rent," *Natural Resources Journal,* October 1974.

world supply of nickel and cobalt are mined by U.S. companies.[19] But U.S. companies anticipate profits from these metals as a result of deep sea mining.

French and German mining companies have interests in this field that differ slightly from those of U.S. companies. In France, Le Nickel seeks to hold on to its world market share; its interest is thus defensive. West German companies seem to be primarily interested in the processing end of the industry.

The governments of the United States, the USSR, and Japan also hope to mine the nodules as a means of obtaining security of supply, considering that nickel, cobalt, and manganese are all vital in steel production.

At present, the United States can rely exclusively on domestic supplies only for molybdenum; all the other minerals contained in the nodules must be partially imported, and nickel and cobalt are not mined at all in the United States. While part of the U.S. manganese supply comes from mines owned at least in part by U.S. steel companies, most of it comes from Brazil and Gabon, where there is the possibility of future nationalization.

Japan is likewise dependent on foreign supplies. The USSR has abundant land resources of these minerals, but they are not all located in close proximity to its steel production in Asiatic USSR. Mining the nodules of the deep sea would be a substitute for improving the USSR's land-based transportation system.

All of these would-be miners, particularly the Americans, want exclusive rights to designated areas of the ocean floor, as current technology for nodule mining has to be custom-designed for a particular mining site and might not be reusable elsewhere. More important, exclusivity is considered necessary to recover the expenses incurred in site selection.

Designation of exclusive mining areas is being sought either through national legislation or through international treaty. Judging by the draft bills introduced on their behalf in the U.S. Congress, the miners are

19. Because of the limitation on the total size of the nodule industry caused by the nickel market, the arguments of the companies in favor of domestic legislation that they will have a measurably favorable effect on the U.S. balance of payments are false. They will supply only a small proportion of U.S. nickel consumption, and the direct effects will be too small to be of significance. In addition they will be partially offset by converse indirect effects.

willing to pay nominal lease fees for their exclusive rights, but only if both their investment and a rate of return are guaranteed. If there is to be an international regime for nodule mining, the miners would prefer only a registry system, through which, for a nominal fee, national claims to ocean areas can be recorded and respected.

The mineral exporting countries, however, fear that because the deep sea nodules might contain cobalt, copper, manganese, and nickel in proportions that differ from current patterns of supply, ocean-based production could swamp land-based production and change relative prices. Some of these countries have proposed an international authority for the deep seabed that would capture a good portion of the economic rent. The authority would itself be a mining agency, or would be responsible for regulating production in order to avoid or mitigate negative changes of the mineral prices in the world markets. Alternatively, the authority could compensate countries who suffered from sea-based competition.

Regime Alternatives for the Seabed

In view of the characteristics of the manganese nodule industry and the differing interests of various countries in nodule exploitation, it is not surprising that there remains much international disagreement on the design of an international regime for managing the deep seabed. The Law of the Sea negotiations have narrowed the range of choice. The real alternatives can be grouped in three categories.

International Registry

In order to prevent claim jumping and reduce inadvertent conflict over parts of the ocean floor, states could agree to notify the international seabed authority of their intention to explore and/or exploit a particular site (or to charter corporations to do so), and to wait for clearance from the authority before proceeding. The international authority might be designed to give virtually automatic clearance upon finding that a site was not yet being worked; alternatively, it could be given certain regulatory functions incident to its principal function as a registry. The claimants to particular sites, for example, could be required to indicate a willingness and capability to adhere to antipollution rules; they might also be required to present evidence of an actual find before being registered for exploitation, to have the appropriate technology, and to be assured of adequate financial backing. Some variants would require the registered enterprise to work at a specified rate of production. The essential feature of a registry system, however, would be its neutral character: It would lack authority to discriminate among various claimants or to deny registration on other than the specified operating requirements agreed to by member nations in advance. Thus, an international registry system would provide a very thin layer of coordination over what would be essentially an extension of the national management regime into the deep seabed.

The objections to the registry system come mainly from developing countries, which fear that it would give virtually carte blanche to a small number of technologically advanced countries and multinational corporations to stake out the seabed for their own profit. They argue that it would provide a stimulus to those currently possessing the technological know-how to register as many claims as possible before others developed the technology. Unless substantial revenue-sharing obligations were imposed on the exploiters, the developing countries contend, nothing would be left of the concept that the resources of the deep seabed are the common heritage of mankind.

International Allocation

A system in which an international institution would select the areas to be explored and exploited and grant licenses to corporations or states on the basis of internationally agreed criteria would be more in accord with the common-heritage idea. These internationally acceptable criteria might be based on considerations of equity as well as of efficiency.

There are a variety of schemes for implementing this general design. Efficiency of production is probably best served by allocating leases to sites or blocks by auction to the highest bidder, and by requiring another auction after a specified period. This would mean that virtually all of the blocks would go to the wealthiest and most technologically advanced countries and corporations. The lease payments would ensure that at least some of the economic rent would go to the international agency. The rest would go to the nodule miners and consumers.

To spread the economic rent directly among more countries, the authority could limit the number of blocks that could be auctioned off to any one country or corporation. Alternatively, it could distribute blocks at random to all the countries of the world. The latter scheme might be supplemented by a requirement that the site be worked within a specified period (or else it would be put up for auction). Most countries that lag technologically, except those that wanted to restrict mining of the seabed to protect their land-based mining industries, would in any case have incentives to sublease exploitation rights to enterprises technologically capable of handling the job in order to obtain revenues. Either of these schemes would permit more countries to share the economic rent from nodule mining, but would reduce the share going to the international authority by lowering the amount it might receive from the auctions.

Any of these international allocation systems could retain for the international authority considerable regulatory functions, which could be exercised in the course of granting or withholding leases to areas of the seabed. Lessees would hold temporary title to their assigned areas as custodians of the common heritage, bound by international rules for conservation, ecological care, and revenue distribution. Revenue could be collected for the international community from license fees, from auctions, or from taxes on the royalties from production.

An International Public Enterprise

The international institution for the seabed could itself conduct the explorations and exploitation of the minerals on the ocean floor. The deep seabed would remain undivided, and all profits from its resources would go to the international community for financing the ocean regime, other community projects, and redistribution to developing countries.

If the international institution were to be engaged directly in exploring, mining, and processing the minerals—with its own staff and equipment—it would need to be provided with a large and powerful bureaucracy. It is doubtful that the members of the international community could provide such an enterprise with sufficient functional autonomy from the international political arena to overcome the inefficiencies characteristic of international bureaucracies. These cumbersome organizational requirements would be reduced somewhat by having the international authority manage work on the deep seabed through contracts to corporations, states, and international consortia as suggested in the draft negotiating text. Even so, the prospects are slight that direct management by the international authority would be efficient, if the world's experience to date with international institutions is any guide. An attempt to install such a regime of direct management might only reduce the economic rent that might otherwise be collected by the international community.

Recommendations

Managing the deep seabed in ways that would most faithfully implement the concept that the ocean is the common heritage of mankind, maximize revenues for the international community, and yet not require a politically unworkable degree of supranationalism seems to us to point to an international authority that would lease mining sites to states or firms on the basis of competitive bidding. The international authority would also set environmental regulations and other limits on mining to prevent interference with other uses of the ocean. Leasing provisions would be designed to maximize the economic rent collected by the international authority from private corporations and states.

This leaves open an issue that has been given considerable attention, both in theory and in the Law of the Sea negotiations—namely, whether leases should go directly to the firms engaged in deep sea operations or to governments which could then contract with research or mining firms.[20]

The purported advantages of having the international authority lease exploration and exploitation blocks to national governments are: that it would lodge responsibility for regulating the research and mining activities and for collecting revenues with the only actors on the world scene with a demonstrated ability to perform such functions; that it would give developing countries a sense of sharing equitably in the seabed (assuming some means, perhaps random, were instituted to allocate blocks to countries on bases other than bidding) through management of their own blocks; that it would reduce to insignificance the ability of land-based producers to prevent other countries from mining the ocean floor; and that it would reduce the requirements for a heavy international bureaucracy.

The purported advantages to leasing directly to firms are: that it would reduce the conflicts between nations over rights to the seabed and avoid extending a crazy quilt of national jurisdictions throughout the ocean; that it would strengthen the authority of the international

20. See Evan Luard, *The Control of the Sea-bed: A New International Issue* (Taplinger, 1974), pp. 174, 218–23.

seabed regime by eliminating the thick national political and bureaucratic layer between it and those who are actually working the seabed;
that royalties would be returned directly to the international community, lessening the amount that would be siphoned off by national governments; and that it would provide for a greater degree of competition
among the companies—and, therefore, presumably efficiency—in producing the minerals, since they would be bidding against one another
for preferred sites to be leased by the international regime (in contrast to
the national leasing system, where control over the preferred sites would
be widely dispersed among the nations of the world, and the national
governments would therefore be under competitive pressure to offer the
most favorable terms to those few corporations able to conduct such
mining).

These arguments reflect differences over who should collect the economic rent. The justifications for leasing to nations appear to reflect a
desire to expand mineral production as far as possible, giving more
of the rents to companies and consumers. If the international authority
for the deep seabed leased sites directly to companies, it would maximize
the economic rent it obtained—particularly if the authority could limit
the number of sites leased. The nodule mining industry is likely for quite
some time to limit its total output to keep the price of nickel from falling,
so wide-scale leasing of sites would not necessarily lead to a very large
increase in output. It is more likely to have the pernicious effect of lowering the revenue the international authority would receive.

In short, the market for sites is likely to be a buyers' market, unless
the international authority is able to control the number of sites leased
each year. Efficient production and maximization of economic rent from
those sites would be served by putting a fixed number of sites up for
nondiscriminatory, competitive bidding. Whether companies or nations
are allowed to bid for the sites seems less important than limiting the
total number leased.

Such an international allocation and leasing system implies an international institution with two specialized bodies, perhaps three, and one
plenary body. A separate technical body composed of economists and
technologists might be established to determine the revenue potential
of ocean mining. Their evaluation would be based on estimates of the
mining capability of the firms, on site surveys, and on estimates of
changing market conditions. On these bases, it would periodically determine the location and number of sites to be auctioned. Another body

might administer the auction and leasing. Perhaps a third would redistribute leasing revenues, but this function might be retained by the plenary body. The plenary body, composed of all countries, and acting on the basis of one country, one vote, would appoint the specialized bodies and set general policies.

When decisions made by the mining authority adversely affect other ocean users, or when other users interfere with the activities of the deep seabed that are authorized by this institution, the conflicts would be referred to a comprehensive ocean authority for resolution.

CHAPTER SEVEN

Scientific Research

The clash between the traditional principle of open access to the ocean and the extension of national sovereignty is particularly sharp with respect to the prerogatives of ocean scientists. Ocean scientists argue that their unimpeded access to all parts of the oceans is vital to the accomplishment of their work. The scientists' case is based largely on the familiar notion of the physical indivisibility of the ocean. It stresses the fluidity of the waters, the mobility of sea life, and the artificiality even of the geologic divisions of the ocean (continental shelf, continental slope, ocean floor, abyssal plain). Oceanographic investigations cannot proceed effectively, they argue, if scientists are prevented from following their lines of inquiry across all artificial demarcations, especially political jurisdictions. Most governments of coastal states, on the other hand, want authority to control all activities, including scientific research, both within territorial waters and in any resource zones that may be created.

Oceanic research has also become entangled in the dispute over global issues of distribution. Coastal states of the Third World argue that scientific research off their shores has operated to the benefit—both commercial and military—of the rich countries, often at the expense of the poor countries.

In response to the growing efforts of governments to limit their activities, ocean scientists have advocated drawing a distinction between basic or pure research and applied research. The scientists are willing to accept some political controls on applied research, but they want basic research to continue unfettered. The rebuttal, particularly by spokesmen for the developing countries, is that it is often impossible to know the real purposes of research projects conducted by foreign countries.

They argue—correctly—that the actual activities and equipment used in both kinds of research are frequently indistinguishable. The big oil companies not only conduct basic research on their own, but are also perhaps better equipped than anyone else to apply effectively the results of oceanographic research conducted by others. The U.S. Navy has many projects that, by scientific definition, could be defined as basic research, but there are notorious cases of military intelligence ships of the USSR and the United States (and also of other countries) using marine science as a cloak to cover more dagger-like activities.[1]

Both sides in this debate have validity, but some compromises will have to be made if the larger public interests are to be served. The difficulty in discerning the real purpose behind some research activities stems in part from the fact that the same scientific data often reveal basic information about marine phenomena *and* improve the ability of commercial or military users to pursue their goals.

Thus, data on ocean currents can reveal information of commercial value about fish populations. Data on the movements of the earth's plates under the ocean (plate tectonics) reveal basic information about the forces within the earth and how they have shaped continents, and can also yield direct information on potential mineral sites. No less true, however, are the scientists' claims that expansion of oceanographic knowledge can serve larger public interests, and that the phenomena under study cut across political boundaries. An examination of the larger public interests at issue, and how they would be affected by various regimes, may provide a basis for suggesting an alternative to both the regime of open access favored by most scientists and the regime of prior consent demanded by most developing coastal states.

Social and Economic Values Served by Ocean Science

The scientists' case for maintaining their free access to all areas of the oceans rests on the premise that substantial international benefits result from the research in the ocean. The most important of these purported benefits are better pollution control, improved forecasting of the weather and climate, more efficient exploitation of ocean resources, and the growth of scientific knowledge itself.

1. For example, the Navy claimed that its electronic surveillance ship *Pueblo*, which was captured by North Korea, was engaged in environmental research.

Pollution Control

Probably the most important function of ocean science is its potential for adding to knowledge about the sources and impacts of ocean pollution, and thereby increasing the prospects for its control. Much remains unknown about the complex interactions of the various chemicals in the ocean—those there naturally and those injected by man—with the living matter of the oceans.

Much current research is designed to determine the effects on marine organisms of petroleum, halogenated hydrocarbons (such as DDT and PCBs), trace metals (such as mercury, cadmium, arsenic, selenium, zinc, cobalt, and antimony), and man-made nutrients (particularly inorganic phosphorous and nitrogen compounds). "It is absolutely essential," maintains John Knauss, "that we succeed in unravelling these puzzles if we are to treat the possible threat of ocean pollution in a rational, timely, and systematic way."[2]

Forecasting Weather and Climate

Much scientific research in the ocean is also aimed at increasing our understanding of global and regional patterns of the weather and climate. Improved forecasts are important for reducing loss of life and property at sea from waves, storms, and ice. Better knowledge of the interaction of meteorological and oceanographic factors is needed to anticipate the movements of hurricanes, which can inflict severe damage upon coastal states. Knowledge of changes in the patterns of ocean circulation is essential to long-range weather forecasting and warnings of impending climatic disasters.

Efficient Exploitation of Ocean Resources

Assessments of what kinds of fishing will give the maximum sustainable yield depend upon dynamic models of the life cycles of many species of fish and the interactions among species. These models need to be based on detailed biological investigations of the ocean, and on research into the patterns of ocean currents so as to be able to predict where the upwellings will occur, and thus where the fish will be.

Successful drilling for the hydrocarbon resources and hard minerals

2. John A. Knauss, "Development of the Freedom of Scientific Research Issue of the Third Law of the Sea Conference," *Ocean Development and International Law Journal,* vol. 1 (Spring 1973), p. 103.

of the sea is critically dependent upon advances in ocean geology, which in turn depend heavily upon access by oceanographers to all areas of the ocean floor and upon the ability to employ acoustical and other measuring devices.

The Expansion of Knowledge

In most Western societies, scientific activity is considered socially valuable in its own right. Widely regarded as the most powerful means at man's disposal for understanding the universe, scientific investigation has been accorded a degree of freedom from political regulation allowed few if any other human pursuits, while at the same time receiving substantial public subsidies. Even in the USSR, where education, art, philosophy, and religion are totally subservient to the needs of the state as determined by the Communist party, scientists are encouraged to determine their own lines of inquiry without having to demonstrate social utility at every step.

Marine science, being part of the overall scientific enterprise, can legitimately claim the same social value and the associated privileges and official encouragement.

The Increasing Political Control over Ocean Scientists

Until the mid-1960s, scientists were generally free to pursue their research in the oceans without having to notify or obtain the consent of governments, unless they were operating within territorial waters. The 1958 Geneva conventions concerned with the high seas, the territorial sea, and the continental shelf set forth the legal rights and obligations of states in the oceans. They included regulations for conducting scientific research. Article II of the Convention on the High Seas embraced the principle of freedom of the seas, which was generally regarded by those states then concerned with the oceans as including freedom of scientific research as recognized by the general principles of international law.[3] The Convention on the Continental Shelf prohibited "any interference with fundamental oceanographic and other

3. Convention on the High Seas, 13 U.S.T. 2312, T.I.A.S. 5200. Article II lists four specific freedoms, which are included under freedom of the high seas—navigation, fishing, laying submarine cables and pipelines, and flying over the high seas—and then refers to the other freedoms "which are recognized by the general principles of international law."

scientific research carried out with the intention of open publication." It required consent from coastal states for research concerning their continental shelf and undertaken there, but added that the coastal state could not normally refuse its consent if the request was from a qualified institution and was for "purely scientific research in the physical or biological characteristics of the continental shelf."[4]

The convention, however, did not come into effect until 1964. Informal arrangements between scientists and institutions were relied upon to facilitate access to coastal waters. For research undertaken in the territorial sea or inland waters, consent was normally required from the coastal state. Before the mid-1960s, such requests were normally granted.

Since the mid-1960s, marine scientists have seen the freedom to conduct scientific research increasingly restricted. As the technology has matured for exploiting the continental shelf beyond 200 miles, thereby extending the legal limit of the continental shelf (as provided by the 1958 Convention on the Continental Shelf, which says that the legal limit should vary with exploitability), marine scientists have been compelled to obtain consent to explore larger areas. In addition, the unilateral extension of their territorial seas to 200 miles by some coastal states has posed the difficult question for U.S. marine scientists of whether to obtain consent for conducting research within these broader territorial seas or risk damage to their vessels by coastal states.

There has been no coherent pattern for handling requests to engage in scientific research in coastal waters. Scientists have increasingly had to rely on bilateral governmental arrangements to obtain access to foreign coastal waters. The U.S. government, for example, has asked research vessels flying its flag to obtain clearances through the Department of State for research in the coastal waters of other countries. The data available, while incomplete, suggest that there have been a number of impediments to granting access for such scientific research.[5] Experi-

4. Article V, sections 1 and 8, Convention on the Continental Shelf, 15 U.S.T. 471, T.I.A.S. 5578. This provision generated legal controversy as to whether it applied to research conducted over the continental shelf but not touching the continental shelf.

5. A study of the data on requests to the Department of State from 1967–72, by Judith Kildow, indicates that there were thirty-two incidents of difficulties in refusals. According to Kildow, "A review of those incidents indicates several apparent principal causes for the difficulties—all of which have some political basis. Of the thirty-two recorded cases, military security reasons ac-

ence indicates that relying on ad hoc bilateral governmental clearances will not be sufficient for facilitating basic ocean research that is in the international interest and for accommodating the interests of coastal states that have to grant access to their coastal waters.

The 1970 General Assembly Resolution on the Seabed and Ocean Floor was less than a ringing declaration in support of freedom of scientific research. Section 10 provided that "States shall promote international cooperation in scientific research exclusively for peaceful purposes," and listed three ways in which they could promote such cooperation: by participating in international programs and encouraging cooperation in scientific research by other countries; by publishing research programs and disseminating research results; by cooperating "in measures to strengthen research capabilities of developing countries, including the participation of their nationals in research programs."[6] The U.S. Draft Convention on the International Seabed Area of August 1970 included the provisions that were later adopted in the General Assembly resolution and an additional provision stating that "each Contracting Party agrees to encourage, and to obviate interference with, scientific research."[7] This provision is more favorable to scientific research than the language of the General Assembly resolution, but it does not affirm freedom of scientific research.

The Ocean Scientists Defend Their Interests

Marine scientists have tried to influence the evolution of the regime affecting their work through various organizations, primarily the Inter-

---

counted for twelve, bureaucratic delays for nine, concern over resource exploitation for five, and six cases had strictly political or special causes." Judith A. Tagger Kildow, "Nature of the Present Restrictions on Oceanic Research," in W. S. Wooster, ed., *Freedom of Oceanic Research* (Crane, Russak and Co., 1973), p. 14.

6. Declaration of Principles Governing the Sea-Bed and the Ocean Floor, and the Subsoil Thereof, beyond the Limits of National Jurisdiction, GA Res. 2749 (XXV), December 17, 1970. The text of the resolution appears in *International Legal Materials*, vol. 10 (January 1971).

7. Draft United Nations Convention on the International Seabed Area, United Nations Committee on the Peaceful Uses of the Sea-bed and the Ocean Floor Beyond the Limits of National Jurisdiction, UN Doc. A/AC.138/25 (August 3, 1970), p. 6.

governmental Oceanographic Commission (IOC), which is linked to the United Nations Educational, Scientific, and Cultural Organization (UNESCO), and the Scientific Committee on Oceanic Research (SCOR), which is part of the International Council of Scientific Unions (ICSU).

The International Council of Scientific Unions has long been concerned with the problem of facilitating the mobility of ocean research vessels. As early as April 1964, ICSU adopted a resolution expressing concern about the potential restrictions on scientific research in the oceans. In response to the Continental Shelf Convention, ICSU adopted a resolution proposing that ICSU itself establish the criteria for acceptable ocean research. Agreements could be worked out, preferably on a regional basis, to give those conducting ocean research free access to particular areas.

The primary contribution of the ICSU to facilitating ocean scientific research has been the formation of SCOR, which has organized international oceanic research programs, in which many countries have participated. In June 1968, the SCOR Executive Committee adopted a statement supporting freedom of scientific research and denouncing the restrictions that result from expansive interpretations of the Continental Shelf Convention. But this and subsequent statements proposed by SCOR have had no discernible impact on the issue.

The Intergovernmental Oceanographic Commission has been the principal international forum for efforts to extend freedom of ocean scientific research. The IOC was formed in 1960 to promote scientific research in the oceans. It has had considerable success in intergovernmental coordination of ocean research. But it has never been able to clear with the international community measures that would facilitate access for scientific researchers to coastal waters. It has served mainly as a forum for discussion of the need to protect marine science.

Representatives of the USSR at the IOC have been, with U.S. scientists, the most vociferous champions of scientific research. In 1967, they proposed that the IOC seek approval of a general convention embodying principles for safeguarding marine scientific research. A legal working group was set up to explore this possibility, but such a convention has not been adopted. In September 1969, after a heated controversy between the developed and the developing nations, the IOC revised its statute to provide that one of its purposes was to promote freedom of scientific investigation.

The 1969 session of the IOC also brought about a fundamental change of emphasis in the role of the coastal state in marine scientific research. Resolution VI-13, "Promoting Fundamental Scientific Research," endorsed the concept of clearances from coastal states to conduct scientific research, and encouraged genuine participation by scientists from coastal states in the proposed research programs off their coasts.[8]

Until recently, marine scientists have been reluctant to press their case politically. The new response of some U.S. marine scientists, as Lauristan King has noted, is to try to become political advocates for marine science in the enlarged forum for the oceans.[9] Marine scientists now have representatives on the U.S. delegation to the Law of the Sea Conference. They have been trying to demonstrate their relevance and usefulness, and to dissociate themselves from those elements that may adversely affect their image in other countries. They have picked up the oil pollution issue, which concerns many countries, and are showing how their own research efforts can help alleviate oil pollution and other environmental pollution problems. They are beginning to engage in discourse with the developing countries, and to explore possibilities to help these countries use the oceans to appease their opposition to research in marine science.

A Possible Compromise

The challenge in determining a regime for marine research is to work out arrangements that promote scientific research beneficial to all peoples, and at the same time recognize the interest of the coastal states in controlling access to the waters off their shores, and the particular interests of the developing countries in sharing in the benefits of research. One approach might be a two-tier system to govern ocean scien-

8. The text of the resolution appears in the appendix to William T. Burke, "Marine Science Research and International Law," Law of the Sea Institute, University of Rhode Island, Occasional Paper no. 8 (September 1970; processed). For a summary of the debates on Resolution VI-13, see Report of the U.S. Delegation to the Sixth Session of the International Oceanographic Commission, Paris, September 2–13, 1969.

9. Lauristan R. King, "Oceans Policy and the Political Education of United States Marine Scientists," paper presented at the Symposium on Oceans Policymaking, American Association for the Advancement of Science, Washington, D.C., December 27, 1972.

tific research that distinguishes between kinds of *agencies* conducting the research, rather than attempting to separate so-called basic science from applied science.

Scientific research conducted, chartered, or authorized by international ocean institutions or international environmental institutions would be free of any unilateral coastal state restraints. The fact that the research was being conducted under international auspices would essentially serve as a waiver for the consent of coastal states to conduct the research off their shores. Such international research would be subject to internationally agreed upon provisions, which would make the results of the research immediately available to all states and other interested parties; would set guidelines to ensure the participation of coastal states in the research if they wished; and would provide for special technical assistance to states in interpreting the results of the research, if they so desired.

For all other scientific research, coastal states would have the right to require that researchers obtain their consent before sending vessels into their territorial seas or resource zones. This would apply to other states, to private persons, and to all corporations. Coastal states would have the right to insist on their own participation in the research activities, immediate access to the data from the research, and technical assistance in the interpretation of the data.

Such a two-tier approach probably would encourage the internationalization of all research designed to further understanding of the processes of the ocean and to preserve the marine environment.

The promotive side of such a regime would be designed to stimulate coastal developing countries to build basic and applied marine science programs. This would involve technical assistance by international organizations and developed countries in the form of education and training of local educators, scientists, and technicians; experts to examine and assist with particular problems; and provision of scientific instruments and related equipment, technical journals, and data. Assistance for such programs would need to be sustained on a long-term basis as a means of ensuring that the programs become firmly established and are resistant to periodic changes in national budgetary policies.

Effective marine science programs also require access to proprietary technologies that are available only in the international commercial sector. These may be obtained by purchase, by participation in joint ventures or similar arrangements, or by hiring experienced people as employees or consultants. Such a transfer of technology in ocean science to developing countries could be funded by requiring enterprises engaged in exploiting the marine resources in territorial waters to provide or fund such programs directly. Alternatively, if states adopt revenue sharing as the price for those wishing to exploit marine resources, some of these funds could be allocated to such programs.

Efforts might also be made to establish and expand regional multinational institutes and programs in ocean scientific research, such as, for example, the Cooperative Investigation of the Caribbean and Adjacent Regions. Regional efforts such as these could integrate the efforts in ocean research of various countries, perhaps by encouraging the participants to agree to specialize in different areas of marine science, or by establishing a marine science institute in one country that would utilize the combined resources of the region to purchase expensive equipment and support for a broad-based marine research program. The objective of this program would be to allow countries that would otherwise not have sufficient funds to establish large marine science capabilities to share in the research and training benefits and to use the institute for specific projects of national concern.

CHAPTER EIGHT

Toward a Durable Regime for the Ocean

The preceding analysis of the problems of ocean use in specific sectors—military and commercial transportation, fishing, petroleum and hard mineral exploitation, and scientific research—casts doubt on the durability of current attempts to achieve orderly management by dividing the sea into sovereign national jurisdictions. The most prevalent alternative to the nationalist approach has been sectoral. Each sector (say, commercial shipping or salmon fishing) would evolve its own rules, decision processes, and institutions. Some would require regional, others virtually global, institutionalization. This functionalist, sector-by-sector response to the dramatic increase in ocean uses, which resulted from the technological revolution after the Second World War, was championed by the U.S. government in the 1950s and 1960s. It was the basis of the initial U.S. approach to revising the law of the sea. But many of these efforts to cooperate on a functional basis, like the national management solution, have tended to be overwhelmed by the multiple interactions among ocean users.

In short, the ocean is quintessentially a realm of material interdependence—international and intersectoral interdependence. Thus, an ocean regime, to be durable, will need to provide substantial coordination and management on both international and intersectoral bases. The trend of recent years toward more and more national appropriation of the ocean, as reflected in the Law of the Sea Conference, cannot provide the basis for sensible ocean management unless it is substantially overlaid by processes of international accountability across sectors.

Summary of Sectoral Findings and Recommendations

This recapitulation of our functionally specific recommendations will underscore the inadequacy of the sectoral approach to handle the growing conflicts between different kinds of users. The discussion leads again to the question of basic regime alternatives, and points to the requirements of a comprehensive regime for management of the ocean.

Navigation—Summary

Viewed as a self-contained problem area, the navigational difficulties resulting from the proliferation of shipping, the increase in size and speed of ships, and the generally increased congestion of important waterways can be handled by negotiations and deliberations among the shippers themselves and between navies. Ship equipment and maintenance standards, maritime personnel training requirements, and navigational rules of the road typically have been formulated under the aegis of the Inter-governmental Maritime Consultative Organization (IMCO). IMCO facilitates the accountability of shippers to one another for their use of common waterways. Enforcement of IMCO conventions has been largely the responsibility of the state under whose flag a ship is chartered. The maritime interests are in the main satisfied with the IMCO-centered system for managing navigational problems, and tend to resist any limitations on use of the ocean other than those negotiated through IMCO.

Major pressures have been building up, however, to hold the shippers accountable to a wide array of public interests, and to reflect this widened accountability by giving either coastal states or international forums, in addition to IMCO, more authority over shipping standards and navigational rules. These pressures have their sources in a number of developments: the growth of transoceanic transport of petroleum, and the resultant fear that oil spills will injure ocean ecologies; increased mining, industrial, and recreational activity in coastal zones, which give interests other than shipping competitive claims to the use of ocean space; and growing reliance on sea-based weapons, military installations, and surveillance, which gives coastal and straits states a strong national security rationale for asserting control over navigation near their shores.

No longer can navigation (even through waters that are presumptively international) be taken for granted as an established right. It has come to be generally accepted that navigational rights carry with them reciprocal duties. Today the most controversial questions are not so much the substance of navigational rules, but who should be the makers and enforcers of those rules.

The trend, reflected in deliberations of the Law of the Sea Conference up to the point of this writing, is to accord coastal states competence, at least in their territorial seas, to make rules and regulations on navigational safety, including the designation of sea lanes and traffic separation schemes; the protection of coastal-zone installations; the protection of cables and pipelines; conservation of fish; preservation of the coastal environment; oceanographic research; and fiscal, customs, immigration, and health and sanitary regulations. Subject to the right of coastal states to make such rules, ships of all states are to enjoy the right of innocent passage through the territorial seas of other states.

States with large maritime fleets tend to oppose such broad grants of navigational regulatory authority to coastal states on the grounds that the shippers' need to adapt to a wide variety of often conflicting local requirements would raise prices to shippers and consumers. Those who share this view want IMCO to be the source of standardized navigational requirements.

Some environmentalists worry about the effects on regional or global ecologies from ship accidents or negligence in the territorial waters of those states whose local requirements are too lax. They, too, want coastal states to conform to international standards, but they suspect that the traditional responsiveness of IMCO to the shippers' interests makes it inappropriate for ensuring that shippers will be held accountable to wider public interests. In response, IMCO supporters point to recent modifications in the organization's structure and decision processes that are supposed to give more weight to the interests of the environmentalists and the nonmaritime coastal states.

The prospect of the extension of territorial seas to at least twelve miles from shore puts under national jurisdiction more than 100 straits that were previously in international waters and therefore freely transited by merchant and naval vessels. While the leading maritime states have been willing to compromise with the new assertiveness of coastal states toward regulation of navigation in territorial seas generally, they have been adamant on preserving international rights of unimpeded transit through straits of commercial and military importance to them. The straits states, however, have been no less adamant in asserting their rights of self-protection, particularly in view of the fact that the chances of collisions and ship groundings are most severe in straits. The way the straits issue is resolved is of special interest to the two superpowers, whose global military reach depends on being able to project their strategic and tactical naval forces through these narrow waterways.

Navigation—Recommendations

No navigational regime will be durable that does not establish a balance between coastal interests on the one hand and maritime and naval interests on the other. A treaty should delineate rights and duties of coastal states and of those who must navigate through or above waters near coastal states. Specially designated international waterways, including straits important for international commerce, should be presumed free for international passage; and rule-making and implementation in these waterways should be primarily the responsibility of the international community. The regulation of maritime passage within other recognized national areas should be primarily the responsibility of the coastal states. A procedure for international consultation and dispute resolution should be mandatory for the involved parties if national rules interfere with one another and if international and national rules conflict.

The alternatives of virtually total regulation of navigation by coastal states within their national jurisdictions or virtually complete international regulation of all ocean navigation appear to us to be politically unrealistic. The major maritime users regard ocean transit as an aspect of their national security and economic well-being too vital to allow to become a privilege they can exercise only at the sufferance of individual coastal states. The major maritime countries, being also military powers, would attempt to impose their rights of transit by force if they were systematically denied by coastal states. But the major maritime users can no longer simply impose their wills on uncooperative coastal states with impunity. Many of these coastal states, while militarily inferior, possess at least spoiling capabilities, which could render some of the narrow waterways unpassable. As long as many coastal states insist on retaining certain prerogatives of local control, neither international negotiation nor the threat of force is likely to take away all of these prerogatives. The most that realistically can be hoped for is an international bargain between the maritime users and the coastal states, delegating responsibility for regulating navigation to international and national authorities.

Where there are to be internationally agreed and implemented norms for safety and ecology, particularly in the form of navigational rules for the specially designated international waterways and specifications for ship design, the international community will need some means of enforcement. Consideration should be given to an international agreement permitting only internationally licensed ships to use the ocean legally and lodging the responsibility in IMCO (with oversight from a more representative and comprehensive general ocean institution) for assessing fees or special taxes on the basis of tonnage, ship size, and type of cargo. Collection of license fees and enforcement of licensing will probably have to be a responsibility of the coastal states, but the international regulatory institutions should probably be accorded as many inspection rights as can be internationally negotiated to determine adherence to standards of ship design.

Fisheries—Summary

The worldwide problem of overfishing has its source in the regime of open access and free use, with its norm that only capture confers ownership of fish. Such a regime does not permit an enforceable limit on the total catch from a stock. Unless some maximum allowable catch is established, with provision for dividing the catch internationally, restrictions on gear and fishing seasons and the like are apt to stimulate the improvement of fishing technology to speed the rate of capture.

Countries that have fishing operations far from their own shores—the USSR, Japan, Portugal—want fishing rights allocated among nations at least partially according to historic use of stocks. But this would tend to leave current patterns basically unchanged, and would not deal with the problem of overfishing.

In response to the threat of overfishing, many coastal states have unilaterally asserted ownership of the fish nearest their shores, proclaiming fisheries zones that extend well beyond their internationally recognized territorial waters. The United States, attempting to fashion a fisheries policy acceptable to both its own coastal and long-distance fishermen, has proposed that fish be allocated to the nearest coastal state to the limits of its ability to harvest them. (Because of the difficulty of defining ability, the U.S. variant might become an allocation based on technological prowess.) The basic problem of the national management approach, however, is that stocks cannot be controlled throughout their range or throughout their life cycle; this prevents a national authority from limiting the total catch from a stock. Moreover, without international agreement on the criteria for use of stocks, there is no rein on a nation that prefers the current gains from overfishing, despite its long-range effects. Where such attitudes govern one state's use of a stock that occupies the fishing territories of several states, there is a serious potential for conflict.

Fisheries—Recommendations

A global fisheries commission will be needed to manage global stocks such as whales, tuna, and the resources of Antarctica. The commission might also absorb the scientific and informational services of the United Nations Food and Agriculture Organization (FAO) that are concerned with fish.

Existing regional fishing authorities should be strengthened and new ones established to make binding allocations of regional stocks among the countries of a region. Allocations should be a percentage of the maximum sustainable yield of that stock. The maximum sustainable yield should be set by a nonpolitical scientific institution attached to the global fisheries commission.

The alternative to the international approach to fisheries management is national ownership and management. While the national approach is most likely to be endorsed by the current Law of the Sea Conference, it is not likely to be a sustainable method because of the great interdependencies of the resources.

Offshore Oil and Gas—Summary

Two kinds of basic difficulties are created by the expansion of oil and gas drilling offshore: the problem of dividing the continental margins among the adjacent coastal states; and the problem of reconciling hydrocarbon exploitation with the uses of ocean space for other activities, particularly shipping and fishing.

The problem of dividing the continental margins among the coastal states is a matter of reaching agreement on how to extend baselines. Although the UN Conference on the Law of the Sea is likely to arrive at some formula, there will be cases of oil pools that cross national boundaries, and these will result in some inefficiencies and conflict, as each of the joint owners attempts to increase its own proportion of the oil from the pool.

The conflicts of oil production with other uses of the ocean are likely to cause even greater problems. Fixed oil rigs pose a hazard to ships if navigational systems are not working properly, or if the rigs are not accurately shown on maps. Collisions can be expensive for shippers because of damage to equipment and lost cargoes, and the resulting spillage of oil into the ocean poses ecological hazards. The risks are highest on the continental margins, where vessels converge on their way into ports and as they pass through straits. The continental margins are also the location of the largest stocks of exploitable fish; the fish are threatened by oil spills from collisions and from drilling accidents. Also, pipelines linking oil rigs with the shore can snag fishing nets, and the force with which the nets are towed can sometimes rupture a pipeline.

Offshore Oil and Gas—Recommendations

The number of international agreements required to allocate oil pools demonstrates the need for strengthened machinery to resolve disputes. To prevent collisions between oil drilling platforms and vessels performing other ocean activities, international agreement is needed on a system of registration and marking of oil rigs. Moreover, the risk to the ecology of the ocean that is posed by weak environmental controls suggests the need for agreement on the requirements to be imposed on hydrocarbon drilling. Some international inspection and enforcement will be needed to implement these agreements. Since there is currently no international organization with the appropriate powers, these functions might also be assigned to a comprehensive ocean authority.

Hard Mineral Mining—Summary

The hard minerals of greatest international interest in the ocean are the manganese nodules located on the deep ocean floor beyond the continental margins. The nodules contain manganese, nickel, copper, and cobalt. They are ubiquitous, but not uniform in quality. Almost all of the promising mining sites are more than two hundred miles from shore and therefore beyond the territorial waters of most coastal states. Although UN resolutions have affirmed that these are international resources, there has been substantial disagreement over the criteria to be applied in according exploitation rights to countries and corporations.

Most of the developing countries want to have nodule mining controlled directly by an international authority. Some countries want the authority to do the actual mining. Several of these countries are now mining on land the minerals contained in the nodules, and fear that ocean mining could disrupt their present markets; they would like the international authority to be able to restrict exploitation of the seabed. The notion of an international agency to actually conduct the mining appears to be politically unrealistic. Such an agency would require personnel, technology, and funds from the industrially advanced countries to start operations, and many of those countries appear unwilling to cooperate with a regime whose policies might be dominated by developing countries, which want to control the mineral market.

The few countries that have the technology to mine the nodules want only minimal limitations on their access to the seabed. Their preference is for a regime under which countries would only register their claims to specific sites, and other countries would agree to respect the claims, thereby preventing claim-jumping. Such a scheme could probably work if a small group of countries—those capable of mining the ocean—agreed to it. There is considerable pressure by the ocean mining industry on the U.S., Japanese, and French governments to institute such an arrangement without waiting for universal international agreement. This approach, however, would outrage almost all of the developing countries, which might try to retaliate on other ocean matters—say, by placing heavy restrictions on maritime navigation in straits and even in extended coastal zones. Consequently, during the course of the Law of the Sea negotiations, the potential miners have shown a willingness to forgo insistence on completely free access to the seabed, and have accepted the principle of some (at least nominal) rent to be paid to the international community in return for the right to mine.

Hard Mineral Mining—Recommendation

A compromise that might satisfy some of the demands of the developing countries, while continuing to provide adequate incentives to potential miners, would establish an international authority with power to auction leases to a limited number of mining sites each year. Countries or companies that purchase development rights to the sites would also pay a royalty on their production as is done on land. Revenues from the auction, and perhaps also from royalties on production, could be used by the international community to assist the developing countries. The international authority would also apply environmental standards to nodule mining, and would enforce rules designed to minimize interference with other ocean users.

The authority probably should have a plenary assembly of universal membership, operating on the basis of one nation, one vote, to underline the fact that the deep seabed is owned by the entire international community. The operations of the authority would be best directed by an executive council designed to represent categories of countries (ocean miners, land miners, and consumers) fairly. The council should appoint internationally recruited technicians to verify site surveys, revenue reporting, and adherence to environmental standards.

Scientific Research—Summary

The greatest progress in scientific research occurs when scientists are free to study ocean phenomena wherever they occur. But because so much of even basic research yields information that is of immediate commercial or military value, less capable countries see unlimited access for scientists as a way for the developed countries to maintain or even increase their economic and military advantages. For this reason, they have been asserting a right to prior consent to all scientific research conducted on or over their continental margins.

The developed countries, on the other hand, argue that at least basic scientific investigations, as distinguished from applied research, should be unhampered by such requirements. To support this point of view, they cite the gains to the international community from increasing knowledge about the ecological and climatic roles of the ocean. The problem with this approach, however, is that the distinction between basic and applied oceanography lies not in the nature of the activity itself, but in the use to which the information gathered is subsequently put.

Scientific Research—Recommendations

Since marine science is very important for developing workable environmental controls and for forecasting weather and climate changes, there is a high international interest in facilitating it. In order to permit the flexibility that is important to many marine science projects, open access might be given to work specifically sponsored by international agencies. Prior consent of the coastal state could be required for all other scientific investigations. Coastal states would be free to impose whatever restrictions they wished upon research that was not sponsored by international agencies.

It would also be desirable to use the international oceanographic projects to train the scientists of developing countries, by requiring that a percentage of any expedition's personnel be from the affected coastal state.

Reconsideration of Basic Regime Alternatives

In our opening chapter on the ocean, the regime alternatives of open access and free use, national management, and international management were outlined briefly in terms of their inherent logic. Having analyzed the management needs for specific types of ocean uses, we can now better assess the suitability of each kind of ocean regime for ordering the growing interaction of ocean uses.

Open Access and Free Use

A basic problem with the regime of open access and free use is its assumption that interference by users with one another will be an exceptional rather than a normal occurrence. Technological developments and the expansion of scientific knowledge about the ocean have undermined this assumption. Even those who use the water solely as a medium of transportation can no longer argue convincingly that their use does not affect its availability to other users. It is now widely understood that many navigational users do indeed affect the condition of the water. Moreover, the expansion of nonnavigational uses such as mineral exploitation, fishing and aquaculture (fish farming), and oceanographic science—often in areas of navigational congestion—is bound to increase international conflict between those who use the ocean primarily for transit and those who require relatively stationary facilities.

If neither national nor international authorities have internationally recognized management responsibility for specific ocean resources and areas, conflicts over rights of use are likely to be more prevalent, and the parties will be tempted to resort to coercion to maintain their special interests. There is little if any assurance that the resolution of conflicts of interest under the open access, free use regime will be efficient, equitable, or ecologically sound.

In the first place, if confrontations are necessary to resolve disputes, then claimants to resources or areas over which there is contention will have to maintain coercive capabilities to come out ahead in the confrontations. The cost of maintaining such a capability will be reflected in the form of higher prices to the consumer.

Second, if economic and/or military might establishes and maintains the right to use the resources of the ocean, even fewer corporations or states will be in a position to enter the competition, and the opportunities for the formation of oligopolies or cartels will be that much greater.

Third, under a regime of open access and free use, there is little incentive for initial users of a resource to limit their exploitation in the service of conservation or distribution. There are not likely to be adequate restraints on their transfer of external costs (e.g., degradation of ocean-based food supplies, pollution of recreational beaches) to neighbors or others whose normal uses of the ocean may be affected. Under this regime, benefit is calculated by the user in terms of returns on his investments over costs that are almost totally internal—that is, intrinsic to the activity or project itself. The user pays nothing to the international community for the use of this common property; he has no obligation to compensate other users for degrading valuable ocean resources; nor does he have any obligation to share any of the benefits accrued from use of the resources. If a compromise must be made between one use and another, say, petroleum extraction and tourism, individual states are free to make their own determinations as they see fit, even though the consequences may substantially affect a neighboring country's petroleum resources or coastal environment. Moreover, under the open access and free use regime, the absence of a responsible collector of economic rent for use of the resources means that conservation objectives and the benefit of future users will remain outside a user's calculation of costs and benefits, and will therefore be undervalued.

These externalities would be inconsequential in an economy of abundance. But as the scarcity of ocean resources becomes evident, a new political economy for allocating the externalities appears warranted.

National Management

It is doubtful that the objectives of assuring responsibility for the care of the ocean and creating the juridical stability conducive to its efficient exploitation can be attained through a national management approach. The ocean cannot be managed effectively in an artificially divided condition. Activities in the ocean, especially with advancing technology, have become ever more part of a de facto regime of global interdependence. Different rules for use at different points on the ocean highway would retard the transport of needed commodities and raise the costs to consumers. Low standards of ecological care in one part of the ocean can affect food-nutrient conditions in other parts, and perhaps also the regional and global climate.

To move the increasingly anachronistic terrestrial system of nation-state sovereignty to the sea may superficially appear to be an attractive solution to the problem of authority; but even under the most optimistic assumptions about territorial assignments, a national regime would at best be only a half system of ocean management.

The outward-creeping jurisdictional claims of recent years, the result of technological developments opening larger portions of the sea to exploration and exploitation, are unlikely to abate during the coming decades. Thus, there is no reason to assume that today's entitlements will be congruent with tomorrow's capabilities. Moreover, if one's national title is established by creeping farther out or deeper, power will still be the essence of the law of the sea.

Perhaps confrontations between rival claimants will be averted by giving legal recognition to claims of jurisdiction based upon physical pre-emption; but those without the ability to stage the technological and economic seizures are likely to become embittered at the obvious inequities.

Where conservation and ecological care of ocean resources require highly coordinated or joint action by many countries, a system of allocation that rewards coercive strength is unlikely to foster cooperation from the intimidated. In addition, the instability of prevailing jurisdictional boundaries that this system would produce over the long term is unlikely to encourage conservation by those currently in possession of the resources.

In sum, an ocean regime modeled on the nation-state system that is traditional on land will be ill-equipped to arbitrate volatile jurisdictional conflicts or to accommodate overlapping uses on the basis of what is best for ocean ecology or for general human welfare, and it portends increasing international conflict and bitterness on the part of those who cannot prevail.

International Management

It seems clear from our recapitulation of the open access and national management regimes that a considerable degree of international management is required to deal adequately with both the scarcities and the indivisibilities (intersectoral and international) of ocean resources. In its most matured application, an international regime for the ocean would assume that the entire international community owns the oceans; users would be held accountable to one another and to the community as a whole for anything they do to one another in the ocean or to the ocean itself.

The problems with the international management approach are chiefly political. Most countries are nation-states of recent vintage, the majority having attained independence from one or another of the European empires only since the Second World War; others are struggling to maintain internal cohesion against ethnic or religious groups insisting on greater local autonomy. The leaders of most developing countries in particular tend to be jealous guardians of national sovereignty and to resist international limitations on their freedom of action. It is no accident that those coastal states that are developing countries tend to be highly nationalistic about control of offshore resources. They are anxious to preserve their political autonomy against foreign encroachments and also to keep for themselves the potentially large income gains from exploitation of the resources of the continental margin. They feel that the insistence of the maritime countries on international prerogatives in the margin areas is in part a device by which the more technologically advanced countries and corporations can maintain advantageous access to the lucrative resources, now that the coastal states are asserting extended national jurisdictions. Their suspicions that the maritime countries are really practicing a policy of "what's mine is mine, what's yours is international" are reinforced by the objections of the maritime countries to international regulation of deep sea mining beyond the continental margins. Indeed, when it gets down to cases, the industrialized countries are no more ready than the developing countries to subject their ocean activities to authorization by international bodies with broad membership.

In fields in which there is a consensus that international organizations do have a role to play, there is likely to be considerable disagreement about the structure of those organizations. This is especially so in organizations with broad membership, such as those contemplated for managing the mining of the deep seabed or for the coordination of ocean uses. Membership in these organizations will include countries of differing ideological persuasion, types of economy, and levels of development. The maritime countries with advanced technologies, perceiving that they will be in the minority in the plenary assemblies of most ocean organizations, usually favor executive councils weighted on the basis of financial or industrial indicators, and usually favor assembly procedures that restrict the opportunities for the majority to impose its will on the technologically advanced countries. For example, those countries and corporations anxious to begin mining the minerals of the deep seabed are opposed to proposals that the authority for the deep seabed have strong assembly powers and that assembly decisions be taken on the basis of one nation, one vote.

These political difficulties are substantial but need not be regarded as insurmountable obstacles to international management. The interdependencies of ocean uses make it necessary for any durable ocean regime to require considerable international accountability and coordination. The task of diplomacy, therefore, is to fashion substantive and institutional bargains between countries, taking into account not only the technical characteristics of particular uses, but also variations in the number, location, and economic and political power of the relevant nations and affected populations.

A Strategy for Implementing the International Management Concept

A politically prudent approach to international management would not simply reject the arrangements for use of the ocean emerging from the Law of the Sea Conference and other multilateral and bilateral negotiations—as, for example, in the areas of fisheries, navigation, and arms control. Rather, it would attempt to build on them by devising processes for accountability to manage the overlap and interference between the evolving specific sector and local management efforts. But this effort would be directed by the philosophy that the national and multinational arrangements are only temporary delegations of authority by the whole international community for managing parts of the common heritage. Local management should serve the interests of the whole community. Thus, implementation of international management can be perceived as a two-stage strategy: (1) functional pluralism overlaid by (2) more integrated multinational and multisectoral accountability, including machinery for the resolution of disputes and, if possible, a comprehensive authority for management of the ocean.

Functional Pluralism

The first stage of international management should support the evolving mixture of user arrangements. Some of these are being established and maintained unilaterally (such as the regulatory procedures set up by Canada under its 1970 Arctic Waters Pollution Prevention Act), some bilaterally (the procedures for oceanographic notification and sharing of results negotiated between the U.S. Department of State and particular coastal states), some multilaterally (such as the arrangements for exploitation of the oil in the North Sea), and a few globally (such as the navigational standards promulgated through IMCO). Forums and memberships are determined on a functional basis according to what is most negotiable in today's political marketplace. At the outset at least, it must be expected that some of the arrangements and institutions for particular ocean uses will overlap, and in some sectors there will be little if any regulation in the broad public interest of the traditional pattern of open access and free use.

This evolving pluralism allows for flexibility and experimentation with varied forms. It takes as its starting point the existing complex of ocean institutions and law and the ongoing negotiations in the Law of the Sea Conference, and uses them as a guide to what can realistically be expected over the next decade or so.

The current rate and extent of evolution of international management of the ocean, however, will probably not lead to sufficient coordination of rules and institutions, unless statesmen willing to give ocean management high priority actively guide the evolving patterns. Functions that are highly interdependent are unlikely to be coordinated adequately with one another. Left to its own momentum and direction, today's ocean diplomacy is unlikely to create an adequate web of accountability arrangements to take in commercial and military navigational interests, coastal ecology, and fishing interests. Yet in many parts of the ocean, various combinations of these interests will simultaneously attempt to use the same areas and resources. Functional or regional institutions are unlikely to give adequate protection to some ecological systems or to allow efficient exploitation of some resources, since the evolving institutions will have spans of control too narrow to allocate the external costs. This structural deficiency will be particularly glaring in cases such as overfishing or ocean dumping, where users of ocean resources do not themselves expect to suffer, and are content to pass on the costs to neighboring societies or future generations.

The need, therefore, is to supplement the evolving functional pluralism with an active effort to achieve increased multilateral and multisectoral integration.

Integration of Ocean Management

The second stage of international management would actively attempt to stimulate countries to international accountability. International forums would reflect the widest scope of ocean users and their current and emerging interdependencies. This would not involve imposing any structural unity on the inherent plurality of ocean uses. It would, however, actively promote effective international regulation where it is necessary to the conservation and equitable use of ocean resources, and it would require that users in conflict with one another have their confrontations in international forums rather than, so to speak, on the sea.

We urge, in effect, a return to the original animating concept of the Law of the Sea Conference, and a long-term institutionalization of the negotiating process that the Conference initiated.

The comprehensive terms of reference and universal membership of the Law of the Sea Conference were initially opposed by the United States and other maritime powers, on the grounds that not all ocean issues were of equal concern to all countries and that, therefore, each discrete issue should be deliberated by a particular set of countries. The maritime states, being a small minority, were understandably anxious to insulate as many issues as possible from negotiating forums in which all states would be participants. They were also concerned that controversial issues not be a drag on those issues that were close to resolution.

The hope of negotiating issues discretely, however, was no more realistic politically than it was congruent with the interdependence of ocean uses. The U.S. government soon perceived that its only chance for obtaining international agreement to preserve important navigational rights was to concede to the coastal states wide zones of economic jurisdiction. Similarly, the maritime states perceived that offering the developing countries a major claim on the revenues from international mining of the deep seabed, and a substantial role in its management, might be part of the quid pro quo required to reduce the more extreme demands of coastal states for absolute sovereignty out to 200 miles from shore. An approach that linked issues in this way underlay the comprehensive draft ocean treaty the United States submitted to the United Nations in 1970 and subsequently characterized the general posture of the U.S. delegation at the Law of the Sea Conference.

The difficult deliberations in the Law of the Sea Conference have underscored the fact that a durable resolution of differences over the limits of territorial waters requires that agreements on the international rules that are to be applied *within* the territorial waters and on the regime for the ocean areas beyond national jurisdiction be negotiated simultaneously with agreements on international revenue sharing and procedures for the settlement of ocean disputes. Ultimately, what is required is nothing less than a constitution of mutual rights and obligations for the ocean.

As pointed out in chapter 2, it seems doubtful that the current Law of the Sea Conference will be able to put together a package of compromises that will command sufficient international consensus to enable it to serve as the constitution for the ocean. This has led some analysts to conclude that the integrated approach to devising an ocean regime was misguided, and that the international community should return to sector-by-sector negotiations.[1] We consider such judgments premature. The founding of a new public order for the ocean can hardly be accomplished by one conference or a single treaty. The effort must be expected to occupy statesmen for most of the remainder of the century, for it has become deeply entangled with other chronic international problems of the contemporary period: reconciling the requirements of national security with the need to contain the arms race; finding rational, just, and peaceful ways to allocate the world's supply of energy, food, and industrial raw materials; searching for syntheses between the competing demands for economic development and ecological care; narrowing the economic and political gaps between the poor and the affluent peoples; and, in general, managing the increasing interaction of nations.

Indeed, the shortcomings of the Conference are due in large measure to the failure by top policymakers in the United States and other countries to recognize how central the Law of the Sea issues have become to the overall pattern of international relations, and to give the negotiations the priority they deserve. This failure has left more room for special interest groups to affect the negotiating positions of various governments

1. See, for example, Robert E. Osgood, "U.S. Security Interests in Ocean Law," *Ocean Development and International Affairs: The Journal of Marine Affairs,* pp. 1–36; see also Ann L. Hollick, "What to Expect from a Sea Treaty," *Foreign Policy,* no. 9 (Spring 1975), pp. 68–78.

than is normally the case with highly visible international negotiations on, say, international arms control or the monetary system.[2]

A more integrated approach by the United States and other maritime powers would be required to develop attractive quid pro quos for the nationalistic coastal states (in the form of revenue sharing, decision-making power in international forums, and technology transfer), which might avert the fragmentation of ocean space into nearly sovereign national economic zones that now seems the likely outcome of the Conference.

Whatever the outcome of the present Conference, however, it will not be the end of the elaboration of a new law of the sea. If the Conference were to break down completely, the unilateral assertions of national jurisdiction and grabbing of ocean resources would compel various nations to negotiate new rules and regulations, if only to stabilize the new territorial status quo. But in view of the facts that some ocean resources will continue to transcend territorial jurisdictions, and that some ocean uses will continue to traverse them, continuing processes for adjustment of uses and for conflict resolution will be required. Alternatively, if the Conference does produce a comprehensive Law of the Sea treaty, it is likely that it will be so full of ambiguities that its implementation will require still more ocean lawmaking. If, as seems most likely at this writing, the Conference produces an uneven result—some specific agreements on certain matters (say, territorial sea limits), vague agreements on some matters (navigational rights and duties), and no agreement on other matters (the design of an institution to regulate deep sea mineral mining)—then the need will be all the greater for a continuing process of negotiation and dispute resolution.

MACHINERY FOR THE SETTLEMENT OF DISPUTES. The key to maintaining the peace in the ocean will be the willingness of members to submit their disputes to international settlement and to respect the decisions of the international machinery for settling disputes. In order to encourage the utilization of the international machinery and thereby build respect for its role, we favor a flexible structure of tribunals and panels that parties can use on a voluntary basis. The outline of such a flexible approach was developed in the Informal Working Group on Settlement of Disputes at the Spring 1975 session of the Law of the Sea Conference

2. Seyom Brown and Larry L. Fabian, "Diplomats at Sea," *Foreign Affairs*, vol. 52 (January 1974), pp. 301–21 (Brookings Reprint 282).

in Geneva: Parties to a proposed convention on the settlement of disputes would agree, in cases where a dispute could not be resolved bilaterally, to accept the jurisdiction of special, internationally recognized boards of arbitration, a special Law of the Sea tribunal, or the International Court of Justice. A case brought against a signatory party would have to be brought before the forum chosen by that party.[3] We would interpret the workings of a special law of the sea tribunal as essentially the same as those we are suggesting for the comprehensive ocean authority described below.

A COMPREHENSIVE OCEAN AUTHORITY. The need to institutionalize the process of bargaining over jurisdictions among different kinds of ocean users, and to readjust periodically national and international prerogatives, points to the desirability of establishing an overarching ocean authority. At the start, the ocean authority could be seen as a permanent forum, under whose aegis special committees would form and re-form, and particular negotiations and resolutions of disputes could take place. Over the long term, this forum might develop supranational powers to set and enforce policy for the use of the ocean and to establish binding guidelines for the more specialized agencies governing use of the ocean. But at first, the authoritativeness of the general ocean institution would have to come less from formal grants to it of supranational powers than from the voluntary respect members and states gave its deliberations and decisions. Implementation of its decisions would still be largely the responsibility of the governments of member countries, and of multilateral authorities in regions with well-developed patterns of cooperation.

Any number of institutional designs could implement this concept. The following sketch is meant only to be illustrative of the kind of institutional structure that would be appropriate to today's need for a full-time negotiating, coordinating, and adjudicating forum, and yet be adaptable for the performance of more substantial supranational functions if and when the members find this desirable.

The institution could be designed around four major organs. *Plenary:* a permanently sitting general assembly of virtually universal membership, to make and revise basic rules of ocean use. *Coordinative:* an executive council composed of representatives from sectoral and regional

3. Department of State, Office of Law of the Sea Negotiations, Third United Nations Conference on the Law of the Sea, "Informal Single Negotiating Text and Text on Settlement of Disputes," A/Conf. 62/WP.8/Pts. I, II, and III and SD (May 9, 1975), SD, p. 2.

organizations (such as IMCO, fisheries commissions, the mineral mining agency, oceanographic boards), and elected representatives from the general assembly. *Adjudicative:* a special judicial body to resolve disputes (providing consultation, mediation, and arbitration) with empaneled experts and ad hoc commissions to service disputes in particular fields, such as mining of the seabed, navigation, or fishing. *Administrative:* a secretary to provide administrative and information services for the assembly, the executive council, the specialized ocean institutions, and the marine tribunals.

Most ocean affairs will continue to be conducted under the direct authority of national governments, so the plenary, coordinative, and adjudicative processes of the comprehensive ocean authority are for the time being best regarded as consultative. Where problems of ocean use arise between particular kinds of users, committees of the relevant parties could be constituted to obtain a consensus on procedures and compromises and then report back to the general assembly and executive council; the latter bodies would not have to take formal action.

In the assembly, each country could have one vote, but the membership could be divided into categories of countries with particular characteristics, and majorities within these categories could be required (with varying formulas) for certain kinds of decisions. This could ensure that the assembly would find it very difficult to take decisions contrary to the vital interests of particular types of ocean users, and that substantive decisions actually taken would be supported by a majority of states. Routine matters could require a majority of all members present and voting, plus a majority of members in more than half of the special categories. Decisions of extraordinary importance could require two-thirds majorities in all membership categories. There are, of course, many variants in between.

The basic design of voting in the executive council should weight votes in favor of the categories of ocean users most directly affected by the pending issues. This purpose could be achieved by varying the formulas for voting majorities and by providing for separate categories of membership in the general assembly to elect their own representatives to the council.

In sum, the major need is for *processes* to accommodate the proliferation of ocean users, to reconcile their often conflicting patterns of use, and generally to make them accountable to one another and to the international community at large for their use of this common resource. The means to achieve such international accountability are institutional in the broadest sense—namely, patterns of interaction ranging all the way from commitments among groups of nations to consult with one another, to agreements to be bound by international adjudicatory mechanisms in cases of dispute, to agreements to subordinate national actions in particular fields to the decisions of supranational organizations.

The eventual buildup of supranational authority in most fields requires a foundation of general success with accountability processes involving primarily consultation and voluntary adjustments of behavior. We recommend a comprehensive ocean authority as an institution to facilitate the consultative processes, but also as an aegis under which thicker patterns of institutionalization can take place when the conditions are ripe in particular fields and among particular sets of countries.

CHAPTER NINE

Alternative Regimes for Activities in Outer Space

Outer space would seem to be specially suited for a regime of open access and free use. Infinite in dimensions, and its main resource—space itself—presumably immune from depletion, this nonland realm would seem to have no need of political management. The hope that outer space would be preserved for peaceful use appeared to require only that the superpowers avoid interfering with each other's spacecraft. In recent years, however, the countries with advanced space capabilities have been increasingly under pressure to submit their activities to international scrutiny and participation.

The Changing Context of Outer Space Issues

Space diplomacy is becoming politicized. This is primarily the result of three trends: the growing emphasis on earth-oriented applications of satellites; the widening circle of involved governments and private interests; and the waning of cold war bipolarity.

Growing Emphasis on Earth-oriented Applications

In the early years of the space age, space activities were predominantly exploratory, but scientific experiments with military potential were given priority. Scientists designed and tested satellite systems that could more accurately determine relative positions on the earth (thus enabling more precise targeting), that could send and receive signals, and that could collect data about the weather and climate more comprehensively than could systems operating from the ground or from aircraft. The satellite experiments of the late 1950s also had meteorological and communications applications. Progress in applying space technology to these and other fields accelerated during the early 1960s, initially within the U.S. space program and later within that of the USSR.[1]

As satellite technologies to perform these functions were perfected, scientists and engineers realized that the same technologies could also serve a variety of civilian uses. Further technological developments brought the costs down to a level at which it became evident that satellites could perform a number of civilian functions more cheaply than alternative technologies.

The quickening pace during the 1960s of applications with civilian potential laid the technological foundation for the new period of space diplomacy that emerged full blown in the 1970s. Early experimental satellites were transformed into vehicles for operational programs, and the number, variety, and capacity of operational programs increased.

Before 1965, the United States had launched sixteen satellites for communications purposes; twice that many were put into orbit during the next six years. Nine weather satellites were deployed before 1965; twice that number were launched during the next six years. By 1965, three geodesic satellites (essential for earth mapping and targeting of long-range ballistic missiles) had been launched into space; nearly five times this number were launched between 1965 and 1971. Before 1965, a dozen ocean navigation satellites had been launched; by 1971, another dozen were in orbit.

There was no experimentation with satellites designed primarily to survey earth resources before 1965, but after that their potential attracted considerable attention. The first manned U.S. spacecraft to orbit the earth in the early 1960s—the Mercury series combining visual and instrument observation—had given strong hints that the space program could yield important benefits through surveys of the earth. The growing American interest in using spacecraft to gain information about the earth led to experiments with weather satellites and highly sophisticated experimental satellites, which in turn led to the first earth-resources tech-

1. An overview of early American and Soviet applications experiments can be found in Charles S. Sheldon II, "Peaceful Applications," in Lincoln P. Bloomfield, ed., *Outer Space: Prospects for Man and Society* (Praeger, 1968), pp. 37–74.

nology satellite (ERTS-A, now called Landsat 1) in 1972 and the placement of instruments to survey the earth's resources on Skylab, the first
manned laboratory in orbit, in 1973.[2]

The USSR also began to emphasize applications in the 1960s, but at a
somewhat slower pace than the United States. Soviet nonmilitary satellite programs typically lagged about eight years behind equivalent U.S.
missions. (Soviet earth-oriented applications for military purposes also
lagged several years behind.)[3]

The Widening Circle of Involved Actors

Although the development of sophisticated space satellites has been
almost totally dominated by the United States and the USSR, other
countries are beginning to carve out lesser roles in space use.

Canada, some countries of Western Europe, and Japan all experimented in the 1960s with various satellites for astronomical and physical
research. During the latter part of the decade, various industrialized
countries began to develop space technologies with applications to
earth, including meteorology, communications, and earth-sensing.

By the early 1970s, European governments, advanced nations in the
Pacific, and Canada had gained the status of lesser space powers, and
some of the more technologically capable developing nations were also
pressing forward with space programs. At the present time, in addition
to the United States and the USSR, Italy, France, Australia, the United
Kingdom, Japan, and China have achieved at least some limited capability to launch satellites into orbit. Simpler launch technology, able to

2. For the programs developed in the 1950s and 1960s, see the National
Aeronautics and Space Council, *Aeronautics and Space Report of the President: 1971 Activities* (GPO, 1972), pp. 116–19. Descriptions of the resource
surveys carried out by Landsat 1 and Skylab, as well as of all currently active
and planned U.S. applications, are found in *1974 NASA Authorization*,
Hearings before the Subcommittee on Space Science and Applications of the
House Committee on Science and Astronautics, 93:1 (GPO, 1973), pt. 3,
pp. 38–111.

3. *Soviet Space Programs, 1966–1970*, Staff Report prepared for the use
of the Committee on Aeronautical and Space Sciences, S. Doc. 92-51, 92:1
(GPO, 1971), p. 297. See also *Soviet Space Programs, 1971*, Staff Report
prepared for the Committee on Aeronautical and Space Sciences, Supplement, 92:2 (GPO, 1972); and Philip J. Klass, *Secret Sentries in Space*
(Random House, 1971), esp. pp. 72–129.

boost objects into the upper atmosphere, is available to other countries, including Argentina, Canada, Egypt, India, Israel, and West Germany. Most of the countries possessing orbital launch capabilities are also able to build spacecraft of one kind or another.

In addition, there has been a substantial increase in the number of countries or special interests relying on space-technology services. More than eighty nations are now members of INTELSAT (International Telecommunications Satellite Consortium), which provides global telephone and television relays. Nearly every nation takes part in the extensive satellite network that gathers and exchanges data under the auspices of the World Meteorological Organization.

Advanced test programs in earth sciences are under way that will give satellite services added significance for many users. Dozens of nations are now collaborating with the experiments with the earth resource satellites and Skylab instrumentation that the National Aeronautics and Space Administration (NASA) developed in the early 1970s, and the data from these projects is openly available to all nations for resource planning and other uses.

The 1970s have seen the spread of satellite broadcast or broadcast-relay systems within nations, and perhaps among regional partners. Specialized users of satellites for sea communications and navigation are actively developing new systems, and international air carriers may subsequently use satellites.

Many private companies in the resource, communications, and transportation industries now use satellite services. Many also produce and sell the associated hardware or software in a growing international market.

The Waning of Cold War Bipolarity

Space diplomacy in the first decade after the launch of *Sputnik I* (1957) was essentially a part of the competition between the superpowers. Both felt the need to justify publicly their experimental and military activities in outer space after they had occurred, but not to clear such activities in advance with the international community.

At the opening of the space age, the United States and the USSR both saw their prestige heavily involved in the space competition. Both saw important connections between progress in civilian and military space technologies. "The extension of the Cold War was virtually assured by the nature of space technology and the state of political relations between the powers conducting space activities."[4]

How far the extension of the cold war into outer space would go, and how much militarization of outer space it would require, were central international policy questions during the early years of space age diplomacy. The superpowers probed each other's intentions on the use of outer space for military reconnaissance and on the placement of nuclear weapons and other weapons of mass destruction in orbit.

The arms control emphasis that developed in the 1960s began to moderate these cold war preoccupations. In 1962 and 1963, both countries agreed to a policy of no bombs in orbit. The 1963 Nuclear Test Ban Treaty prohibited nuclear testing in outer space. This was also the year that the USSR reversed its standing objection to satellite reconnaissance. These developments paved the way for the arms control provisions of the 1967 Outer Space Treaty, which outlawed nuclear weapons in space, prohibited military installations on celestial bodies, and reserved outer space generally for peaceful purposes.

The 1967 treaty did not entirely demilitarize outer space. But since the late 1960s, most military activities conducted in space by the United States and the USSR have been conducted with each other's tacit acquiescence and with the resigned tolerance of the medium-sized and small powers. The civilian programs are now generating the most international controversy.

The new emphasis on civilian space diplomacy has changed the composition of the negotiating arena. Even on issues of arms control, most nations are far removed from any real influence. A handful of countries took an active part in the negotiations to develop rules for the conduct of space exploration that led to the Outer Space Treaty. Most other nations expressed interest in the development of a regime for exploratory ventures in space. But as long as space activities conferred few general economic benefits, most countries appeared willing to leave space affairs primarily in the hands of the superpowers. Only with the maturing of space applications directed toward civilian life on earth, and with the calming of the cold war itself, have a large number of nations begun to perceive that space diplomacy directly affects their in-

4. Arnold L. Horelick, "The Soviet Union and the Political Uses of Outer Space," in Joseph M. Goldsen, ed., *Outer Space in World Politics* (Praeger, 1963).

terests. Debate over the uses of outer space now engages the majority of nations—as active participants, not simply passive spectators. Many countries are showing greater determination to challenge the policy preferences of either or both of the superpowers, precisely because the interests at stake in many fields of satellite applications are less tied to national security or military competition.[5]

The policy differences between the United States and the USSR on some issues of space applications are sometimes seized upon by other countries to advance their own interests, and to play off one superpower against the other. Because of the larger changes since the fading of the cold war that have undercut global bipolarity, both superpowers have lost much of their previous ability to rally support for preferred space policies from allies and friends through appeals to bloc or ideological loyalties. The result is an arena for space diplomacy that features the superpowers in a mixed pattern of agreement and contention with each other; the noncommunist industrial countries divided along the lines of their varying political and commercial interests; and the developing countries coalescing in opposition to the high-technology powers on some issues, while on other issues variously aligned with one or more of the industrial powers.

INTELSAT as an Early Reflector of the Changes

INTELSAT is an early manifestation of the new emphasis on space applications, and it also mirrors the changing political realities of the present transitional period. The formative negotiations culminating in the 1964 INTELSAT agreements engaged fourteen countries—principally the United States, plus the other industrial nations that together accounted for nearly all the world's international communications. (No communist states participated.) The United States had the competitive motivations, the most advanced communications technology, the sole satellite launching capabilities, the necessary private capital (in COMSAT—Communications Satellite Corporation—accounts) to sup-

---

5. Reflecting on the INTELSAT renegotiations of the late 1960s and early 1970s, one analyst observed, "Neither the United States, the Western European states, nor the less-developed countries saw their vital national interests at stake. . . . The principal issues were disagreements among partners rather than fights between enemies." Jonathan F. Galloway, *The Politics and Technology of Satellite Communications* (Lexington Books, 1972), pp. 156 and 158.

port a global system, and strong domestic support for the concept of a global commercial enterprise.[6] In most important respects, INTELSAT was to be a "U.S. bird."

In its early stages, the European nations were anxious to invest money in INTELSAT, and thus to gain a real voice in its management. The United States, however, deliberately kept the proportion of European funding low, and insisted on the policy veto it enjoyed under the 1964 arrangements. The United States justified its coolness to European generosity by the fact that U.S. public funds had in large measure paid for the research and development costs for communications satellite technology. The European nations were left with apparently little choice but to negotiate as a bloc within INTELSAT for the best possible terms to preserve what little voice they had in the new system, and to press the United States to keep certain aspects of the system open to possible future negotiation, in the hope that their bargaining position would become technologically and politically stronger in the intervening period.

For the United States, the cold war rivalry still dominated its foreign policy in the early 1960s. Fear that the USSR might duplicate its 1957 Sputnik feat, achieving an operational first in space communications, was a major stimulus to the acceleration of U.S. space communications technology and to the vigorous assertion by the United States of a position of leadership in any new international communications venture. U.S. insistence on voting procedures that favored countries with heavy international communications traffic, on commercial operating criteria, and on other operating guidelines of the institution virtually ruled out participation by the USSR in the original INTELSAT. In all, the U.S. position had the effect of inviting the USSR to decline overtures aimed at securing its participation in the new arrangements.[7]

6. For general background, see Richard R. Colino, *The INTELSAT Definitive Arrangements: Ushering in a New Era in Satellite Telecommunications*, Monograph no. 9 (European Broadcasting Union, 1973); Galloway, *The Politics and Technology of Satellite Communications;* and Brenda Maddox, *Beyond Babel: New Directions in Communications* (Simon and Schuster, 1972), esp. pp. 65–141.

7. For the early U.S. views on international arrangements for a new satellite system, see especially Murray L. Schwartz and Joseph M. Goldsen, *Foreign Participation in the Communications Systems,* Rand Corporation Memorandum RM-3484-RC (1963). See also Thomas L. Shillinglaw, "The Soviet Union and International Satellite Telecommunications," *Stanford Journal of International Studies,* vol. 5 (June 1970), pp. 199–226; and

The vast majority of the world's nations remained on the sidelines of international space diplomacy in the early 1960s—however much the two superpowers were inclined to see their own space policies as instruments for winning the loyalty and political support of nations in the Third World that had not developed space technology. But by the time the interim arrangements for INTELSAT were renegotiated between 1969 and 1971, the political and technological premises that had shaped most of the earliest years of the space age had begun to recede. By then INTELSAT was functioning as a sort of international common carrier, and the balance of power had shifted somewhat away from the United States. This had happened as a result of the relative decline in the U.S. share of world communications, the emergence of a political front of industrial nations bent on reducing what they saw as an unduly prominent U.S. voice, and the expansion of membership in INTELSAT to more than eighty nations. The changed nature of INTELSAT and the more cooperative patterns of superpower policies are reflected by the decision of the USSR, reported early in 1974, to build an earth station enabling it to operate with the INTELSAT space segment, as China now does on a nonmembership basis.

Thus, the definitive INTELSAT treaty, which is now in force, reflects some of the newer trends that are beginning to reshape the diplomacy of space applications. While these trends may have only limited impact on the structure and operation of INTELSAT, whose basic outline had been set relatively firmly by its activities under the initial arrangements, they promise considerably more influence in those newer fields where basic institutional, legal, and policy decisions have not yet been made.

Regime Alternatives

The growing use of outer space and the resulting awareness that the way it is used could affect political and economic relationships on earth

Stephen E. Doyle, "An Analysis of the Socialist States' Proposal for Intersputnik: An International Communication Satellite System," *Villanova Law Review*, vol. 15 (Fall 1969), pp. 83–105.

How receptive the USSR would have been to participation in INTELSAT if more favorable terms had been available is not known with any certainty. Soviet officials did show some tentative exploratory interest in the pre-1968 period.

have stimulated considerable international effort, most of it in the United Nations, to elaborate rules for using this realm. The different approaches to rule-making imply three different types of regime: open access and free use; national management; and international management.

Open Access and Free Use

Under the prevailing regime, most satellites are launched simply on the basis of unilateral decisions by countries that have the capability to do so. Users of space resources, such as the frequency spectrum and the geostationary orbit, pay no rent to anyone for their privileges. Services by the space powers to other countries take place for the most part on the basis of bilateral arrangements negotiated ad hoc with particular clients.

Limited exceptions to this pattern are the International Telecommunication Union (ITU), under whose aegis the use of frequencies is coordinated according to rules to minimize interference, and INTELSAT, which although an international consortium, does not preclude countries from unilaterally performing identical space communications functions.

The basic regime of open access and free use of outer space is based on the assumption that clashes of interest among space users or those affected by their activities would be exceptional occurrences rather than pervasive features of space politics. This regime has been legitimized by the space law that has emerged since the launching of Sputnik, and it draws primarily on maritime law for its concepts.

Thus, the chief U.S. negotiator of the Outer Space Treaty called the language in Article I, which claims outer space as the "province of mankind," a sort of "freedom-of-the-seas" provision.[8] President John F. Kennedy referred to outer space as "this new ocean." The legal regime for Antarctica was also invoked as a pertinent analogy. (The signatories to the Antarctic Treaty, negotiated in the late 1950s, had agreed to hold in abeyance any claims to Antarctica, and to open the area to exploration and scientific research, to use the region for peaceful purposes only, and to permit access on an equal, nondiscriminatory basis to all states.)

The analogies to the ocean and Antarctica, combined with a variety

8. *Treaty on Outer Space,* Hearings before the Senate Committee on Foreign Relations, 90:1 (GPO, 1967), pp. 69–70.

of other legal precepts, became the core of the consensus between the two space powers that was incorporated into various general provisions of the Outer Space Treaty.[9] Nations that were exploring in space would have open access to and free use of all parts of this nonland environment; but they would not have the right to appropriate any part of it, to exclude or interfere with other users of outer space, or to escape responsibilities for their own or their citizens' actions in space. The space powers, however, would retain jurisdiction and control over their national vehicles and personnel in space. The treaty, in effect, placed relatively few constraints on the exploration of outer space by the space powers and preserved for both of them the opportunities to accelerate their ventures into space either competitively or collaboratively, while leaving the international community with virtually no active regulatory authority over the major programs of space exploration then under way.

Article I of the treaty reflects the growing interest of countries in the potential economic returns from the use of outer space. "The exploration and use of outer space, including the moon and other celestial bodies, shall be carried out for the benefit and in the interests of all countries, irrespective of their degree of economic or scientific development, and shall be the province of all mankind."[10] But this obligation is accepted by the space powers on the general assumption that it will not really burden their programs and, in any case, that they themselves will determine unilaterally how it is to be implemented.[11]

9. See Ivan A. Vlasic, "The Space Treaty: A Preliminary Evaluation," *California Law Review*, vol. 55 (May 1967), pp. 507–19; and Thomas R. Adams, "The Outer Space Treaty: An Interpretation in Light of the No-Sovereignty Provision," *Harvard International Law Journal*, vol. 9 (Winter 1968), pp. 140–57. The relationship between an Antarctic legal regime and the requirements of outer space was assessed prominently in Philip C. Jessup and Howard J. Taubenfeld, *Controls for Outer Space, and the Antarctic Analogy* (Columbia University Press, 1959). A representative sampling of the legal writings of this period, and of the use of analogies to the law of the sea, can be found in *Legal Problems of Space Exploration: A Symposium*, prepared for the use of the Senate Aeronautical and Space Sciences Committee, 87:1 (GPO, 1961). Legal thinking in the USSR on questions of space law during the late 1950s and the first half of the 1960s is reflected in a legal review, G. P. Zhukov, *Space Law*, translated from Russian.

10. Outer Space Treaty, 18 U.S.T. 2410, T.I.A.S. 6347.

11. During the Senate ratification hearings on the 1967 Outer Space Treaty, pressures were mounted to attach a formal reservation to the effect that Article I would not obligate the United States to share its space technol-

National Management

A division of the larger environment of outer space into zones for national management is not a live option. Unlike the ocean, and to a lesser degree the weather and climate, the space environment itself (except for the electromagnetic spectrum and the geostationary orbit) is not congested, damaged, or inequitably used. Eventually, when technology allows for space colonization and economic exploitation of the planets and other celestial bodies, there could be attempts by some countries to appropriate particular areas. With respect to most of the uses of outer space examined in the present study, the choice is still between national unilateralism—in effect, a continuation of open access and free use—and multilateral accountability to various countries *on earth* for the effects of activities performed in space.

There is, however, growing agitation, mainly from some developing countries, to allocate scarce frequency and orbit resources on a more or less permanent basis to particular countries. The arguments for such national assignments of frequencies and orbital arcs are that it would prevent interference among users, and that it would also preserve some of the resources for countries that cannot now use them because they lag technologically, but may find them already preempted in the future if the prevailing regime of first up, first use remains the criterion for assigning the resources.

International Management

The rationale for international management of the uses of outer space is based on the premise that this realm belongs to mankind and that all users are therefore accountable to the international community for any disadvantages their use might inflict on others. Some also argue that any benefits gained must be shared.

---

ogy or benefits against the wishes of this country (most concern was over the implications for communications and reconnaissance satellites). The State Department forestalled any such formal reservation by assuring the senators that Article I did not entitle any country to "a free ride," and by agreeing to accept the following language in the report from the Committee on Foreign Relations: "Nothing in Article I, paragraph 1, diminishes or alters the right of the United States to determine how and to what extent it shares the benefits and use of its outer space activities." *Treaty on Outer Space*, Hearings, p. 74.

International management is currently being considered for certain kinds of space satellite functions: the distribution and analysis of data acquired from remote sensing activities; international broadcasting via satellite; maritime communications services; and frequency and orbital use. In each of these fields, some groups of nations feel at a disadvantage with the regime of open access and free use, and are pressing for substantial multilateral oversight of the activities of the space powers.

CHAPTER TEN

Remote Sensing of the Earth from Outer Space

The principal area of international controversy surrounding the remote sensing of the earth by satellite concerns the distribution and use of data acquired by satellite. Some countries have objected to the open distribution policy practiced by the United States on grounds that it interferes with their sovereign control over the development and use of their natural resources. Those nations capable of performing the remote sensing services are themselves questioning free distribution now that such programs are no longer only experimental. They argue that such a regime cannot equitably distribute either the benefits *or* the costs of these programs.

The Purposes of Remote Sensing by Satellite

Reconnaissance satellites have achieved increasing importance for early warning and arms control as military reconnaissance systems based on land have become more vulnerable to political changes. The present study, however, is concerned with the civilian uses of the remote sensing technologies.

From the early 1960s onward, remote sensing for civilian use was conducted from weather satellites, from scientific satellites, and in fact from virtually all unmanned spacecraft. In at least one instance, a large fault system in the western United States was first discovered from a weather satellite photograph. A concerted push in the United States for a satellite program with the primary mission of sensing conditions on earth gained added impetus in 1967–68, when a group of leading U.S. specialists at

Woods Hole prepared a study on space applications.[1] This massive study focused attention on the need for systematic development and testing of technology to develop satellites capable of remote sensing and associated data-handling systems that could be useful for such fields as forestry, agriculture, geography, geology, hydrology, meteorology, and oceanography. During the same period, Soviet space technologists left considerable evidence that, although the USSR appeared not to have dedicated a satellite to detecting earth resources, they had conducted related experiments on data gathered by various manned and unmanned spacecraft, and diverse resource and environmental policymakers had developed considerable interest in data gathered from space.

In most essentials, the Woods Hole recommendations became the basis for the remote sensing experiments performed with data from the first earth-resources technology satellite (ERTS-A, or Landsat 1), launched by the National Aeronautics and Space Administration in 1972. A second satellite, called Landsat 2, was launched in January 1975.

Experiments conducted on data collected by remote sensing devices have been performed by more than two hundred scientists from fifty-two countries, and the ERTS data have been widely distributed. At one point during 1974, the U.S. data distribution center was receiving 5,000–7,000 inquiries a month from around the world. The United States distributed data on request to more than 13,000 petitioners outside the United States in 1973; extractive industries constituted the largest single group of users.

A post-ERTS progress report for the National Academy of Sciences has, in cautious scientific language, concluded that "the potential benefits of remotely sensed earth resource survey data to society appear to be significantly greater than the costs of deploying and operating the ERTS type system."[2] Among the sectors of remote sensing on which there is preliminary evidence of such promise are:

—mapping areas of the world that are difficult to map by conventional methods, and producing maps that record dynamic changes in the conditions and use of the earth's surface;

—geologic mapping of land masses as one of the initial steps toward commercial exploration for minerals and fossil fuels;

1. *Useful Applications of Earth-Oriented Satellites*, Summaries of Panel Reports (National Academy of Sciences, 1969).

2. *Remote Sensing for Resource and Environmental Surveys: A Progress Review* (National Academy of Sciences, 1974), p. 2.

—monitoring patterns of land use, as in rural and urban environments and in coastal zones;

—monitoring geologic hazards and assessing the results of natural disasters;

—forecasting crop yields;

—controlling pests;

—monitoring rangeland;

—surveying soils;

—surveying water resources, identifying the ecological health of bodies of water, monitoring hydrometeorological conditions in the atmosphere and on the earth's surface;

—monitoring the ocean's surface and subsurface conditions to facilitate control of ocean resources and ocean pollution, or gathering data on the state of the ocean pertinent to ocean navigation.

A UN review after the launch of ERTS-A confirmed that remote sensing from space satellites "has very great potential for meeting national, international, regional and global requirements for data relating to the earth's natural environment."[3]

At the time of this writing, no country or group of countries has made a commitment to set up a fully operational earth resource sensing system on the ERTS pattern, although some interest has been shown in a possible European system. The future of the U.S. remote sensing program is itself somewhat clouded by scientific, technical, and financial obstacles, and by internal policy disagreements within the U.S. governmental bureaucracy and among potential users.

Nevertheless, the technology for remote sensing from satellites is here to stay. Several remote sensing satellites are in orbit today under U.S. auspices, and there appears no reason to believe they will all be discontinued in the foreseeable future. In addition to Landsat 1 and 2— for which several successor spacecraft for remote sensing are envisaged on an experimental basis—NASA flies remote sensing satellites for the National Oceanographic and Atmospheric Administration (NOAA), a synchronous meteorological satellite for environmental investigation purposes, Department of Defense satellites for meteorological purposes, and an advanced weather satellite. In the planning stage are others, including a special oceanographic satellite to be called Seasat. NASA

3. "Report of the Working Group on Remote Sensing of the Earth by Satellites on the Work of Its Third Session," UN Doc. A/AC.105/125 (March 13, 1974), p. 7.

plans to use some future manned space shuttles to conduct further, probably improved, remote sensing tasks.

Remote Sensing Technology

Orbiting satellites are only the most recent platforms from which the earth can be remotely sensed. Sensing from satellites is technically no different from that from aircraft, rockets, balloons, or earth-platforms mounted with sensing equipment, whether its purpose is to identify the electromagnetic energy emitted naturally by the earth's features and resources or to read reflected or scattered energy sent from the platforms. The energy is emitted, reflected, or scattered at distinctive wavelengths by each particular surface or atmospheric feature, which can be analyzed for its unique signature. Remote sensors read these distinctive signatures with instruments or cameras sensitive to radiation.

Satellites offer singular advantages for remote sensing of the earth and its weather system, notably in their ability to get pictures of larger or remote areas, with uniform and repetitive coverage. Depending on what an observer is looking for, a spacecraft can be equipped with different types of sensors able to see different phenomena, or able to see them with greater and lesser precision or resolution, and able to function under different environmental conditions.

No single sensing satellite will be able to provide all potential users everything within the current state of the art. Like ERTS, future satellites will be design compromises. Thus, the question of who determines the design of the satellite and its programs has economic consequences.

The agriculturalist may need frequent coverage with high resolution through special sensors. The weather analyst needs synoptic coverage with other sensors, and perhaps a satellite capable of collecting data from land or ocean platforms to be used in conjunction with the other data. Geologists need a satellite that passes over target areas at a given time of day, when lighting conditions are most favorable. Oceanographers need satellites that traverse particular ocean areas that might not be directly under the path of those programmed primarily for land users. The two environments are not best covered with the same categories of sensing devices.

The observation capability of a satellite is determined in part by the orbit of the spacecraft, by the timing of its passage over specific portions of the earth, and by the wavelengths its equipment is built to read. The sensed data is either relayed directly to receiving stations in line of sight, thereby giving nearly instantaneous, or "real time," coverage, or stored in a tape recorder for later relay to a ground station over which the satellite will pass.

A tape recorder on board can give potential global coverage with a minimal number of ground stations. Not having one means that global coverage can be acquired only if many stations to receive data are in place around the globe (one estimate is that fourteen stations will give nearly global coverage). Once the information is received on the ground, it is preserved on tape, which can be transformed into photo images, computer data, or both.

The processing of data from satellites is itself a complex and multi-stage job that needs to be tailored exactly to the eventual purpose of the observation in question. In many instances, data gathered by satellite must be supplemented by data from aircraft or other sources, including on-the-spot observation, before the ultimate user of the information can get the full refinements of observation that are needed to make the satellite data most useful.

Political and Economic Issues

Early in the 1970s, several Canadian specialists who surveyed the rapidly evolving satellite technologies for earth sensing told a prominent international gathering of scientists and technologists that "the development of a global remote-sensing information system has far-reaching implications that are political as well as technical and economic." They urged the nations of the world to begin to think carefully about the international arrangements that would be required to implement this developing capability. "Ultimately," they maintained, "new international organizations may be required to deal with the technical, administrative, and operational activities of global sensing."[4] Many nations would agree

4. J. M. Harrison, L. W. Morely, and A. F. Gregory, "Planning for a Global Remote Sensing Information System," paper presented to the International Astronautical Federation, Brussels, 1971, quoted in *Panel on Science and Technology: Remote Sensing of Earth Resources*, Proceedings of the Committee on Science and Astronautics, 92:2 (GPO, 1972). This was not the first indication of international political concern, but about this time such concern became more widespread.

with the Canadian scientists that the technology has far-reaching implications, but those implications seem to have changed over time.

The earlier concern was largely political: that remote sensing of earth resources threatened to impinge on national sovereignty. Traditionally, nations have been able effectively to control foreign access to their natural resources. The resources under their jurisdiction could neither be surveyed nor used without their concurrence. Although in recent decades much information about resources worldwide has become universally available through conventional research and dissemination, most nations have continued to affirm an essential right of sovereignty over their natural resources—a principle embodied in countless declarations of international law and practice. With the advent of resource surveillance from aircraft, host country prerogatives were retained: airspace was considered an extension of landscape, and foreign overflights, whatever their purpose, were considered illegal unless the state under surveillance consented.

Early in the space age, however, satellites orbiting the earth were treated differently. Then, the space superpowers were able to arrange a laissez-faire outer space regime (free use, open access, neither power restrained from exploring space for peaceful purposes or from conducting military activities in space, except for the orbiting or stationing of weapons of mass destruction).[5] At the time, most nations saw only gains from allowing the early generation of U.S. and USSR weather satellites to circle the planet freely, with the data thus obtained to be openly distributed as agreed internationally. In practice, the international community acquiesced in and promoted the overflight of national territory by remote sensing satellites without requiring national consent.

But the development of satellites designed explicitly to sense earth resources introduced a new element. Now the control over information about its resources that each country had traditionally enjoyed was being eroded by satellite technology, even though the spacecraft were being deployed legally and in full compliance with accepted international procedures.

When NASA launched the experimental Landsat 1 in 1972, there were some efforts, mostly at the United Nations, to promote international legal declarations asserting that the accepted principle of sovereignty over natural resources included sovereignty over information concerning those resources. Some members of the UN Outerspace Com-

5. Outer Space Treaty, Art. IV, 18 U.S.T. 2410, T.I.A.S. 6347.

mittee wanted to reopen the whole question of how the accumulated regime of space law might be changed to take account of the development of earth-oriented remote sensing technologies. Some states argued that a specific rule prohibiting satellite sensing without consent be adopted internationally, and that it apply not only to land areas, but to the areas of the ocean that were certain to fall within the jurisdiction of national resources as a result of the Law of the Sea negotiations in the 1970s. Thus, in 1974, Brazil, with Argentine support, asked the UN to adopt a resolution requiring prior consent for remote sensing.[6]

In the several years following the launch of Landsat, however, the United Nations failed to engage in any wholesale reconsideration of space law. The pertinent debates at the UN and various UN expert studies have left the legal situation for remote sensing essentially unchanged. The UN deliberations have focused on clarification of the capabilities of the technology, and on suggestions for special international arrangements to handle the data gathered by the technology.

Future discussions are likely to concentrate on the ways to allocate internationally the benefits and the costs of remote sensing activities. Three aspects of remote sensing programs are likely to be the focus of these discussions: control over satellite design; the relationships between the satellites and national or regional data receiving systems; and the system of data distribution.

Control over Satellite and Sensor Design

Today the space segment of the experimental remote sensing systems is nationally owned, financed, and managed. It is an open question whether this pattern can, or should, persist for future systems with operational services.[7]

6. UN Doc. A/AC.105/22, February 4, 1974.

7. Rigorous definition of "operational" is recognized by experts to be somewhat difficult. U.S. spokesmen occasioned political controversy in the United Nations when they attempted to neutralize the demands of other countries for a share in the benefits by insisting that the U.S. programs were still "experimental." We are satisfied to accept the UN working definition: an operational system is one that provides an ongoing service based on a continuing requirement from interested users. We also acknowledge that some data available from the early experimental programs can in effect be used operationally because the user needs the data once only, or very infrequently, and does not need repetitive or variable coverage. This is the case, for example, for some (though not all) types of mapping and geology work with satellite pictures.

As the technology becomes more readily available and more easily understood and used, different groups of nations (or different cross-national groups of users) will want somehow to assure themselves that the chosen design of that technology satisfies their special interests, or at least does not ignore them. The experience of ERTS demonstrates that different communities of users are best served by the characteristics of different systems.

Contention among users may be generated by expected improvements in spectral resolution—permitting finer discrimination among different energy wavelengths. These improvements may force choices about what bands a satellite will sense, and here different users may disagree, as the various bands are of differing value for the various uses.[8]

Disagreement is also possible over whether to include on the satellites active sensors or more passive ones.

The recognition that there are significant and not always easily reconcilable differences among users in their preferences for design of future satellites is reflected in calls by U.S. domestic users for more user participation in the choices and design of future satellite sensing systems. Foreign users, too, have begun to press for participation in decisions about systems affecting them.

Data Reception

To be a part of a worldwide operational remote sensing system, nations must invest heavily in data-handling and data-processing equipment and expertise. The ultimate users—the various domestic resource managers and bureaucracies—need to gear their work to the use of data from satellites. In all, this means that substantial and singular national commitments must be made to satellite data systems. Such commitments have already been made to weather satellite systems and are being made by some countries to earth resource systems.

In particular, interest is accelerating in the establishment of national or regional stations for receiving or distributing data similar to that

8. While the present state of the art would permit increases in spatial resolution (sharpness of detail) by a factor of three or four (military sensors have given much sharper detail than ERTS), little actual increase in spatial resolution is expected. Few uses would be served and many might be harmed, for improved spatial resolution can be achieved only by changing other parameters of the system.

collected by ERTS. Three stations exist in the United States, one in Canada, and one in Brazil. Four others are in varying stages of construction in Italy, Iran, Zaire, and Chile. Still others are planned or are under consideration in Argentina, Canada (its second), Venezuela, the Federal Republic of Germany, Norway, Spain, Kenya, Pakistan, Thailand, Indonesia, Australia, Japan, and perhaps elsewhere.

NASA has recognized the need for coordination among users by forming an ERTS Ground Station Advising Committee to facilitate communication. NASA, however, will retain the right to make all final decisions.

It is unclear whether the NASA advisory group will supply sufficient coordination for the user nations to be comfortable over time with a system dependent for the space part of the venture on one country alone. No nation that wholly owns, finances, and manages a global system like ERTS can reasonably be expected to design that system around the needs of foreign users when they conflict with the needs of domestic constituencies. There is also a risk that the sole providing nation could be forced, say by domestic economic constraints, to cut back satellite services, or even to eliminate them entirely. This risk is not fully eliminated by the provision in NASA's agreements on ground stations to share their costs. Political or security considerations could lead to service interruptions, or to threatened interruptions, or the design of the system could be changed unilaterally, with adverse financial and service effects on countries dependent upon the system.

The potential instabilities do not augur well for international operations over which no nation can or should have exclusive responsibility as, for example, satellite sensing services for ocean space and worldwide monitoring of the environment. Yet multiple, duplicative remote sensing systems would be wasteful.

A functioning satellite system for remote sensing is an example of what economists call a public good. If data is already being relayed to the ground, the cost of the relay does not depend upon the ultimate number of users of the data. There is thus no economic reason to orbit more than one set of satellites to perform the various remote sensing tasks; neither ground stations nor on-board tape recorders need to be duplicated for many users to be able to receive the data.

These considerations point to the desirability of a system involving satellite hardware, on-board tape recorders, and ground stations designed to minimize the cost of providing remotely sensed data to a global audience. Such a system is not likely to be the same as the system that returns remotely sensed data at the lowest cost to the nation providing the hardware. The recognition that there are complicated interdependencies between the design and costs of the space segment and data receiving systems was reflected in a request by the Scientific and Technical Sub-Committee of the Committee on the Peaceful Uses of Outer Space that the UN Secretariat prepare:

A study on the organizational and financial requirements of a future operational space segment for global coverage to be internationally operated, owned and financed. This study would include both a brief outline of possible technical configurations and a presentation of organizational and financial alternatives for an international cooperative venture. It would also need to make and state certain assumptions regarding user requirements and priorities and regarding technical constraints on the system.[9]

Data Distribution

In addition to the issues of how best to provide the equipment that is used in space, and of how to coordinate that equipment and the receiving station systems, there are concerns about the method and terms of data distribution. Some countries remain wary about the use of data generated by satellite, fearing that the information will be used to their detriment by hostile states, competitors, or corporations. As more experience is gained with data from Landsat 1, however, the primary concern is over gaining access to data at the lowest possible cost.

Currently, the data generated by U.S. civilian satellites are handled according to a policy of open distribution. Since the launching of ERTS, NASA has made the data obtained from this system available to anyone requesting it, at a modest price calculated to cover only the costs of duplicating the imagery or tapes.

The agreements negotiated with those countries building ground stations require them to make the data available to all who ask at a reasonable price. The agreements also permit the United States to begin charging the ground stations a fee for the privilege of receiving the data, beginning one year after the launch of Landsat 2.

The major advantages of an open data policy are that it is self-operating, the selection (presumably) being made by the consumers, and that everyone benefits by the greater availability of information

9. *Draft Report of the Scientific and Technical Sub-Committee on the Work of Its Twelfth Session*, UN Doc. A/AC.105/C.1/L.70/Add. 1 (April 30, 1975), p. 6.

about the earth. In addition, open distribution of the data may stimulate the introduction into countries lagging in technology of innovations and skills associated with the analysis and application of the data. Private entrepreneurs specializing in analyzing the data could market their services more effectively by using photographs of the intended buyer's terrain to illustrate the usefulness of their services.

It is necessary, however, to note that there is not now (nor will there be) complete disclosure by any of the countries with satellites capable of earth sensing. Military reconnaissance from space uses the most advanced equipment with the highest power of resolution, and a country capable of operating in space may not always wish to have other countries know either what information it is able to gather or exactly what intelligence it has. There is no way of completely assuring other countries that data gained through unilateral military surveillance is not being given on a selective basis to particular countries or to private corporations.

The distinction observed internationally between data gathered from space for national security and that gathered for other purposes has already become blurred. U.S. personnel have had access to the superior meteorological data gathered by the United States Air Force weather satellite for national security and are working to integrate it with data from ERTS to produce sophisticated economic intelligence on projected crop yields throughout the world. The U.S. government has promised to make available to all countries economically relevant data that have been gathered from military satellites. Other countries are nevertheless likely to remain suspicious that they are not getting all the data.[10]

In addition to the possibility of unequal access to data, considerable international concern surrounds the inequality of capabilities for using data. While both poor and technologically advanced countries benefit from the open dissemination of data on earth resources derived from space satellites, the advanced countries and private corporations have far greater capabilities than the poor countries to interpret and use the data. The industrialized countries have advantages in using the information about their own and other countries' resources to exploit natural

10. Consideration has been given by the U.S. government to consolidating satellite programs within the Department of Defense. One proposal would put all U.S. weather satellites under the Department of Defense to save the costs of separate military and civilian operations. Some members of Congress have suggested that other satellites observing the earth, including the earth resources program, could be shifted to the Department of Defense.

resources on land and sea, to plan their own economies based on this information, and to bargain for concessions from developing countries. For example, some developing countries are concerned that the data could be used to their detriment when others have knowledge of the potential crop yield of a developing country and the developing country does not know how to use the knowledge, or when mining companies use the data to locate potentially economically significant mineral deposits and the developing country is not party to this analysis or its implications. The open availability of data from ERTS, however, permits such countries at least to hire consultants to analyze the same data, thus potentially reducing the disparity at the bargaining table between the poorer countries and mining companies.

These concerns are probably excessive, but they are not without foundation. In the case of commodities, knowledge derived from satellite data could lead either to highly informed, short-term speculation on the commodities market, at the expense of those who do not have the same knowledge (such as developing countries, farmers, etc.), or ultimately to a substantial reduction in high risk speculation on futures in the commodity market. Normally, mining companies would need aerial surveys and site testing in addition to the data obtained by satellite before they would invest in the potential mineral deposits. This need offers developing countries some opportunity to protect their interests by enacting stringent laws governing access to them. The satellite data, however, constitute an important component of the knowledge base, and there is a natural concern over the terms on which countries may gain access to it. Hiring private consultants to analyze raw data from remote sensing sources can be an expensive proposition, particularly if the expertise is concentrated in only a few countries.[11]

A Preferred Regime for Remote Sensing

It is tempting to be sanguine about the future of remote sensing policies on the basis of post-ERTS discussions at the United Nations and elsewhere. One interpretation of these discussions is that they have

11. U.S. officials, in urging the UN Space Committee to support arrangements that would facilitate the acquisition and open dissemination of remotely sensed data, revealed in 1975 that U.S. mining companies, using computer-assisted data analyses, have been able to gain information on potentially lucrative mining sites earlier than the countries housing these sites. See "U.S. Probe Uncovers Copper," *Washington Post*, February 22, 1975.

effectively disposed of the principal political and economic issues raised by remote sensing. According to this view, the international community accepts the rights of the space powers unilaterally to deploy remote sensing satellites to achieve global coverage, so long as they make the data available to nations interested in using it on a nondiscriminatory, open basis. There is still, however, considerable discussion of systems. The best arguments, from our perspective, point to some degree of internationalization, sufficient to ensure collective decisionmaking among concerned nations when international coverage is involved.

The Basic System

Wholly national systems for remote sensing may create pressures for other countries to mount their own programs, if only for purposes of prestige, even though such duplication would not add significantly to their knowledge of their own or global resources. Some form of internationalization of the relationships between the space equipment and the ground station may therefore be the only way to provide remote sensing in the least costly way. Internationalization could mean simply having the space segment launched and run by a single nation, but with formal agreements with receiver countries to ensure its continuation and provide for joint financing. This would involve more international accountability than currently exists, but would mean a minimal amount of international management. Another alternative would have the basic system run by an international organization established specifically for this purpose. Internationalization would require predominant financing by the technologically advanced or wealthy nations, no matter which variant was instituted, and these nations would therefore require commensurate management responsibility for the system to be at all feasible.

There is already evidence in the United States of some reluctance to give foreign nations a free ride on systems paid for by the U.S. taxpayer. An example of this is the provision in agreements on ground stations that permits fees for future access. Agencies such as NASA may eventually develop their own preferences for joint international financing. Budget pressures are sure to increase on remote sensing programs, which have never been high priority or large budget items anyway. And NASA may see some advantage—as it has in other international space activities—in securing other nations' financial commitments as insurance against congressional pressures to cut back.

A farsighted approach would have the U.S. government sponsor the idea that remote sensing via satellite is an international public service rather than a commercial operation. This would imply institutional arrangements for international oversight of the design and operation of future remote sensing systems. Those who provide the technology and the money would retain a weighty if not necessarily determinative voice, but without denying less advanced nations a meaningful role in systems management.

Anticipating some degree of internationalization, early consultations with other countries are needed—while the technology is still in the so-called preoperational phase—to establish the general guidelines for organizing and financing future sensing on a multinational basis. It is not too early for international discussions on fundamental designs—how many systems should perform which functions, what kinds of performance compromises can offer the most service to various users at the least cost, how multiple systems (which seem unavoidable) are to be linked up and coordinated, and so on. In this respect, the NASA ERTS Ground Station Advising Committee is a step in the right direction, even if it is not the total answer.

Distribution and Use of the Data

Concern over the existing system of data handling has given rise to several suggestions for new approaches. One method would obligate the state or international consortium launching the satellite for a particular country to provide imagery only to that country (and possibly to organizations that are members of the UN family). States would receive any film frame concerning their own territory. A variation on this scheme would give the photographed country priority of access to the imagery for a limited period (say, ninety days), after which it would be openly available. For estimates of crop production, where very prompt receipt of the information is necessary, priority of access would be valuable. For other purposes—mapping, for example—that do not depend upon highly variable data and repetitive sensing, priority of access probably would make little difference.

Another variant, possibly of interest to some developing countries, would make the data available to specified international organizations, perhaps only upon the consent of the country that is the object of the remote sensing. Whereas some states may be reluctant to have their neighbors acquire the photographs directly, they may be willing to have international experts assist them in analysis, which could be made generally available when completed. Substantial administrative problems would attach to any attempt to assure that other countries did not obtain access to the data during the period of its analysis by the international experts.

The principal disadvantage of attempts to legitimize selective distribution is that it is unlikely to work even if funneled through international organizations. Although it would theoretically allow the satellite operators and the state that is the object of the remote sensing to have a monopoly on much useful data, the opportunities for clandestine transmission of the data to other interested states would be considerable. Consequently, it is unlikely that the satellite operators and the sensed states could negotiate selective distribution arrangements that were mutually satisfactory.

A better approach to the problem of differential ability to analyze raw data is to improve the open distribution system. The advantages of the policy of open distribution could be maintained and some of its apparent disadvantages to developing countries alleviated if the benefits of the data could be brought to those states that are the object of remote sensing but are not in a position to use the data optimally without special assistance. Such an international program would have two central objectives: to ensure that developing countries receive the data and are able to have it analyzed and interpreted for their own needs; and to help ensure that these countries are able to use the information effectively in their own planning and in their relations with states and private bodies that may be using the same data.

These objectives might be furthered through a disinterested service, probably under UN auspices, to help analyze and interpret data procured by remote sensing systems. The international user service would make available expert advice for determining the applicability of the data to the particular problems of a country and for analyzing and interpreting the data for some purposes; it would provide assistance to countries if they wished to choose a consulting firm to analyze the data; and it would help establish indigenous programs to analyze and interpret remote sensing data. Funds could be made available to developing countries, either on a multilateral or bilateral basis, to acquire the expertise with which to analyze and interpret satellite photography or to hire others to do so. An international service of this sort is favored by a few countries, including the United States.

The proposed international user service would receive a free copy of all the data gathered by any satellite designed to sense earth resources. The U.S. government has offered in the past to make a copy of all its ERTS data available to an appropriate international body, but domestic forces have been pushing for the nationalization of satellite information. They may succeed in getting the government to withdraw the offer unless counterpressure is brought to bear. The USSR has supported the idea of providing a copy of remote sensing data on earth resources to an international center, but on a voluntary basis.[12]

In sum, unilateralism by the space powers, even if accompanied by a nondiscriminatory policy for distribution of data, would seem likely to perpetuate feelings of inequity and resentment on the part of many countries. Attempts to restrict access to the data might result in an economically inefficient system in which there were competing sensing systems and a new version of political spheres of influence. There might also be adverse effects on international programs in which states now share the data from remote sensing satellites, such as the World Weather Watch and the Global Atmospheric Research Program. The approach that appears to us most consistent with the "common-benefit" objectives of the Outer Space Treaty has the powers capable of operating in space supporting institutionalization of international arrangements of primary benefit to the poorer countries.

12. Where states have established or plan to establish ground stations to receive data direct from satellites, it may be most efficient to establish regional user services. The regional operations could also provide training programs to develop indigenous expertise in analyzing and interpreting the data received by the ground stations and applying it to problems in the receiver states.

CHAPTER ELEVEN

Television Broadcasting via Satellites

New and prospective technological developments have led some governments to fear that they might lose control over what their citizens see if broadcasters deploy systems for beaming television signals via satellite directly to the ultimate viewer, without conventional retransmission on land. Depending on one's point of view, these developments give rise to new opportunities to build the community of man or pose fearsome threats to independence. Both the hopes and the fears, however, are nourished by considerable misunderstanding and uncertainty about the state of the art of direct broadcast technologies.

The confusion about direct broadcasting technology and its future warrants a survey of the state of the art, particularly as it may affect the crucial political question of government control over signals beamed to their countries. We can then distinguish between those political issues that are based only on technological fantasies and those that do reflect this technology's capability for changing relationships between societies.

Characteristics of the Technology

Up to now, the main business of international communications satellites has been to provide what specialists call distributional or point-to-point communications channels over long distances. Telephone, telegraph, and television signals are sent by an earth station to a satellite, which in turn amplifies and retransmits them to another earth station. From there they are sent by a microwave tower or cable to an ultimate user. The satellite substitutes, as it were, for a giant microwave tower in the sky. So far as television is concerned, present technology does not allow signals beamed from space to be received directly; normal television system reception requires an intermediate step after the signals have been brought down from the satellite. This means that national governments, or at least local authorities in charge of the receiving stations, retain control over what people within their jurisdiction see on their screen.

In order to beam a television signal directly via satellite to a distant viewer without conventional terrestrial retransmission over land, three conditions must be met. First, a satellite must be available with sufficiently high power to deliver a signal to reach the intended receiver. A high-powered signal in effect compensates for the absence of the complex earth stations that normally take a weaker signal and pass it on to ultimate viewers. For such a system, cost and performance adjustments must be made between the size and complexity of the satellites and receiver terminals; generally, the smaller the receiving terminal, the larger the satellite. Second, there must be a proper fit between the technical characteristics of the signal sent and the receiving equipment used. The broadcasts must meet standards for picture (lines per inch and signal scanning), for transmission (signal modulation and spacing between sound carriers), and for channels (radio frequency and assigned bandwidth).[1] Third, the receiving sets must also have unoccupied channels on which that signal can be received.

Direct broadcast systems can fall into either of two broad classes, although the distinctions between them may not be completely unambiguous in all conceivable direct broadcasting systems.

The first class, involving *community reception,* is well within the competence of current technology, and is being tested experimentally in the United States and seriously considered for future deployment in a number of developed and developing states. In the community system, receiving terminals of moderate size and complexity are coupled

1. An informed, broad technical overview of the state of the art in high-powered communications satellites is A. M. Greg Andrus, "A Survey of High Power Communications Satellite System Technology," paper presented at the International Conference on Communications, Sponsored by the IEEE Communications Society and the Philadelphia Section of IEEE (June 19–21, 1972; processed). The technical requirements for direct broadcast systems, including the design of both spacecraft and receiving units, are outlined in CCIR Study Group Draft Report 215-2 (rev. 1972), *Systems for Sound and Television Broadcasting from Satellites.*

with much more powerful satellites than those now being used by the International Telecommunications Satellite Consortium (INTELSAT). The receiving terminals and associated equipment are small enough to be mounted on the roof of a village center or schoolhouse, or some other facility permitting television viewing by sizable groups of people. Present experiments are using antennas seven to ten feet high. Tests under way with this technology are delivering signals directly to as many as several thousand community receiving units of extremely simple design. Other experiments are matching direct broadcast satellites with fewer but considerably more complex community installations.

The second class of direct broadcasting is geared to *individual or home reception.* The receiving unit here could conceivably be either an ordinary television set with an antenna, of the kind now in mass production around the world, or an individual television receiver specially augmented to receive direct broadcasts, so the satellite must be correspondingly more powerful; how much additional power is required depends on the precise technical characteristics of the signal that must be delivered. There are technological problems still to be resolved in the design of spacecraft, in on-board electronics, and in techniques for delivering the signal, but none of the outstanding problems calls for knowledge much beyond the present or anticipated boundaries of advanced satellite engineering. Prevailing technological assumptions project very high costs—launch vehicles required to lift such heavy satellites into stationary orbit would alone run into the $200–$300-million range, roughly ten times the launch costs for one of today's INTELSAT-class satellites. These costs for payload and design might be substantially reduced, however, by sophisticated augmentations of present-day television receivers, or by dissemination of the new generation of home receivers now being built in some advanced industrial nations especially to receive direct satellite broadcasts.

While forecasts on the maturing of the required technologies continue to vary, for purposes of assessing alternative international and institutional responses to the concerns raised by various governments, the basic UN forecast of 1969 should suffice: television broadcasts via satellite directly into conventional unaugmented home receivers are highly unlikely before 1985; television broadcasts via satellites directly into home receivers with special augmentation equipment could be technologically feasible in the late 1970s (work is now under way on sophisticated receiver hardware for such systems in Germany and Japan, and other nations are actively considering such systems); television broadcasting into community receivers is within the current ability of technology.

Political Implications of the Technology

So long as a government or its subordinate authorities can maintain essential control over the installations for community reception, performing a sort of gatekeeper function, the entry of unsolicited programs can be prevented. Even where there were extremely large numbers of community installations, the advantage would rest with a government determined to control, rather than with an intruder trying to penetrate. Moreover, the possibility for government counteraction is believed by some experts to be a sufficient deterrent to potentially intrusive broadcasters.[2] Thus, by supervising the technical design of community installations and exercising normal administrative authority over local communications systems, national governments can generally maintain control over what their citizens see on television broadcasts relayed by satellite.

Government control over broadcasting to individual receivers, whether augmented or unaugmented, would be far more difficult than over broadcasts to a community installation. Control might require, for example, restrictions on the import or production of augmentation equipment, or alteration of sets so that they can receive only government signals, or a monopoly of all available channels by signals originating on land and not capable of being overcome by those from an unwanted satellite broadcast. Intrusive television broadcasting across international boundaries, particularly if it is intended to reach many countries at once, is likely to present the prospective broadcaster with major technical hurdles, largely because of the need to make television signals compatible in all respects with technical characteristics of the specific receiving units used by the intended audience.[3] Moreover, while it is technically feasible to convert a satellite-broadcast program to meet the varied

2. This is the argument of French experts in Abram Chayes and others, *Satellite Broadcasting* (Oxford University Press, 1973), p. 29. This volume is a useful overall assessment of how British, American, Japanese, and French experts anticipate dealing with direct broadcasting to community systems.

3. Observers sophisticated about these technical obstacles have underlined the point by saying that the immense diversity of basic technical standards in the world's television systems serves as a kind of "universal contraceptive" against intrusive direct satellite broadcasting on any large scale.

standards of recipient sets without the cooperation of host governments, the required alteration of broadcasting equipment, whether through greater sophistication or heavier payloads, involves high costs.

All this implies substantial built-in invulnerability to direct television broadcasting on a massive international scale—meaning that countries continuing to use televisions with the technical characteristics currently in worldwide use will not be *technically* vulnerable to intrusive broadcasting until the most high-powered and exotic capabilities for direct broadcasting from satellites to individual receivers are available.

A country that either augments its present television receivers to accommodate direct broadcasts or adopts new types of receivers capable of receiving broadcasts directly from satellites may be increasing its potential vulnerability to unwanted satellite broadcasting by bringing its national television system within reach of this technological capability. For prospective broadcasters, the technological constraints, when combined with differences in time zones and language around the globe, point to direct television broadcasting to a specific country or perhaps to a specific region as potentially more attractive than any kind of universal programming.

Direct radio broadcasting using satellites would probably also be burdened by technological obstacles because of the types of radios now in use internationally. These technical problems are reduced when the state receiving the transmission cooperates by adopting types of radios geared to direct satellite broadcasting. Educational systems using this technology have been under study in the past. If user charges come down, international radio broadcasters might well use satellites to relay programs to the existing worldwide network of transmitters on land that relay signals to radios. But intrusive radio broadcasting via satellite to these same radios, even if the proper incentives made it technologically feasible, does not seem to present any special advantage. It would probably not be too attractive to international radio broadcasters unless they felt insecure about access to present land transmitters or adequate substitutes.

Responses to the prospects of intrusive television broadcasting may go beyond simple avoidance maneuvers to increase invulnerability, such as retaining control over community systems or manipulating the technical characteristics of receivers and availability of channels.[4] As in the

4. Both of these countermeasures already have some precedent in international terrestrial television broadcasting: East Germany has attempted to prevent reception of West German television programs by installing com-

radio field, *electronic* countermeasures could be available to obstruct the broadcasts beamed from satellites. Any one of several alternative jamming methods would entail expensive equipment and considerable technical complexity. Probably only the two major space powers could claim, for many years to come, an ability to destroy physically an offending satellite. Only a handful of advanced nations appear capable of developing electronic antisatellite capabilities. The majority of countries, including many of those that are most worried about the harmful effects of direct satellite broadcasting, would have difficulty obtaining jamming capabilities without outside help. Depending on the technical characteristics of the television receivers in question, even countries with less sophisticated technology can use land transmitters to beam signals nationally that are difficult to override or capture by a satellite-based signal aimed at unaugmented receivers.

Existing Legal Constraints on Direct Broadcasting

The fundamental law for outer space, the 1967 treaty, is silent on the question of direct broadcasting, although its provisions are pertinent. An effort by Egypt, with Brazilian support, to insert an article concerning direct broadcasting into the Outer Space Treaty met with failure. The article would have imposed a moratorium on the use of direct broadcast satellites until such time as worldwide regulations for technology and program content had been established by international agreement. Most governments, including the United States, contented themselves at the time with the position that the issues deserved further study and discussion.

Thus far, the existing legal constraints on direct broadcasting emanate from the International Telecommunication Union (ITU), the UN specialized agency responsible for developing technical regulations for international broadcasting and securing voluntary compliance with them from member nations. As a result of decisions endorsed by the ITU in 1971, satellite broadcasting has been brought under the provisions of a

---

munity antenna systems that receive only domestic broadcasts. Israel changed from VHF to UHF to keep out unwanted VHF-transmitted signals from neighboring Arab states. Other countries have also tried to effect import restrictions or other equipment controls to insulate citizens from foreign television programs.

fairly extensive corpus of technical and administrative regulations.[5] The most important of these is Radio Regulation Number 428A, which provides:

In devising the characteristics of a space station in the Broadcasting-Satellite Service, all technical means available shall be used to reduce, to the maximum extent practicable, the radiation over the territory of other countries unless an agreement has been previously reached with such countries.[6]

The British government and others have suggested that this rule should be regarded as tantamount to a formal consent requirement for direct broadcasting from all receiving countries.

The argument is that, in accepting the 1971 ITU regulations, a country has obligated itself to consult with those it may affect by a broadcast satellite system; and although the regulations were designed primarily to deal with the technical problem of interference with other communications from signals broadcast by satellite, receiving countries in practice could use rule 428A to decide they did not want to receive certain transmissions. As of this writing, the U.S. government formally maintains that 428A is only a technical regulation covering avoidable radiation that physically interferes with other communications services, but some U.S. lawyers see the possibility of relying on procedures to avoid radiation as a way to defuse the controversial political issues.[7]

The Political Controversy

The technological constraints on television broadcasting via satellite to populations against the will of their governments should, perhaps, have obviated the need for heavy international regulation of this particular use of outer space. But the political issue has been joined at the level of conflicting grand principles—freedom of information versus national sovereignty—in a way that makes it difficult to find technical means to allay the sensitivities of the various parties. It may be correct

5. Gerd D. Wallenstein, "Make Room in Space: Harmony and Dissonance in International Telecommunications," pt. 1, *Telecommunication Journal,* vol. 40 (January 1973), pp. 29–46; and pt. 2, *Telecommunication Journal,* vol. 40 (February 1973), pp. 95–102.

6. Quoted by Abram Chayes and Paul Laskin, *Direct Broadcasting from Satellites: Policies and Problems* (American Society of International Law, 1975), p. 20.

7. Ibid., pp. 21–22.

to say that direct broadcasting is not a real issue in technical terms, but the political fuss over hypothetical applications of direct broadcasting is now part of the international scene, and it provides the various technical options with highly charged ideological symbolism.

An appreciation of the evolution of the political controversy, therefore, helps to understand any attempts to induce international cooperation in the use of this technology and the widest dissemination of its benefits.

A demarche by the USSR pushed the issue of international regulation of television broadcasting via satellite into worldwide prominence in late 1972. Foreign Minister Andrei Gromyko asked the UN General Assembly to endorse a treaty that stipulates: "Direct television broadcasting to foreign States is to be carried out only with the express consent of the latter." All states would be granted the legal right to "utilize the means at their disposal in order to counteract illegal direct television broadcasting of which they are the object." This provision would extend legal protection to jamming offending satellites, to shooting them down, or to neutralizing them electronically. The USSR went beyond saying simply that nonconsensual broadcasting is prohibited, and proposed restrictions on program content, making the following kinds of direct broadcasts illegal: those "detrimental" to the maintenance of peace, those entailing "interference" in domestic affairs of states, those that propagandize "violence [and] horrors," or undermine "the foundations of local civilization [and] culture," and those serving to "misinform the public."[8]

The most vigorous defenders of international "freedom of information" were quick to respond to Gromyko. Frank Stanton, then vice chairman of the Columbia Broadcasting System and a key adviser to the United States Information Agency, spearheaded a public exposure of the issue when he saw—correctly—that the State Department was trying to avoid a head-on confrontation in the diplomatic arena. Stanton argued, "Delaying tactics, pleas that haste is unnecessary or further study is required are entirely out of place when the fundamental principle of free speech is at stake. There can be no temporizing. You don't negotiate free speech. The United States must do all within its power to block the path to international censorship." "Any other course," he insisted, "would be unworthy of our national heritage. When liberty is

8. UN Doc. A/8771, August 9, 1972.

threatened, when freedom of thought is challenged, the policy of the United States must be resolute and uncompromising."[9]

The USSR makes no secret of the fact that its opposition to unregulated television broadcasting by satellite rests partly on a wish to avoid exposure to satellite-based television such as Radio Liberty, Radio Free Europe, or the Voice of America. Even, perhaps especially, during an emerging détente, the USSR takes as a paramount foreign policy objective the protection of its sphere against electronic intrusion of Western ideas and influences, as a counterpart to tightening ideological harnesses internally against political opposition and dissent. Conceivably, a large part of the USSR's motivation in proposing its satellite television treaty to the United Nations was to buttress its case in the European political and security negotiations of the early 1970s—particularly at the Conference on Security and Cooperation in Europe—where the Western push for freer human contacts and exchanges of people and ideas across the old dividing lines of the cold war became a prime point of confrontation between the USSR and Western governments.

The General Assembly did not accept the Soviet treaty proposal of 1972. Instead, it endorsed a compromise devised by some European states authorizing the United Nations to elaborate general principles to govern transnational direct broadcasting, with a view to the eventual conclusion of one or more international conventions on the subject.[10] The U.S. government was unwilling to accept this compromise,[11] and cast the lone vote against it in the General Assembly—with 102 nations voting in the affirmative. U.S. officials argued that the compromise did not support the principle of international free flow of information strongly enough and that it prematurely set a course toward principles or a treaty, when neither was currently warranted by the state of the technology for direct broadcasting. At the same time, over U.S. opposition, the United Nations Educational, Scientific, and Cultural Organization (UNESCO) also adopted in 1972 a declaration of principles for satellite broadcasting, culminating several years of efforts by France and a coalition of developing nations. While generally less restrictive than the USSR draft treaty and more promotive of the potential social value of

9. Frank Stanton, "Will They Stop Our Satellites?" *New York Times*, October 22, 1972.

10. UN Doc. A/RES/2916 (XXVII), November 14, 1972, p. 4.

11. See Statement of the United States, First Committee of the General Assembly, in Press Release USUN-125(72), October 20, 1972.

direct broadcasting technologies, the UNESCO language also calls for "prior agreements concerning direct satellite broadcasting to the population of countries other than the country of origin of the transmission."[12] Subsequently, in 1973, Sweden and Canada took an intermediary position by introducing a draft treaty calling only for the consent of countries that were to receive broadcasts. There were no references to program content in their draft treaty, which has become the focus of much of the UN debate.

The task of attempting to formulate a consensus on legal principles was assigned to a working group of the Legal Subcommittee of the Committee on the Peaceful Uses of Outer Space. The March 1975 report of the working group showed some convergence from the polar positions of 1972, but as yet nothing approaching a consensus that could form the basis for a draft treaty acceptable to the United States, other industrialized countries, the USSR, and most of the developing countries. To the extent that there is an emerging consensus, however, it would seem to be that the essential question now is *how* to regulate television broadcasting across national boundaries, rather than *whether* to do so.[13]

Granting the need for some regulation, the U.S. government remains in favor of Article 19 of the Universal Declaration of Human Rights, which asserts the right "to receive and impart information and ideas through any media regardless of frontiers." U.S. representatives to the United Nations Working Group on Direct Broadcasting Satellites have steadfastly maintained their adamant objections to a prior consent treaty, branding it as a device to impose censorship on international broadcasts. One of their most telling arguments has been that a prior consent rule would give some countries a handle for preventing even the domestic broadcasts of neighboring countries, let alone for interfering with regional international arrangements. As one U.S. official put it rhetorically:

How would a country deal with a challenge to its own domestic direct broadcast satellite system by a neighboring country objecting to some undesired

12. UN Doc. A/AC.105/109, February 12, 1973. The Soviet draft treaty and the UNESCO declaration are compared in Charles Dalfen, "Direct Satellite Broadcasting: International Responses," paper prepared for delivery at the Conference on International Communications and Institutions, Ottawa, Canada (March 24, 1973; processed).

13. Legal Subcommittee, Committee on the Peaceful Uses of Outer Space, "Draft Report of the Chairman of Working Group II," UN Doc. PUOS/C.2 (XIV)/1/Add. 3, March 4, 1975.

spillover? Could one country in a specific geographic area veto the operation of a regional system by refusing to consent to the arrangement because of spillover? Do countries supporting the prior consent principle assume they can make convenient exceptions to exclude some countries in a region? Furthermore, if the countries in a particular region decide they do not wish to have a prior consent restriction on regional broadcasting, would it be possible simply to make an exception to a global principle? Have countries which may desire domestic or regional systems weighed the viability of relying on such exceptions based on subjective distinctions between unavoidable or unintentional spillover on the one hand and intentional broadcasts on the other?[14]

By making the spillover problem a central issue, perhaps *the* central issue, the United States seems only to have let loose a boomerang, which has returned to its own feet in the form of suggestions by other countries that the Americans apply their technological expertise to developing technical means for avoiding unwanted spillover. Studies now under way at the ITU and by national governments may resolve the issue to some extent if they show, as expected, that the state of the art allows the use of various techniques to reduce spillover: beam shaping and satellite stability; reduction of signal amplitude in border areas, coupled with the use of more sensitive receivers and higher gain antennae in those areas; antenna directivity and shielding in the direction of unwanted transmissions; assignment of separate frequencies to adjacent countries; use of receivers requiring special decoding in order to receive the unwanted transmissions.

Alternative Approaches

Some degree of accountability by the broadcasters to those societies that may receive the broadcasts (either by design or inadvertently) seems to be a premise from which negotiations are proceeding in the United Nations. The main alternatives appear to be a consultative regime, a prior consent regime, and an agreement regime.

Consultative Regime

The least onerous regime, from the point of view of the United States, would obligate broadcasters to consult with those who would be receiving the program, both in advance and during the life of a program, to

14. Statement by Lee T. Stull at the Fifth Session of the United Nations Working Group on Direct Broadcast Satellites, March 13, 1974. United States Information Service Press Release.

minimize technical, political, and cultural conflicts such programs might occasion.

From the point of view of most of the developing countries, the USSR, and countries like Canada and Sweden that have been attempting to work out a compromise, such a regime would leave too much leeway to the broadcaster countries, for it would not establish the presumption that broadcasts offensive to the recipient countries are illegitimate.

Prior Consent Regime

Most countries still favor prohibiting all television broadcasts relayed by satellite that have not been approved in advance by the countries receiving them. But this would amount to prior censorship beyond that practiced by the U.S. government for domestic programs and would probably contravene the First Amendment to the Constitution. The prior consent regime would also allow countries that were not the target of a broadcast to veto programs from which they accidentally received radiation, even though the programs had been agreed to by the United States and particular recipient countries. The United States would surely refuse to be bound by any such prohibitions, and thus a regulatory system incorporating these features would only undermine progress toward legal accountability in broadcasting. The United States would probably continue to broadcast internationally, and other countries would have to resort to jamming to prevent unwanted broadcasts from penetrating their jurisdictions.

Agreement Regime

The partially contrary objectives of facilitating the freest international exchange of ideas and information while supporting a climate of mutual respect and accountability in the field of space broadcasting could, in our opinion, best be reconciled in a regime that incorporated the following features:

1. *A general international convention would stipulate that broadcasting via satellite into foreign countries should be with the agreement of the involved countries.* (The convention would incorporate existing ITU rules on technical coordination with all receipient countries to minimize unavoidable spillover.)

Such a convention would be consistent with the central tenets and operating requirements of American international information policies.

These policies include a commitment to open up the largest possible number of information channels across international boundaries. Most of these channels would not transmit information to foreign populations against the wishes of their governments. Rather, they would be used to facilitate communications involving consensual relations with foreign governments accepting U.S. information sources and personnel—relations estimated to account for more than 95 percent of all of the government's international communication activity.[15] Thus, basic U.S. policy on international communications, rather than rigidly insisting on freedom of information, would shift toward encouraging a working network of agreements with other countries. We are convinced that uncompromising U.S. insistence on an absolutely open regime for satellite broadcasting would work contrary to present arrangements and would impede extension of any eventual capabilities for direct broadcasting. In this sense, we assert that acceptance of a cooperative international regime for satellite broadcasting will enlarge—not diminish—prospects for the free flow of information internationally.

In contrast, intrusive satellite broadcasting would do substantial harm to the international information programs of the United States. The technological limitations of worldwide television broadcasting would raise major financial and practical obstacles. Aimed at adversaries that are advanced nations, intrusive broadcasting probably would not be immune from jamming; the return on the use of such an expensive, politically volatile, and vulnerable tool would seem marginal at best. It is therefore not surprising that communications professionals in government international broadcasting circles in the United States and Great Britain give some evidence of acknowledging this.[16]

The recommended regime would acknowledge that the central international political problem raised by direct satellite broadcasting is to control the misuse of this technology by governments. Credible scenarios for future direct broadcasting, other than by agreement with govern-

15. L. John Martin, "Effectiveness of International Propaganda," *Annals of the American Academy of Political and Social Science*, vol. 398 (November 1971), pp. 62–63.

16. This is not to imply, however, that the weight of leadership in the relevant organ of the U.S. Information Agency, the Voice of America, would favor this course of action. For many years, the USIA has, in its congressional testimony, left open the door to satellite broadcasting. See also the *26th Report: United States Advisory Commission on Information* (GPO, January 27, 1973), esp. pp. 22–23 and 39.

ments affected, are difficult to construct. They might include broadcasting to community receivers that temporarily escape government control, or to individual receivers capable of being reached directly by satellite. Overall, the conclusion seems inescapable that for the foreseeable future only governments would have enough incentives and wherewithal to employ intrusive broadcasting direct from satellites, and they would do so chiefly for information and propaganda purposes. Private corporate use of broadcasting, circumventing government control, for purposes such as advertising, is unlikely to be technologically practical or commercially attractive because of the costs involved, the audience limitations for many forms of direct broadcasting, the ready availability of alternative advertising methods, and the risks of provoking hostility and perhaps economic countermeasures from local governments. Likewise, the international television industry appears to have every strong incentive to utilize direct broadcast capabilities only in conjunction with consenting authorities or other recognized public or broadcasting authorities.

2. *Appropriate codes of conduct and guidelines for program content would be developed by nongovernmental and specialized multilateral broadcasting associations.*

In a diverse world community with deep-rooted differences about the acceptability of various categories of information, the prospects of successful intergovernmental negotiations to achieve universal agreement on program content are small. Whatever agreement might be achieved would probably allow only for the blandest programs. An alternative is to formulate the multinational arrangements through the professional broadcasting associations. This mode of arranging for international programs already has been used extensively and successfully. A large number of nations have endorsed an expanded role for such organizations in establishing the ground rules for international broadcasting.

This suggestion is based on the observation that the tension between promoting international freedom of information and respecting legitimate national interests will be best resolved not in the grand clash of legal principles formulated and defended absolutely in treaty negotiations, but in the less formal institutional and collaborative structures among broadcasters who are committed to serving both principles as fully as possible in broadcasting operations. Intergovernmental oversight arrangements, perhaps negotiated among countries in a region, might be required to assure *compliance,* but the basic collaborative framework should be among the professional broadcasters. These preferences assume that the broadcasters will be vigorous defenders against unnecessary program censorship, and equally vigorous adherents to the transnational cooperation already integral to their profession.

The broadcasting organizations, too, can generally marshall both highly specialized technical expertise and the support of their governments to develop solutions to politically sensitive subjects, such as the spillover of signals across national borders and the allocation of decision-making power among partners in regional or other multinational systems for regulating satellite broadcasting.

To be sure, there are considerable disparities internationally in the extent to which broadcasting associations are in fact entities separate from their governments. But even in countries with pervasive state socialism, the broadcasting associations constitute technical interest groups, with their own needs determined by their functions. Indeed, the prescription advanced here assumes that ties between broadcasters and government are sufficiently thick to ensure that arrangements among broadcasters are responsive to the overall intergovernmental consensus on the future course of direct satellite broadcasting.

3. *The U.S. government and other technologically capable countries would indicate their willingness to explore international arrangements that would help developing countries gain access to and benefit from direct satellite broadcasts intended for educational and other welfare purposes.*

We recognize that in many cases direct satellite broadcasting may not be the most cost-effective way to distribute information to countries, particularly to countries with high population densities that are relatively evenly distributed geographically. Larger countries with populations in remote areas may regard the technology as cost-effective.[17] Technologically advanced countries, however, should be prepared to assist in facilitating the use of direct broadcasting from satellites where countries do regard it as an effective and desirable communications medium.

It is not clear precisely what form such encouragement should, or

17. For an excellent comparison of the cost-efficiency of direct broadcasting from satellites and other alternatives, see R. C. Butman, G. W. Rathjens, and C. Warren, *Technical Economic Considerations in Public Service Broadcast Communications for Developing Countries* (Massachusetts Institute of Technology, 1973).

could, take There has been some discussion in scholarly and other forums of the possibility of launching regional satellites for direct broadcasting. These would have periods of time allocated to individual countries for whatever programs they desire. One member of the UN Secretariat has suggested that an organization for direct broadcasting by satellite be established under UN auspices to coordinate satellite programming and to facilitate international participation in the use of the technology. Such institutional arrangements for promoting the beneficial applications of the technology to countries desiring it would be difficult to negotiate, but it is not too early to begin consultations with potentially interested countries.

CHAPTER TWELVE

Maritime Satellites

Our discussion of ocean issues revealed a general public interest in improving the communications available to oceangoing merchant fleets. An international consensus appears to have emerged in the maritime community that satellite-centered systems would be the best means of attaining the needed improvements. The consensus breaks down, however, over the nature of the institutions to be given authority to manage maritime satellites. With the great material and security interests involved in ocean navigation and communications (oceangoing merchant fleets transport approximately 90 percent of the world's traded products), and the consequent high political interest being exhibited by the major powers in the institutional design of a global system, both the process by which the design issues are resolved and the structure of the resulting institutions are bound to have considerable influence on the overall regime for affairs of outer space.

Functional Needs for Maritime Satellites

As much as 93 percent of all communications with ships at sea is still conducted at an average speed of eight words per minute, using the Morse code technique developed in 1838. The remaining 7 percent of communications with ships is mostly via radiotelephone, used primarily by fishing and passenger vessels. Radio message delays of six hours in each direction of transmission are common. The world's 390 or so shore-to-ship stations—generally used by vessels of the same nationality as that of the station—can only maintain twenty-four-hour contact with ships within 200- to 300-mile distances. Fleet managers can be out of contact with their vessels for twenty-four hours or longer under certain transmission circumstances.

These outdated communications capabilities have become increasingly anachronistic in the 1970s in the face of the drive to modernize cargo handling and ship design that is now energizing the world shipping industry.[1] The traditionalists who used to dominate the industry long resisted suggestions to modernize their communications, contending that shipboard communications other than those needed for safety were an economic liability. Today, however, there is increasingly wide acceptance of the view that better communications are needed for precise scheduling, quicker loading and unloading, and more timely and comprehensive information on the weather and sea conditions to reduce the possibility of a delay. It is also more generally understood that maritime satellites offer the only mechanisms for accomplishing the desired communications improvements.[2]

The fact that first-generation satellites for ocean navigation have been successfully used by the navies of the United States and the USSR for some years now has been important in eroding the inertia of the traditionalists. Commercial interest quickened when the U.S. Navy Transit System—enabling ships to navigate by listening passively to signals emitted from a chain of low-orbiting polar satellites—was declassified in 1967, and then used modestly by some commercial vessels and oil company survey ships.

In addition, new projections for world shipping and maritime communications have supplanted earlier assessments, which predicted no compelling need for ocean communications satellites. Oil tankers and bulk carriers will undergo huge expansion in fleet capacity and average tonnage during the coming decade. The number of container-type

1. E. P. Fitzgerald, "Maritime Communication Service Requirements," address to the Ninth Annual Meeting of the American Institute of Aeronautics and Astronautics, January 9, 1973 (processed), p. 1.

2. B. A. Mendoza and others, *Maritime Services Satellite System*, Definition Study, Automated Marine International, Prepared for the Transportation System Center of the Department of Transportation, Contract DOT-TSC-98 (August 1, 1971), p. 2. This study was part of a series that served as a catalyst toward broader acceptance of the utility of maritime satellites. See Automated Marine International, *Maritime Satellites: Technical and Economic Planning Report*, Executive Synopsis, Report A.M.I./DC-20 (ES), December 20, 1971.

ships will rise faster than any other category. Tankers to carry liquefied natural gas (LNG) will enter oceangoing trade in greater numbers, though fleet size could vary widely. The number of fishing vessels will expand, and will include more large-scale operations.[3] Most significant for maritime communications is the anticipated increase over the long range of the number of vessels at sea; only 8 percent overall growth in ship population is forecast for the 1969–80 period, but the number of ships at sea at any given time could increase by a whopping 40 percent.[4] This shipping explosion and the congestion it will bring to important sea lanes puts a premium upon more cost-effective communications, more accurate navigation, improved search and rescue, and prevention of maritime accidents. The standard arguments in favor of using satellites to perform these functions can be summarized as follows.[5]

More cost-effective communications. Satellites can offer maritime users global communications coverage on a twenty-four-hour, real-time basis. Their use would relieve present congestion on the medium- and high-frequency bands of the radio spectrum. Message and voice traffic should be quicker, more reliable, of better quality, and cheaper. The result of the use of satellites should be a richer mix of new communica-

3. For current maritime industry projections see R. V. Wiederkehr, "A Forecast of 1970–1985 World Shipping," NATO SACLANTCENT Tech. Report 199, September 1, 1971; and John F. Wing, "Trends in World Shipping," paper presented at the Conference on Bulk Transportation of Hazardous Materials by Water—A Long Range Forecast, Sponsored by the National Research Council of the National Academy of Sciences and National Academy of Engineering, July 9–10, 1973.

4. See Barry A. Mendoza and others, *A Study of Maritime Mobile Satellite Service Requirements, Frequency Planning, Modulation and Interference Analysis,* vol. 1: *National and International Merchant Vessel Population and Distribution,* Automated Marine International, Prepared for United States Coast Guard, Contract DOT-CG-00505A, November 1, 1970; and updating of these data in Robert P. Thompson, "Establishing Global Traffic Flow: A Study of World Merchant Ship Population and Distribution Present and Future," paper presented to the Royal Institute of Navigation, prepared for Celesco Industries, a division of the Susquehanna Corporation, Costa Mesa, California (n.d.).

5. Our discussion below relies heavily on James L. Baker, "Satellites for Maritime Applications," prepared for the Ninth Annual Meeting of the American Institute of Aeronautics and Astronautics (AIAA Paper 73-47), January 8–10, 1973. See also Panel of Experts on Maritime Satellites, *Report to the Maritime Safety Committee,* Inter-governmental Maritime Consultative Organization, doc. MARSAT V/6, September 16, 1974.

tions services, such as the teleprinter copy, graphics, and wideband digital data that fleets with advanced technology will use routinely in the future.

More accurate navigation. Satellites provide important advantages to commercial users, compared with present electronic navigation aids. Satellite navigation systems could follow several basic variations. One satellite overhead could provide ranging information in conjunction with existing on-board electronic navigation equipment. Two satellites overhead would permit independent determination of position. Most elaborate would be a surveillance system, enabling authorities on shore to monitor or control ship movements in the manner of today's air traffic controllers.

Improved search and rescue. Ancillary benefits of better communications and navigation could help to eliminate the search from search and rescue. Only a small fraction of the world's merchant fleet currently participates in a voluntary system of position reporting, and reports are often inaccurate or delayed. These shortcomings could be alleviated by satellite systems, in combination with new devices for distress signaling via satellite.

Preventing maritime accidents. Better communications and navigation could also help reduce loss of life and property damage from collisions, weather damage, and groundings. Worldwide data for the six-year-period ending in 1970 shows a 41 percent rise in ship losses.[6] Environmental hazards from tanker breakups add new concern. While human error is the decisive contributor to maritime accidents, on-board aids and shore-based advisory or control systems could favorably affect accident rates, particularly in congested areas.

Basic Technical Requirements

In its basics, the design of a global maritime communications system could be fairly straightforward. Worldwide coverage will call for at least three spacecraft in stationary orbit over the equator, one for each major ocean basin. Satellite channels would provide two-way links between ships and land telegraphic, telephonic, or data transmission networks. Shipboard terminals of a modest size would send and receive.

6. Thomas O'Toole, "Merchant Ships Sink at a Rate of One a Day," *Washington Post*, August 7, 1972.

Several types of ground stations would be required to control satellites, and to route messages to their destination on land.[7] Details of this concept could differ over a range of engineering and economics options. The satellite could provide only communications services, or navigation as well. No technical obstacles would prevent the satellite from carrying earth sensors—as do some military ocean satellites—although the cost of carrying them and the complexity of their technology would discourage interest on the part of those with commercial stakes in a communications system at the lowest possible cost. The satellite size could vary, as could the precise communications services it provided, the standards of channel quality it met, and the complexity and cost of the shipboard terminals required to use the system. The numbers and location of associated ground stations could also vary. Technically, the network of earth stations probably need not exceed a few for each ocean, but the total may well be higher because maritime nations will press for their own stations, perpetuating existing patterns of national maritime communications via national shore stations. The system, furthermore, could be dedicated to maritime users only, or could be shared with other users, such as international airlines, for normal communications or for emergency signaling.

Our objective here has not been to endorse or criticize the technical validity of these forecasts and arguments. On a variety of technical and economic grounds, specialists still hold contrary views about the need for and inevitability of maritime satellites. For our purposes, what is important is that maritime policymakers and satellite technologists have already pushed the issue beyond the level of mere technical debate onto the politically charged level where choices need to be made among the alternative systems for international management that are likely to be deployed.

Deployment Prospects and Problems

The Communications Satellite Corporation (COMSAT) ocean satellite service was designed initially to serve primarily the U.S. Navy. The Navy has supported the COMSAT program as an interim service

7. Most of the ideas for a system under consideration in the international community are briefly described in Inter-governmental Maritime Consultative Organization, "Report of the Panel of Experts on Maritime Satellites" (Third Session, September 10–14, 1973; processed), esp. Agenda Items nos. 3 and 4.

to take care of the urgent need that arose when the Navy's experimental communications satellites in the Atlantic and Pacific began deteriorating seriously in the early 1970s. The COMSAT system would be turned over to civilian users when the new sophisticated system the Navy and Air Force are developing becomes operational.

COMSAT's domestic competitors opposed the COMSAT-Navy arrangement, but the Federal Communications Commission (FCC) authorized it nevertheless, calling for a consortium led by COMSAT and indicating that the arrangement should not be prejudicial to efforts to negotiate international arrangements under the auspices of the Intergovernmental Maritime Consultative Organization (IMCO), the institutional arrangement preferred by the European nations and the USSR. Despite the FCC admonition for restraint on the question of international management, the COMSAT move has been interpreted as a strong bid for U.S. leadership in any subsequent global system. At least this is the charge made in some circles in Europe as well as by maritime communicators on land (both American and non-American), who see their economic interests put at a disadvantage by the COMSAT initiative.[8]

The United States is not the only country that can marshall the technological capability to build maritime satellites and associated shipboard and other equipment. The European nations and Japan are prime contenders. For the time being, however, the United States is the only country with a demonstrated capability to launch maritime-type satellites into stationary orbit over the equator. The USSR may be able to do so in the future, and has promised comparable launch services for cooperative international meteorology programs during the 1970s.

The possibility that the USSR might serve as an alternative source to the United States for launching a European-built maritime satellite has not been lost on some participants in the maritime satellite debate. The United States, through a policy announced unilaterally in 1972, has offered assurances that it will launch other nations' satellites under certain carefully specified conditions on the basis that it would be reim-

8. For a survey of the COMSAT technology and the policy positions of all involved U.S. actors, see *Memorandum Opinion and Order*, FCC 73-397, April 11, 1973; and the supporting COMSAT application dated March 5, 1973; see also Katherine Johnson, "Maritime Satellite Policy Spurred," *Aviation Week and Space Technology*, January 22, 1973; and Katherine Johnson, "Maritime Satellite Plan Faces Opposition," *Aviation Week and Space Technology*, March 12, 1973.

bursed for the cost of launching.[9] Europeans, worried that these conditions could be interpreted to exclude launch services for satellite systems that compete economically with U.S. satellites, have expressed some reluctance—as they have also done in other satellite applications fields—to rely on the existing launch assurances for future maritime satellites.

Accordingly, in 1973, the Europeans agreed among themselves on a space technology package that could someday have large significance in the international maritime satellite field. The package includes a new European Space Agency that would concentrate heavily on space applications (principally European satellite systems for meteorology, air navigation communication, and maritime systems), while at the same time committing major financial contributions to the post-Apollo manned spaceflight program. (The latter joint venture is favored by NASA in the hope that a European commitment will reinforce Congress' willingness to fund the post-Apollo programs in question.)

The Europeans have also decided to proceed as rapidly as possible with the development of a maritime satellite, with the United Kingdom paying more than half the bill and producing much of the electronic equipment for the European-built satellite. While this package also included a new push to develop the European booster capability that has always been a special French interest, it is likely that any initial European maritime satellite would have to be launched by the United States—or, less likely, by the USSR.[10]

International Management Issues

Outside the United States, the preference for management of a global maritime satellite system has been a totally new and independent international organization. Prodded by the USSR, the U.K., France, and

9. See "U.S. to Provide Launch Assistance for Peaceful Satellite Projects," *Department of State Bulletin* (November 6, 1972), pp. 533–34. For an interpretation arguing that the U.S. launch policy was dictated by a COMSAT eager to prevent the sharing of actual launch technology (rather than *services*) with other advanced nations, see Judith Tagger Kildow, *INTELSAT: Policy-Maker's Dilemma* (Lexington Books, 1973), p. 77.

10. For general descriptions of the new European package, see John Walsh, "NASA and ESRO: A European Payload for the Space Shuttle," *Science*, vol. 182 (November 9, 1973), pp. 562–63; and Herbert J. Coleman, "Europe Makes 79% Pledge on Spacelab," *Aviation Week and Space Technology* (August 6, 1973), pp. 15–16.

some of the Scandinavian countries, IMCO established a panel of experts in 1972 to examine alternative designs for an international system to satisfy general maritime communications requirements. On the basis of the work of this panel, an international conference to establish an international maritime satellite system convened in London in April 1975, under IMCO auspices.

Three principal issues have emerged during the course of these deliberations: who should be the participating members of the maritime satellite organization (governments only, or also nongovernmental communications entities such as COMSAT); what should be the basis and distribution of decisionmaking power in the organization; what should be the organization's procurement policy?[11]

The Role of Nongovernmental Entities

At the International Conference on the Establishment of an International Maritime Satellite System, which began in London in the spring of 1975 and was attended by forty-three countries, the United States indicated that it could not participate in a global maritime communications system unless the institutional framework allowed governments to designate private, nongovernmental telecommunications entities to undertake financial, technical, and operational responsibilities, without financial guarantees from the designating governments. Accordingly, the United States proposed two agreements: an intergovernmental agreement to be signed by governments, and an operating agreement to be signed by either a government or its designated entity. Many Western European delegations, the USSR, and the Eastern European delegations opposed the U.S. suggestion, insisting that governments should remain responsible for all activities of their designated entities.[12]

The ensuing discussion at London narrowed the differences on this issue between the United States and the Western European nations to the point at which they could agree in principle that the entity designated by a government should be subject to the jurisdiction of that

11. The range of institutional alternatives and issues that have surfaced in the maritime satellite debate is summarized in Panel of Experts on Maritime Satellites, *Report to the Maritime Safety Committee* (IMCO, September 16, 1974).

12. This description of the international negotiations at the time of the 1975 London conference is based on the "Report of the United States Representative to the International Conference on the Establishment of an International Maritime Satellite System, London, England, April 23–May 9, 1975" (Department of State TD serial no. 57; processed).

government; the rights, obligations, and functions of any such entity should be clearly defined; and in the event of default or withdrawal from the system by the designated entity, the government would assume its capacities, designate a new entity, or itself withdraw. The socialist bloc countries gave no indication of their readiness to accept such an agreement.[13]

Decisionmaking Powers

The United States has been arguing for strong executive power to be lodged in a council, in which investors would have weighted votes proportional to their investment. Under the U.S. plan, an assembly, in which each member state would have one vote, would have the power only to make recommendations and express its views to the council. The council would decide all matters of a technical, operational, or financial nature. The United States has again been in the minority on this issue, as most governments feel the assembly should have more substantial policymaking powers. Most governments, however, accept the idea that membership and voting in the council should be based in part on investment shares.

Procurement Policy

Most countries participating in the negotiations are in basic agreement that the maritime satellite organization should award equipment and service contracts on the basis of open bidding, with primary weight given to price, quality, and favorable delivery time. But there remains some difference over the extent to which the organization should give weight in its selection of contractors to the need to stimulate worldwide competition in the supply of goods and services. The United States, as might be expected, wants consideration to be given to the latter only in cases in which a choice cannot be made on the basis of price, quality, and delivery time. Other countries want the organization to make a broadening base of international competition a necessary criterion.

Recommendations

With respect to the role of nongovernmental entities, we support the position that operational responsibility should be lodged in whatever entities each government decides can carry out the maritime communi-

13. Ibid. The negotiations were scheduled to reconvene in February 1976.

cations tasks most efficiently. The role of COMSAT in the INTELSAT organization provides a good model for this type of arrangement. Governments will have to take responsibility for whatever their designated entities do in any case; thus, the question of formal representation by such nongovernmental entities is a false issue. The fuss made over this issue by the USSR and its allies is excessive. But given the prospective international benefits from a unified system, for the United States to make the success of the negotiations hinge upon the acceptance of formal representation by a nongovernmental agency does not seem to us to be sensible.

On the matter of decisionmaking power in the prospective maritime satellite organization, the need to keep heavy participation by the technologically advanced powers in a unified system argues for arrangements that give special weight to those with the largest investments in the system. This can be provided for in the executive council itself if the council is given sufficient autonomy from day-to-day direction by the assembly. The assembly, however, should be accorded broad budgetary and policy authority, and should probably operate on the basis of one nation, one vote (with specified majorities for matters of substantive importance) in order to sustain political support for the organization from the developing countries. The constructive participation in the system by all countries who navigate the ocean is important, for unsafe navigational practices by any country's fleet can be a hazard to the ships of other countries and to the ecological health of the ocean.

We also support a procurement policy that lets contracts for hardware, software, and services on the basis of open bidding, with awards made on the standard efficiency criteria of price, quality, and delivery time. These criteria must be qualified, however, by a requirement to avoid situations of monopoly or oligopoly and to encourage a broadened international base of supply of goods and services. Considerations of efficiency in the short run may argue against broadening the procurement base, but the effectiveness of the system in the long run may depend importantly on developing technological competence in user countries, which could be stimulated by a more liberal procurement policy. Thus, while it is not our recommendation to sacrifice performance efficiencies, we do recommend some marginal sacrifices in short-run efficiency in the costs of running the system.

Effective maritime satellite services, to be sure, are of most concern to the principal maritime powers; relatively few developing nations are likely to be equipped with classes of vessels that can use satellite communications equipment. But there is a good opportunity in this field for the advanced segments of the maritime community to serve the larger public interest in safe navigation and at the same time to facilitate international participation in the management of technology for use in outer space. If successful, this experience in international management could serve as a guideline for future projects in outer space that will require broad international cooperation.

CHAPTER THIRTEEN

Frequency and Orbit

The growing use of frequency and orbit raises issues of allocation and accountability similar to those that have arisen from the use of scarce ocean resources. Users of these resources are increasingly in one another's way. The need for electronic communications for both space and land activities is growing exponentially, putting new demands on the radio spectrum. The growth in space activities also places potential pressure on the geostationary orbit—the tube of space surrounding the earth 22,300 miles above its equator.[1]

Although research and development have continually expanded the usable portions of the frequency spectrum and orbit, thus increasing the available quantity of these resources, incentives both to conduct the pertinent research and to incorporate its fruits have been inadequate. Moreover, the pattern of distribution of these resources among nations is not universally acceptable.

Future newcomers in communications, particularly smaller, less developed countries, fear that the technically advanced countries may be preempting the resources, and some are demanding that the frequency spectrum and orbit be allocated now to reserve some of each resource for each country, regardless of its current ability to use it.

How the world community manages the growing competition for use of the spectrum and orbit will affect the magnitude, distribution, quality, and price of information transmitted electronically. Moreover, the management decisions in this field—which previously were mainly the pre-

1. The area is called geostationary because satellites in this orbit travel at approximately the same speed as the earth rotates and thus appear fixed in space.

serve of the developed countries—will increasingly be affected by, and will in turn affect, overall political relations among the developed and the developing countries.

The Resources

The radio spectrum and the geostationary orbit share certain characteristics as resources. Although the frequency spectrum and geostationary orbit are physically distinct, the number of satellites that can simultaneously use the geostationary orbit depends in part upon the way in which each uses the radio spectrum.

The Radio Spectrum

All electronic communication uses electromagnetic waves that pass through space or along wires. These waves are initiated by passing bursts of electrical currents through an antenna. Electromagnetic waves vary in the number that can be sent per second—that is, their frequency, measured in cycles per second. The higher the frequency, the shorter the length of the wave. The frequency is determined by characteristics of the electrical current passed through the antenna.

The electromagnetic spectrum extends from zero cycles per second all the way up into X-rays (one quintillion and more cycles per second) and beyond. The radio spectrum consists of only a portion of the entire electromagnetic spectrum, specifically the portion that can be used to transmit information. Currently, the radio spectrum extends from zero cycles per second all the way to 100 billion cycles per second. The spectrum is divided into subgroups, based on the way the waves interact with land and the components of the atmosphere. Because of differences in this interaction, various sets of frequencies can be used in different ways.

Use of the radio spectrum is unlike the use of many other resources, because the spectrum is not consumed or destroyed by use. When the signal ceases, the frequency can be used again and again. Various uses do have to be coordinated, however, because two or more signals can be sent in such a way as to prevent the receivers from hearing anything meaningful. When this occurs, the signals are said to interfere. Specifically, interference occurs when more than one user attempts to use the same frequency of the spectrum at the same time over the same area.

When the use of electromagnetic radiation for communications began in the early part of this century, the usable portion of the spectrum lay between 20,000 and 1,500,000 cycles per second. During the past half century, communicators have expanded the quantity of available frequencies to accommodate new users and needs, mostly by extending into progressively higher frequencies on the usable spectrum, for which correspondingly more sophisticated and expensive technology is required.

The advent of satellites expanded the uses of frequency, but so far these new uses require frequencies already used on land. Experiments are being carried out to develop equipment and techniques for satellite communications on frequencies that are not used on land, but no such techniques are yet available. Communications with satellites require the use of frequencies above about 100 million cycles per second. Frequencies lower than these are reflected back to earth by components of the atmosphere.

Technological changes have also made possible more intensive use of much of the radio spectrum, including the part that is usable by satellites. Basically, the changes made it possible to aim signals more accurately (thus using less space to send a signal), to put more information on a given amount of frequency, or to send a given amount of information in less time. For actual users to adopt these technological improvements, however, requires that each individual user install new equipment that incorporates the changes. Such new equipment has generally been more costly for the individual user. Once acquired, equipment lasts for many years. Because of this durability, those who already have installed equipment effectively become a vested interest opposed to rapid expansion in the use of crowded frequencies.

The Geostationary Orbit

The principal advantage of the geostationary orbit is that each satellite can see one-third of the globe from this vantage point. This allows for coverage of the whole earth by as few as three satellites, rather than by the many more required for comparable coverage with satellites in lower orbits. In addition, geostationary satellites do not require tracking by ground stations, as is required by satellites in lower orbit. This reduces the expense of building and maintaining ground stations.

The precision with which satellites can be kept in their original slot within the orbit is one determinant of the total number of satellites that can be placed in the geostationary orbit at any one time. Although satellites in this orbit, traveling at the same speed as the earth rotates, appear stationary relative to the earth, they do not remain perfectly aligned. Over time, they tend to drift within the orbit, and if uncorrected will eventually drift out of the orbit altogether. To correct drifting, satellites are constructed with fuel and rockets that are fired periodically to maintain the satellite positions.[2]

The other determinant of the total number of satellites that can share the geostationary orbit is the way these satellites use the frequency spectrum. Satellite systems that do not incorporate the best techniques for focusing their signals require more space between them and their neighbors. The current Canadian domestic communications satellites (Aniks), for example, require five degrees on either side to prevent frequency interference. Proposals before the Federal Communications Commission for U.S. domestic communications satellites contain a range of spacing of less than five degrees. Spacing of less than five degrees would require more complex equipment on the satellite and at ground stations than is used in the Canadian system.[3]

Not all parts of the orbit are equally desirable. Since a given satellite covers one third of the globe, the most pressured sections lie over those land masses serviced most heavily. Consequently, the push for communications satellite systems in Canada and the United States, and the prospects for additional users among Latin American states, have created allocation problems over North America, and the satellites transmitting weather data in this region have occasionally interfered with satellites surveying resources. Similar problems are possible in the arc of the orbit most valuable for services to Europe and Africa.[4]

In sum, both the geostationary orbit and the spectrum share certain characteristics as resources: the available quantity of either depends upon the technology of the users. Better technology permits more re-

2. Currently, the best available techniques can maintain a satellite within one-tenth of one degree (plus or minus) of the nominal position, and work continues to improve this still further. Standards established by the International Telecommunication Union require drifting of no more than one degree when orbital space is limited.

3. J. Freibaum and J. E. Miller, "NASA Spectrum and Orbit Utilization Studies for Space Applications," American Institute for Aeronautics and Astronautics, Paper no. 74-434, Fifth Communications Satellite Systems Conference, Los Angeles, California, April 22–24, 1974 (processed), p. 2.

4. Ibid.

source use—namely, more satellites in orbit, and more communications upon a given unit of frequency.

Each expansion in usable quantity of these resources is more costly for the individual user because the equipment needed, either to move to new frequencies or to avoid interference on currently used portions of the spectrum and orbit, is more expensive. While neither resource can be consumed (depleted so as to make future use impossible), the use of either requires specific types of costly durable equipment, and the equipment chosen determines, in turn, the total amount of available resource. Thus, vested interests develop to prevent additional uses of either resource in portions of the geostationary orbit or the frequency spectrum that are already heavily utilized. The problem is to establish an allocation system that creates incentives to induce users to upgrade their equipment more rapidly than at present, thus allowing better sharing as particular frequencies or orbital sections become crowded.

The Existing Regime

The existing regime governing the use of frequency and orbit resources, similar to the traditional regime for ocean resources, is based on the assumption that nobody need own them, and that conflicts over their use will be the exception rather than the norm. Unlike ocean resources, however, the innate character of the frequency resource has compelled a fairly high degree of explicit international coordination and accountability in its use.

Similar procedures have been followed for the use of orbital resources. These procedures take place under the aegis of the 100-year-old International Telecommunication Union (ITU).[5] Over the years, this

5. The functions of the ITU are set forth in its constitution, the International Telecommunications Convention, as renegotiated at Montreux in 1965. In the words of the Convention (Article 4), the ITU is mandated to:

(a) effect allocation of the radio frequency spectrum and registration of radio frequency assignments in order to avoid harmful interference between radio stations of different countries;

(b) coordinate efforts to eliminate harmful interference between radio stations of different countries and to improve the use made of the radio frequency spectrum;

(c) foster collaboration among its members . . . with a view to the establishment of rates at levels as low as possible consistent with an efficient service . . .

organization has developed a complex array of institutional and standard-setting arrangements that involve a fairly high degree of international accountability in the use of frequency.

The main allocation activities of the ITU are performed by administrative conferences and by the International Frequency Registration Board (IFRB). The major function of administrative conferences is to revise any or all of the administrative regulations, which are the agreed provisions applying to telephone or telegraph services, or frequency use. The radio regulations constitute a system of agreed allocation of the usable spectrum according to types of use, similar to a system of land zoning. The regulations give priority to particular types of use in various portions of the spectrum. Who actually performs these services is left to the member states. The states submit applications to the IFRB to have particular frequency assignments recorded in its master register. These requests are checked by the IFRB for conformity with all ITU provisions, and are circulated to all other members of the ITU to ensure a lack of harmful interference.

The result of these procedures is essentially a first-come, first-served allocation of spectrum among nations, but actual use of the spectrum conforms largely to the priorities that have been set internationally.

The procedures for registering frequency uses also have provisions for coordinating the actual choice of frequency. In addition, the consultative committees of the ITU serve to coordinate both technologies and policies in the various types of international communications services. These committees work to draw up recommendations for consideration at the administrative conferences.

Private operating agencies and scientific and industrial organizations play an important role in the ad hoc working or study groups of the consultative committees, and, because of the complex and technical nature of the fields, tend to exercise major influence on the recommenda-

---

(d) foster the creation, development and improvement of telecommunication equipment and networks in . . . developing countries by every means at its disposal, especially . . . in the appropriate programs of the United Nations;

(e) promote the adoption of measures for ensuring the safety of life through the cooperation of telecommunication services;

(f) undertake studies, make regulations, adopt resolutions, formulate recommendations and opinions, and collect and publish information concerning telecommunication matters for the benefit of all members and Associate members.

tions of the consultative committees and on the formal decisions of the
IFRB and policy bodies of the ITU.[6]

Defects in the Current Allocation and Coordination System

The ITU system for allocating and managing the use of the spectrum
or orbit has by no means brought us to a crisis, in the sense of impeding
normal international communications.[7] Yet the dimensions of future
pressures on orbital and frequency resources are difficult to predict.
Probably the vast majority of communications technologists today can
find some comfort in the many techniques for conserving frequency and
orbit that are now under development. Indeed, some analysts of the ITU
feel that it serves as a model that could be followed in other arenas.
Thus, the following conclusion of a study recently completed:

Examination of the ITU's working methods . . . reveals an effective, results-
oriented mechanism for international agreement. The procedure is the more
remarkable as it achieves its objectives by accommodation and acquiescence.
There are no clear-cut winners or losers—all participate in what modern system analysts would call a nonzero-sum game. An organization with no chief
executive, no power centre to force decisions, the ITU may be a good model
for international co-operation, consistent with our world's diverse standards of
humanity.[8]

Despite the past success of the existing system, some countries are
pushing for a new method of allocating these resources. In advance of
the 1977 World Administrative Radio Conference to deal with regulations to govern both the orbital and frequency needs of direct broadcasting satellites, several countries indicated that they would demand
that the conference assign orbital positions to the nations in attendance,

6. For more detail, see *The International Telecommunication Union:
Issues and Next Steps*, A Report by the Panel on International Telecommunications Policy of the American Society of International Law, Occasional Paper
no. 10 (Washington, D.C.: Carnegie Endowment for International Peace,
1971).

7. Indeed, the organization has weathered tolerably well a number of
important technological changes in the communications field, and it has belied
the doomsayers who at various times in its history have said that it could not
cope with the pressures of new demands for allocation of the frequency spectrum.

8. Gerd D. Wallenstein, "Make Room in Space: Harmony and Dissonance
in International Telecommunications," pt. 2, *Telecommunication Journal*, vol.
40 (February 1973), pp. 101–02.

rather than perpetuate the first-come, first-served regime. Such a demarche would probably be followed by further redistribution of both orbital and frequency resources at the World Administrative Radio Conference scheduled for 1979.

The impetus behind proposals to alter the existing allocation system of the ITU stems in part from dissatisfaction over the distribution of these scarce resources. Over time, the industrialized countries of the northern hemisphere and Oceania have acquired priority assignments to much of the usable portion of the spectrum. So far, the geostationary orbit has not been fully utilized, but smaller, less-developed countries fear that it will be allocated as was the spectrum. Their concern is that they may be preempted from future orbital use by rapid expansion of the satellite programs of the industrial nations. Similar concern and proposals are also expressed over allocation of the higher frequencies that are just being added to the usable portion of the spectrum.

Dissatisfaction with the global distribution of orbital and frequency resources, however important, is not the sole reason for consideration of alternative allocation systems. Examination of the ITU reveals two types of serious defects in the existing international system for allocating and coordinating frequency and orbit use.

Structural Defects

It has been charged that the ITU is structured so as to be dominated by telecommunications interests, particularly telephone interests.[9] States are represented in the ITU primarily by their communications ministries, which are usually most concerned with telephone and telegraph services rather than educational broadcasts for developing countries, meteorological and ecological data, or navigational signals. Moreover, because of the way technical standards are set, the ITU is dominated by the major communications powers. Technical standards are formally recommended by the International Radio Consultative Committee, which in turn takes its cues from ad hoc study groups whose work is dominated by the few members from the most advanced states, which have the resources and competence to sustain active participation in the highly technical discussions.[10]

9. Abram Chayes, "Current Trends in International Communications Policy," *Indiana Law Review*, vol. 6, no. 2 (1972), pp. 182–89.

10. See David M. Leive, *International Telecommunications and International Law: The Regulation of the Radio Spectrum* (Oceana Publications,

While the principal communications powers rightly exercise major influence over the ITU—influence derived from both their massive stakes in the shape of world communications and from their advanced expertise on which the ITU must depend—the political and psychological effects of this uneven distribution of power have come to be a sore point on many grounds. "In fact," charges Abram Chayes, "it is not too much to describe the ITU as a kind of club or cartel, in which the big communicators meet to work out among themselves their problems of allocation and technical standardization, presenting the rest of the world with a *fait accompli* that they have no choice but to accept."[11] Developing nations have pressed for organizational reforms in the ITU that give greater weight to their voices and special concerns. Understandably, the leading communications powers have tended to resist these demands or accommodate to them somewhat reluctantly—just as they have resisted efforts to give greater power to independent international expert bodies within the ITU structure, apparently preferring to retain decisive roles for national telecommunications entities.

Procedural Defects

Users of the geostationary orbit and the frequency spectrum are subject to few binding international constraints. They pay no fees to any world agency for the use of these valuable world resources. First users of particular orbital spaces or bands on the frequency spectrum tend to be given priority, there being no international mechanism to compel old users to give way to new users or to users of greater social value.[12]

The precedent of giving priority rights to those up there first grows

---

1970), pp. 96–97; G. D. Wallenstein, "International Telecommunication, Where Cooperation Is the Message," *Telecommunication Journal*, vol. 39 (June 1972), pp. 367–69; and Harold Karan Jacobson, "International Institutions for Telecommunications: The ITU's Role," in Edward McWhinney, ed., *The International Law of Communications* (Oceana Publications, 1971), pp. 57–58.

11. Chayes, "Current Trends in International Communications Policy," p. 188.

12. In the recent decisions on domestic communications satellites, the Federal Communications Commission has stated that permission should not be construed as guaranteeing permanent allocation of particular positions within the orbit. It remains to be seen whether any users will in fact be displaced.

out of the recognition that the choice of existing equipment and the attendant capital investment are based on the premise that users will be able to operate over time on a particular segment of the frequency spectrum (and, in the emerging era of space applications, in a particular position in the geostationary orbit). To shift frequencies or orbital position, presumably, would require the original user to bear additional costs.[13] Therefore—according to the traditional rationale—new users should not have equal claim with old users to all segments. Moreover, if the new users might interfere with the established ones, the latecomers should bear the design costs of avoiding interference.

The result of following the rationale that new users must bear any burdens of interference and location costs is inefficient spectrum allocation. For example, maritime mobile satellite services will have to locate on bands that will require larger shipboard antennae than would have been needed at the optimal band.

On the grounds of economic efficiency, the escalating demands for use of the frequency spectrum and geostationary orbit, simultaneously with technological progress permitting increased use of particular portions of each resource, call into question principles for according priority that are used by the existing regime. Without some incentives internationally imposed to institute the equipment modifications that are now technologically feasible, current users will feel no compelling need to change their equipment to make way for others. Moreover, future users of newly accessible reaches of the spectrum will not need to be especially concerned to employ the most efficient capabilities in terms of width of orbital arc or frequency band. "The ITU has traditionally experienced great difficulty in 'clearing' frequency bands for more advanced or different users and in establishing the relative rights of the old and new users."[14] Thus, the resource can be wasted, so to speak, by underutilization or preemption by inefficient users.

13. The costs of adjusting to different frequencies can be very high. For example, the frequency allocations at the 1971 World Administrative Radio Conference did not cover the Indian government's first choice for their experimental educational satellite because some African countries objected that it might cause interference. It was estimated that significant changes in the experiment would cost $3 million. See "U.S. Delegation Expresses Satisfaction with WARC Conference Results," *Telecommunications Reports*, vol. 37 (July 26, 1971), p. 20.

14. Leive, *International Telecommunications and International Law*, pp. 16–17.

The problem of preemption is aggravated by the overregistration of frequencies. In a 1962 survey, only 25 percent of the administrations questioned on recorded assignments stated that their entries were operating in accordance with the notified technical characteristics. After the Second World War, an attempt was made to set up an engineered spectrum, free of the deadwood allocations, but the Soviet bloc insisted on priority rights in registered frequencies, and the attempt failed.

In addition to existing inefficiency in the use of spectrum and orbit, the priority principles and procedures of the present regime lack the flexibility to respond to changing international priorities in communications. Changes in the allocation of portions of the spectrum to categories of services are negotiated among the national communications administrations at the periodic World Administrative Radio Conferences of the ITU, the last of which was held in 1971. Assignments to particular communications services within the categories established by the conferences are made for the most part by the national administrations, and in a few cases by international agencies providing communication services. There is no international agency comparable to the Federal Communications Commission, or the state communications monopolies characteristic of most countries, capable of adjudicating (however imperfectly) among claimants for assignments on the basis of public interest criteria.

Reforms to Increase International Accountability

The concerns noted above, while not felt by all countries or by all who have examined the workings of the ITU, have prompted a number of suggestions for reform. Most of the analysts of the ITU, such as David Leive, Abram Chayes, and Harold Jacobson, have advocated structural and legal reforms that would increase the degree of international accountability in the use of frequency and orbital resources, but they do not address the question of who owns them. These analysts hope that more international accountability will distribute more of these resources to less developed countries, but they do not propose measures to ensure such an outcome.

In addition to examination of the ITU and its procedures, extensive analysis of frequency allocation issues has occurred in discussions of the operations of the Federal Communications Commission.[15] The analysis of U.S. domestic frequency allocation has centered on issues of ownership of the spectrum resources and how to increase the efficiency of their use. Some of the suggested reforms in frequency allocation that have arisen from this domestic discussion might be adaptable to the international system. The disquiet felt by some of the smaller, less developed countries over the distribution of resources resulting from the current ITU system may require reforms that give direct attention to distribution. Any such reforms seem certain to require some agreement on who owns the resources, and on the values to be served by their use.

Structural Reforms

The main target of structural reform proposals is the ITU's central regulatory mechanism, currently located in the International Frequency Registration Board (IFRB). The principal criticism of this body is that it is unable to make independent findings or to take any action against a member without the member's consent. Today, the principal function of the IFRB is to register frequency uses reported to it by national administrations, who are themselves responsible for self-enforcement of ITU technical performance requirements, such as those meant to avoid harmful interference. The many gaps and ambiguities in the international regulations make it difficult for the IFRB to aid in their resolution. The IFRB will conduct studies and make recommendations on request, but it strongly encourages bilateral negotiations and agreements. The board adjudicates only an estimated 5–10 percent of harmful interference cases. Bilateral negotiations may continue to be adequate in the 1970s, but the proliferation of systems that is expected in the 1980s may require a better approach.

Structural alterations might go so far as to give the IFRB (or some newly created organ of the ITU) the functions of a regulatory commission, according it the power to subpoena information; to conduct adversary proceedings (which could be initiated by the board or by a member); to issue orders that have the status of law (i.e., that members are obligated to obey); to enforce ITU regulations; and to impose penalties for noncompliance (perhaps in the form of revocation of licenses to

15. The FCC allocates and coordinates all nongovernmental U.S. frequency and orbital use; the Office of Telecommunications Policy coordinates U.S. governmental use.

operate at certain frequencies). The most prominently circulated reform proposals fall considerably short of such full-scale renovation of the IFRB, but, by implication, at least tend in that direction.[16] The prevailing view among analysts is that the more comprehensive reform variants would not be negotiable unless there were great pressure on national governments to move in this direction as a consequence of a telecommunications crisis.

Another structural feature that should be a target of reform is the overwhelming dominance in the ITU's decisionmaking processes by the technologically advanced countries and/or industrial groups. A structural reform here would involve giving greater general policy guidance and review to plenary bodies to assure that regulatory decisions by the IFRB and related commissions are responsive and accountable to the majority will. This will set the stage for confused decisionmaking, however, unless it is accompanied by a thorough rehabilitation of ITU secretariats, giving them the authority and capability to conduct independent studies and to recommend policy to the plenary bodies. Except for some general suggestions for increases in the technical competence of the ITU staff to facilitate technical information services for the less developed countries, there are now no fleshed-out proposals to this effect under serious consideration by the international telecommunications community.[17]

The present regulatory regime could be improved significantly, some analysts contend, by reformulating the rights and duties of producers and

16. See, for example, the detailed reforms suggested by David Leive, in *International Telecommunications and International Law*, pp. 283–301. Leive sees the overcrowded frequency spectrum as the central problem for international regulation, and recommends an evolutionary approach to increase the powers and improve the procedures of the IFRB. The central elements of his proposal are to increase the flexibility of board actions, allowing it to act without prior approval from the administration concerned, particularly in the modification and cancellation of entries in the registry of frequencies; to strengthen the findings of the board by obligating ITU members to provide data making the findings timely, without prolonged delays and explanations; to increase the power of the board in enforcing the regulations by depriving assignments of recognition if the administration continues in violation; and to increase the role of the board in settling harmful interference disputes and in coordinating actions to forestall disputes.

17. Harold K. Jacobson, "International Institutions for Telecommunications: The ITU's Role," in *Global Communications in the Space Age: Toward a New ITU* (New York: Twentieth Century Fund, 1972), p. 64.

consumers of telecommunications. The legal principles, they argue, need to be clarified and purged of obsolete formulations—particularly with respect to the concept of avoiding harmful interference and the obligations this places on various parties. There should be no presumption of priority use of orbit or spectrum on the basis of past assignment. Instead, the guidelines should spell out criteria for determining who makes adjustments when users come into conflict.

David Leive is pessimistic about the wholesale abandonment of the first-come, first-served principles of the existing regime. He finds it difficult to conceive of alternative criteria that could win general acceptance. Accordingly, he suggests a number of qualifications and limitations to the existing principles for establishing priorities. First, any telecommunications service (except emergency services) not regularly using the specific frequency it has been assigned should lose its priority claim. Second, more weight should be given to the nature and purposes of conflicting uses, and more recognition given to "the fact that the country with the earlier date of notification could more easily adjust its equipment or operations to eliminate the interference or shift to other means of communication not requiring use of the frequency spectrum."[18] Leive concludes: "More ambitious attempts to make the relative importance of or need for the frequency by the parties concerned relevant or controlling factors are perhaps doomed to failure, at least in the near future."[19]

Reforming the Basic Incentive Structure

The need for the new legal principles discussed above stems ultimately from the fact that more people want to use specific frequencies than the available quantity of those frequencies permits. Therefore, some mechanism is needed for choosing among the potential users. Put simply, spectrum is scarce. To be sure, no major use or user of the spectrum has yet been permanently barred because of such scarcity, since technical improvements have permitted more users per band than previously. But serious future congestion cannot be completely discounted. To avert

18. Leive, *International Telecommunications and International Law*, pp. 306–07.

19. Ibid. See also David M. Leive, *The Future of the International Telecommunication Union: A Report for the 1973 Plenipotentiary Conference* (American Society of International Law, 1972).

this, some mechanism is needed either to reduce the number of users of the spectrum or to reduce the amount of use by those users.

The same outcome—a reduction of frequency use by current users—is needed if there is to be any change in the pattern of distribution of these resources among nations. This is true even if an altered distributional pattern occurs only with future additions to the usable spectrum.

Defenders of the present allocation system contend that it can effectively handle all these future problems. They do concede that moderate institutional reforms, of the kind suggested by David Leive, might be required. It appears to us, however, that the uncertain economic and technological projections on the severity of future congestion require a fresh examination of the fundamental premises of the inherited allocation system. It also seems that questions should be raised internationally —as they have been in some quarters within the U.S. frequency management community—about the advantages and disadvantages of changing the basic incentive structures for frequency users. Some government and private communications sectors that have an immediate stake in more efficient use of the spectrum are conducting research on conservation of the frequency spectrum. Present incentives, however, do not appear to be sufficient to avert the serious international problems that may arise as more and more countries attempt to expand their communications systems and as competition for scarce frequencies becomes more intense.

The problem of incentives is largely a problem of economics. Planning for a fundamentally new incentive structure should no longer ignore the benefits lost because the spectrum is not available for some uses (this is what economists call the opportunity costs of the spectrum). As the number of uses for a particular band expand, so does that band's opportunity cost. Allocations could take this into account by increasing the cost of access to those portions of the spectrum that have become more pressured and therefore more valuable. This in turn would encourage planners to seek alternative methods of sending information, or to develop alternative technologies for conserving frequency.

Any system of allocation that could directly increase the cost of access to particular portions of the spectrum would have to rest on some agreement about who owns the spectrum (no one); the current registered users; the countries in which current users reside; or the international community as a whole. The present system is ambiguous on this question. The inability to charge for access is consistent with no ownership; the necessity to clear unused registrations with the registering country implies national or user ownership; yet some of the language in the regulations implies international ownership.

The debate over frequency management within the United States addresses ownership directly, along with the problems of efficiency in the use of the scarce resource. The domestic debate has focused on variants of market systems, which may have some relevance to future consideration of options at the international level.

The Total Market Option

The first proposal was for a total market system. Proponents of a total market approach to spectrum management advocate that the market, not a regulatory agency, be the institution that determines both what *uses* get what parts of the spectrum, as well as which *users* get which frequencies.[20] Most proposals of this sort call for the existing users to be given property rights to the allocations they now have, and to be permitted to sell them, in whole or in part. For existing users, the discovery

20. Proponents of market systems include Ronald H. Coase, "The Federal Communications Commission," *Journal of Law and Economics,* vol. 2 (October 1959), pp. 1–40; and William H. Meckling, "Management of the Frequency Spectrum," *Washington University Law Quarterly,* vol. 1968, no. 1, pp. 26–34.

Largely in response to what is seen as the political impossibility of achieving a genuine market system, Levin has called for the allocating bodies to use market simulation as the major tool of decisionmaking. This means that the allocators would use computers to determine the price for frequency if it were sold, and then to determine which uses and users would be willing to pay those prices—in other words, which uses and users would get the most value from having the resources. See Harvey J. Levin, *The Invisible Resource: Use and Regulation of the Radio Spectrum* (Johns Hopkins Press for Resources for the Future, 1971).

The problem with this approach is that it is almost impossible to get the necessary data to reach the desired conclusions. Shadow prices, the economist's term for what the regulators would be calculating, are very difficult to determine in practice, and, even when determined, there is no mechanism for ensuring that any decisions are based upon them. It is argued that shadow pricing will enable allocators to take into account the economic consequences of their decisions without creating political opposition from those who hold spectrum now. This is because nobody would necessarily be charged the shadow price, but future applications for spectrum would be evaluated on these grounds. It seems likely, however, that if allocators knew the real value of the resource they are now giving away, they would decide to try to charge for it.

that they can sell some of their spectrum for more than the amount needed to buy frequency-conserving equipment is a powerful incentive to make this investment in more efficient frequency use.

For a market system of spectrum management to work, there would need to be a new definition of spectrum rights. This does not seem to be an insurmountable obstacle; at least one attempt has been made for specific segments of the spectrum.[21]

Proponents of a market system for spectrum argue mainly that it would produce more efficient and broader expansion of communications services. In addition, a market system would clarify the criteria for obtaining spectrum rights, requiring not merely ability to pay, but also willingness to pay.

Opponents of a market system for the spectrum object on several grounds. One argument is that it is more efficient to have similar use worldwide of a given band—in other words, fixed services should all use the same bands, whether they are serving China or New York—and that a market would not assure this result. The two principal reasons for wanting like services uniformly situated are that uniformity makes it easier to introduce new spectrum uses into an already allocated band, and that a rule of common usage would permit more mobility for the spectrum users and standardization of equipment.

A second set of objections to a spectrum market system arises from a belief that certain public interests can best be served by a regulatory system. Those who hold this view express concern that a market system would allocate insufficient spectrum to socially desirable uses such as local police and firemen; that public authorities would lose the ability to induce broadcasters to comply with certain kinds of programming standards; and that spectrum would be concentrated in the hands of the wealthy.[22]

Proponents of the market system reply that each of these concerns is

21. See, for example, Arthur S. DeVany and others, "A Property System for Market Allocation of the Electromagnetic Spectrum: A Legal-Economic-Engineering Study," *Stanford Law Review*, vol. 21 (June 1969), pp. 1499–1561.

22. William K. Jones, "Use and Regulation of the Radio Spectrum: Report on a Conference," *Washington University Law Quarterly*, vol. 1968, no. 1, pp. 71–115; Nicholas Johnson, "Towers of Babel: The Chaos in Radio Spectrum Utilization and Allocation," *Law and Contemporary Problems*, vol. 34 (Summer 1969), pp. 505–34.

insufficiently sensitive to the actual workings of market incentives, to the alternative means of assuring public service requirements, to the variety of tools for government regulation of communicators, and to the factors working against excessive concentration of frequency-buying by a financially capable few.

Thus far, the debate over a market system has been largely in response to the notion of instituting such a system for allocating spectrum within the United States. When such a system is considered for international spectrum allocation, three issues comparable to those raised domestically seem pertinent: the problem of common use, provision for certain public services, and problems of distribution. The problem of common use clearly is both national and international.

The need to protect allocations for public services internationally would require that bands be held clear for such uses as SOS calls and radio astronomy. Both activities have no currently available substitute to the use of the spectrum, and the consequences of interference are high for both. Thus, discussion of a market system for international allocation of spectrum would have to exempt these bands from sale.

Perhaps the major issue raised by a total market system for frequency allocation is the question of distribution. Giving ownership of frequency resources to the existing users would initially sanction the existing distribution of these resources. The frequency spectrum is now predominantly registered to the developed countries, so any change in this distribution would require the less developed countries to buy spectrum from the developed countries.

The Zoned Market Variant

In order to preserve the principle of having all like services on the same part of the spectrum, it has been proposed that the spectrum be zoned in a fashion analogous to land.[23] Market operations could continue to function within each zone, but all participants would be bound by the zoning provisions.

While this provision would meet the need for common use, it would not meet the other objections to a market system noted above. Moreover, unlike an unzoned market system, it would not permit the substitution of new uses for old ones as new ones became more valuable. Thus, while it would permit some of the opportunity costs of spectrum to be

23. Jones, "Use and Regulation of the Radio Spectrum," pp. 103–05.

considered in its allocation, it would not help increase the overall efficiency of the use of frequency.

A Fee for Use

Both the problem of the obsolescence of established zones and the problem of assuring certain public values in the use of spectrum can be met by renting out the resource for fixed terms, rather than selling it. In its simplest form, this would mean charging user fees for licenses granted. This suggestion has arisen in the debate about domestic frequency allocation, but it is applicable in principle to the international system as well.[24]

An advantage of such a system is that it would vest ownership of the spectrum in the international community at large, and the international community could thus benefit from rising opportunity costs in the form of rising user fees. For the international community to take full advantage of rising opportunity costs would require setting fees by competitive bidding. This could be done within zones, to keep similar uses on the same bands. If the terms of the users were all concurrent, the licensing authority could rezone whenever prices in one category diverged significantly from other categories. If one service began to pay much less per unit of bandwidth, while other zones experienced high bids, it would serve as a signal to cut the size of the allotment to the first service. The only exception to the auction principle should be those bands used for emergency services and research.

A system of user fees could also avoid the tendency, associated with the market system, for the spectrum to become concentrated in the hands of wealthy countries. The revenues from leasing the spectrum could conceivably be used to try to reduce inequities in distribution of essential communications services to poor states—for example, through a fund to help the poorer countries bid for spectrum rights where they might otherwise be relatively squeezed by the wealthier states. Revenues from the auctions could be added to this fund.

The auction system would not be likely to prevent countries from maintaining as complete a communications system as they can afford. Indeed, countries now hindered by lack of available frequency in pre-

24. A similar approach should be applied to allocation of positions within the geostationary orbit. While not spelled out here, most of the same arguments that apply to frequency allocation also apply to orbit allocation.

ferred parts of the spectrum might be able to obtain some allocation. Use of the system would encourage wider adoption of alternative techniques, such as cable systems, for providing communications services. Unlike an airline system, or other services governments feel compelled to provide for reasons of prestige, communication services such as telephone, television, and radio programs can be provided in several ways.

The ITU as now structured would be ill suited for administering such a system of fees for use. But if the International Frequency Registration Board (or some other organ of the ITU) were reconstituted to strengthen its regulatory powers as suggested above, there is no reason why it could not at the same time be given the responsibility for conducting the rental auctions, collecting the fees, distributing the revenues, and other functions implied by the concept. This structural reform would, of course, require a revision of the ITU convention.

This raises the problem of political feasibility, since the existing system is congenial to the advanced communications powers, and the consent of most of them would be necessary to revise the convention. Charging for spectrum, especially if the charge approximated the opportunity cost of the specific portion involved, would probably change the pattern of who would adopt alternatives to radio transmission. The greatest impact would be felt by those who now have the largest allocations, namely the industrial nations. These countries could find their communications systems very much more expensive to run. Over time, however, some of them could more easily and economically alter their patterns of use of the spectrum by upgrading equipment or by switching to alternative means of communication. Others would have fewer such opportunities. The USSR, for example, might find it more difficult than other countries to cut back on its expanding frequency use, since it has many sparsely populated centers separated by long distances that are linked more efficiently by communications relayed by satellite than by substitutes such as cables. Australia and New Zealand might experience similar difficulty. A system requiring a fee for use of frequency could therefore substantially raise the cost of the communications systems of these countries. The United States and other industrialized countries, however, contain large, densely populated, high-volume markets for communications, which might be served better by cable connections, especially if there is no longer a free ride on the radio spectrum.

Despite the preferences of some countries for the system of free use of the spectrum, the arrangements we have suggested ought to strike most countries of the world as fair, since they would compel frequency users to pay for its use on the basis of its real value to them. Moreover, it would induce all users to adopt frequency-conserving measures, thereby increasing the total supply available to all members of the international community, which in turn should keep the price within reason. Forthright support by the United States for the user-fee system could well engender sufficient international consensus behind it to make it a realistic and negotiable alternative.

CHAPTER FOURTEEN

Toward International Accountability
in the Use of Outer Space

The preceding four chapters have shown that a regime of open access and free use for human activities in outer space is not entirely acceptable to many countries. In each of the fields analyzed—remote sensing of earth resources, direct broadcasting from satellites, maritime navigational satellites, and the allocation of frequency and orbital resources —countries that are less technologically advanced have feared their economic or political interests might be undermined by an open access regime, and they have tried to gain some leverage on the activities of countries with greater capabilities for using the space environment.

Except for frequencies and orbits, the pressures have not been toward staking out national claims to resources, as has occurred in the ocean. Even with respect to frequencies and orbits, the claims of exclusive rights for use are made by very few countries and apply to only a very small part of the total resources available. Most demands in the space field have been for greater accountability of the space powers to the international community.

Remote Sensing

The major issue in the debate over remote sensing of the earth from outer space is how to distribute the data acquired. A satellite designed for remote sensing can supply imagery of almost the entire planet, and this imagery can in turn be used for a wide variety of resource assessments. Because nations differ greatly in their ability to process and analyze the data, some of the technologically disadvantaged nations have expressed fear that other countries and large corporations may be able to use the data to gain economic advantage over them. Some charge that national sovereignty over information about countries is diminished by remote sensing from satellites.

A number of anxious countries have pressed for a system of data distribution that would give countries priority in access to data about themselves or the right to determine who should get access to this data. Our examination of the restricted access proposals shows them to be impractical. The opportunities for surreptitious transmission of data to other interested states would be considerable.[1]

We endorse a continuation of the present U.S. practice of open distribution of the data to all who want it. We also endorse the U.S. offer to provide a copy of all the civilian data to the international community.

To assist the technologically disadvantaged countries with analysis of the data, we recommend that an international user agency be established as a repository of all such data and as a source of data analysis services. It would also be desirable to equip networks of regional ground stations with some capabilities for data analysis. Such regional groups could be eligible for assistance from the international agency.

A future problem in remote sensing may concern the continuing provision of the satellite portion of the service. Currently only the U.S. has a civilian satellite system in operation, from which data is supplied to all who want it upon payment only of the cost of processing the imagery. The satellite portion is paid for entirely by the U.S. government. A problem may arise if and when the United States no longer wants to pay the total costs of the satellite program. Once a wide network of ground stations is established, there may be opportunity to apportion the cost of the space segment among participating countries. It can be argued that the gathering of imagery of a specific area is essentially the provision of a public good, and therefore its provision should not be contingent upon payment of user costs; rather, if there are costs for the service, they should be borne by the entire community. We take no stand on this issue, noting only its potential for controversy.

1. The impracticality of the most restrictive proposals seems to be becoming evident. Forty countries, including Brazil, Argentina, India, France, and the USSR, have sponsored a resolution noting with satisfaction the construction of ground stations around the world and urging consideration of regional centers.

Direct Broadcasting via Satellite

The international controversy in direct broadcasting via satellite centers on this question: should recipient states have the right to determine (a) whether they should be the targets of broadcasts and (b) the content of broadcasts beamed to them? States arguing for a consent regime claim that broadcasts without their consent would be a violation of their sovereignty. The U.S. government claims that a consent regime would seriously interfere with the free exchange of information.

The issue as drawn at the ideological level is a false one. If the United States engages in the debate on those grounds, it may work against the improvements in disseminating information that are made possible by satellite technology. Technical incompatibilities between the television systems of neighboring states and the technological defenses available against unwanted broadcasts suggest that a greater dissemination of information is likely to occur under negotiated arrangements between sending and receiving countries than under unilateral broadcasting.

A general international convention on broadcasting via satellite should stipulate that broadcasting across international borders be with the agreement of the involved countries. This raises the problem of spillover: should a government be able to veto the voluntary arrangements of other countries on the grounds that its citizens are picking up unwanted broadcasts? We contend that where the spillover is unintentional, the government of the country that is accidentally receiving transmission should not be able to void the agreements governing such broadcasting. The broadcasters, on the other hand, should be obligated to consult with the objecting countries and attempt to minimize spillover.

A general broadcasting convention should also endorse the principle of minimal intergovernmental interference with program content. Concurrently, nongovernmental and multinational broadcasting associations should be encouraged to develop codes of conduct and guidelines for program content.

Additionally, countries with capabilities for broadcasting via satellite should encourage international arrangements—especially bilateral and regional—to help developing countries set up systems to use satellite broadcasts for educational or other welfare purposes.

Maritime Communications Satellite System

There is broad international interest in a satellite system to satisfy general maritime communications requirements (i.e., distress, safety, and public correspondence), as reflected in the International Conference on the Establishment of an International Maritime Satellite System, convened in 1975 and 1976 under the auspices of the Inter-governmental Maritime Consultative Organization (IMCO).

The principal international issues concern the institution for managing the maritime communications satellite system. Should the managing organization comprise only governmental representatives, or should a country be able to designate a nongovernmental entity to represent it (such as COMSAT in INTELSAT)? What should be the basis and distribution of voting power in the organization (votes proportionate to members' investment, level of use, or a simple one-member, one-vote formula)? What should be the relations between the deliberative and executive organs? What should be the organization's procurement policy?

With respect to designated entities, we support the position that operational responsibility should be lodged by each country in whatever entities can carry out the tasks of maritime communication most efficiently. We regard the question of formal representation in the international organization as a false issue, since governments will in any case be responsible for whatever their designated entities do. The United States should not make the success of the negotiations to establish the new system contingent upon the acceptance of formal representation by a nongovernmental agency, if indeed this becomes a stumbling block to the treaty.

Voting in the organization should be weighted both on grounds of investment and levels of use in the executive council and on the basis of one member, one vote in the assembly. The assembly should be granted broad authority for policy and budget and the council should be given operational flexibility. Contracts for the hardware and software and specialized operational services should be let on the basis of open international bidding. The actual awards should be made on the basis of the most favorable combinations of price, quality, and delivery time—constrained, however, by the requirement to avoid monopoly or oligopoly and to encourage a broadening international base of supply of goods and services.

Frequency and Orbit Allocation

International concerns are beginning to surface (as in the preliminary discussions surrounding the 1977 World Administrative Radio Conference) over the present system for allocating frequencies and orbital arcs. The present system involves a high degree of international accountability among major users; it is the future distribution of the resources and their efficient use that is of concern.

We favor user fees that would bring the direct costs of using these resources into line with their value (as determined by availability), for this would free some portions of the spectrum that are now underutilized for use by others. Moreover, such user fees would constitute de facto recognition that the spectrum and orbits are internationally owned resources. Finally, the user fees could provide revenue to the international community to be applied to lessen the disparities in communications capabilities among nations.

The administrative responsibilities for a user fee system should be lodged in the International Telecommunication Union.

Toward an Overall Regime for Outer Space

Our review of the problems and potential solutions in each of the specific fields of outer space reveals that there are very few conflicts among the various kinds of uses. The international problems evident in each field of outer space activity are usually specific to that field, even though in some cases there are similarities among the fields. In this respect, outer space differs from the ocean, where the central contemporary issues involve interference between different ocean uses and the need to make exchanges between them.

Because the problems involving the various space activities are specific to individual issues, the overall regime for outer space should be a pluralistic one, characterized by a variety of separate international agreements and institutions. This contrasts with our preferred approach to ocean issues, which calls for a more integrated regime.

If our specific space recommendations are followed, a new international agency would serve as a repository for remotely sensed data and would also assist less capable countries to analyze that data; the International Telecommunication Union would have strengthened powers to allocate resources; a new international agency would manage an international maritime communications satellite system; and a convention on direct broadcasting would regulate satellite broadcasting. INTELSAT would continue to serve as an international link among national communications services.

The desirability of directly managing most problems of outer space in agencies that have single functions does not, however, obviate the importance of coordination among these and other agencies. Remotely sensed data on earth resources are of substantial importance to the United Nations Food and Agriculture Organization, the World Bank, and the World Health Organization. Some of the most important remotely sensed data is on climate and weather patterns, and satellites obtaining such information form part of the network of the World Meteorological Organization. Coordination of the remote sensing activities and data analysis of these agencies is likely to benefit all of them. Similar overlapping of functions suggests cooperation and consultation among agencies and interests involved in regular telephonic communications, maritime communications, and direct broadcasting. Moreover, as the reliance on satellites in these various fields increases, the pressures on scarce orbital and frequency resources may produce a greater need to establish priorities among different types of satellites and to consolidate the programs of different agencies.

Proposal for an Outer Space Projects Agency

The needs for consultation and coordination among the various governmental, international, and private interests involved in space affairs could best be met by the establishment of a permanent international outer space projects agency. This agency would be mandated to facilitate consultation and coordination among the users of outer space by providing a forum in which all aspects of activity in outer space could be discussed. The outer space projects agency would not conduct space projects itself, nor would it serve as a formal authorizing agency for projects. It would be structured primarily to promote widespread, ongoing, substantive discussions among all interested parties. To that end, it should be a universal membership organization that does not rely on voting but on building consensus among the parties with interest in particular issues of outer space. Once a consensus or options are developed on a particular issue, other forums or institutions would serve as the decisionmaking authorities for actual project management. In addition to facilitating consultation and coordination among different kinds of users of outer space, the agency could be the aegis under which special groups lacking an institutional base of their own could consult. It could, for example, offer a forum for nongovernmental and specialized multinational broadcasting organizations to consult with one another on issues of guidelines for program content and codes of conduct.

The success of the agency's coordinating functions would depend critically on the extent to which the space powers funneled their projects through the agency and revised their plans to reflect multilateral consensus developed within the agency. There is of course no tangible international leverage to compel the space powers to do so. It would therefore be most desirable if both space superpowers made such a move simultaneously. Failing this, the United States could make a commitment to work through the agency without waiting for the USSR.

CHAPTER FIFTEEN

Regime Alternatives for the Weather and Climate

Like the ocean and outer space, the earth's weather and climate systems are shared internationally. Changes in the weather and climate that develop in one country frequently circulate to affect the comfort, health, and economic welfare of people in other countries. But the existing international regime for the weather and climate is still largely unstructured, and there are few mechanisms to hold those who might alter local conditions accountable to the other societies they might affect.

Until recently, a laissez-faire regime has seemed appropriate because of two widely held assumptions: first, that the weather and climate are not in any significant way susceptible to alterations by human activities; and second, that even if technological developments changed the first assumption, the weather and climate system are so complex that it would be futile to attempt deliberately to manage their use. Growing scientific knowledge about the weather and climate system, and evidence of human impacts on it, have negated the first assumption. It is now generally appreciated that energy consumption, the distribution of human settlements, deforestation, and the like may have a major effect on international climatic patterns. As yet, scientific and technological developments have only begun to undermine the assumption that the weather and climate system are too complex to manage deliberately; but international interest in weather and climate modification is definitely on the rise. The United States experimented with techniques of rainmaking and cloud alteration during the Vietnam War. And there is growing civilian experimentation in many countries with technologies for affecting rainfall, snow and ice formation, and large storms.

In 1976, the UN General Assembly approved a convention banning the *hostile* use of environmental modification techniques if the effects are widespread, long lasting, or severe. But serious discussions are only beginning among meteorologists and government officials on how purportedly peaceful human interventions in the earth's weather and climate system might best be managed in the public interest.[1]

Essential Characteristics of the Weather and Climate

The global climate system is a product of interactions among air, sea, and land, and of various physical forces, including some in outer space. This global system has many subglobal and local weather systems, and all the subsystems strongly interact. Not only do the local and global levels interact, but the entire complex involves interactions with strong feedback mechanisms among air, water, and land. The global climate system (and its weather subsystems) is thus indivisible in two essential respects: it is constantly in motion and oblivious to political boundaries; it cannot be physically divided into its separate land, sea, and air components.

International Indivisibility

Although the weather of all countries is part of the larger global weather and climate system, the degree to which national weather systems are interdependent depends on various geographical relationships. There are regional weather systems—for example, countries in the northern hemisphere are locked in the same weather arena, while countries in the southern hemisphere share a different weather arena. The weather in Europe, for example, moves across northeastern France, then over West Germany to East Germany—a pattern laden with political significance. Typhoons in the western Pacific move west, toward the Philippines and then either toward Taiwan or northward toward Japan, Korea, and China. The separation of hemispheric weather systems is far from absolute, however; large-scale oceanic and atmospheric circulation patterns assure at least some exchange between the hemispheres. Thus, for example, there is a general flow in the northern winter out of Asia across the equator to Australia. This flow then reverses itself to move back north in the form of summer monsoons.

1. See Edith Brown Weiss, *Man the New Rain God: International Modifications of Weather and Climate* (University of California Press, forthcoming).

The overlapping and interactions of these various regional and local weather systems is of central importance when it comes to devising means of managing them, for any major change can reverberate throughout the larger weather and climate system in ways that are still highly unpredictable.

Physical and Chemical Dynamics

The dynamics of the weather and climate system are not sufficiently understood to predict reliably the effects of human activities on the system. Knowledge in this field, however, is growing rapidly, and some of the essential interrelationships can be specified.

The ocean, the land masses, and the biosphere play major roles in determining the chemical composition of the various layers of the atmosphere. The chemical composition of the atmosphere in turn determines the amount of solar radiation that can pass through the atmosphere to the surface of the earth. Solar radiation critically determines the earth's temperatures.

Carbon dioxide, dust (particulate matter), water vapor, and ozone are four substances known to be important in the transfer of energy between the sun, the surface of the earth, and space. Carbon dioxide is transparent to sunlight but traps heat in the lower atmosphere by intercepting the longwave (infrared) radiation from the surface of the earth that would otherwise escape to space, thus increasing the earth's temperature. Particulate matter (including smog) in the lower layers of the atmosphere prevents solar radiation from reaching the earth's surface, but it also absorbs solar radiation, thereby heating the air. The net result may be either a warming or a cooling, depending on conditions.

There is a layer of ozone in the upper part of the atmosphere (the stratosphere), which, in addition to preventing hazardous ultraviolet light from reaching plants and animals, plays an important role in determining the temperature in the stratosphere and influences surface temperatures to a small extent. Water vapor also affects the climate by absorbing longwave radiation emitted by the surface of the earth and therefore causing the surface to be warmer.

The ocean contributes to both the amount of water vapor in the atmosphere and the quantity of carbon dioxide. It contributes water vapor by evaporation, especially at warm latitudes, and absorbs carbon dioxide at cold latitudes. The colder the water, the more carbon dioxide can be absorbed. Carbon dioxide also takes part in the life cycle of plants, and its atmospheric concentration therefore fluctuates with the seasons, as plants grow in the spring and decay in the fall. The land masses are a source of both dust and water vapor, the latter emanating from the surfaces of lakes and rivers, and particularly from vegetation.

Unintentional Changes of the Weather and Climate

Because so little is known about the processes that occur naturally, it is difficult to analyze the impacts of human activities on the weather and climate. It is clear, however, that agriculture and combustion of fossil fuels have added to the particulate content of the atmosphere. Fossil fuel use also adds carbon dioxide to the air. The carbon dioxide, smog, and dust particles generated by man may be affecting the temperature of the earth. The importance of changes in the average temperature can be seen in the fact that an increase of one degree Celsius in the average temperature at mid-latitudes adds about ten days to the average growing season. A decrease of one degree Celsius has the opposite effect.[2]

According to the report of an authoritative panel of meteorologists, the average temperature of the northern hemisphere increased by 0.6° C. from 1880 to 1940, and has fallen by 1.3° C. since.[3] But the scientists do not agree as to whether pollution or natural fluctuations account for these changes in the earth's temperature.

Increases in both carbon dioxide and particulates can cause warming of the earth's surface. Carbon dioxide traps heat in the atmosphere, thereby increasing the earth's temperature. The concentration of carbon dioxide in the atmosphere in the last century has increased by about 10 to 15 percent.[4] The burning of fossil fuels has caused the increased carbon dioxide thus far, but changes in the condition of the ocean could contribute to future increases. The ocean has a tremendous capacity to absorb carbon dioxide, depending upon the water temperature; the

2. William W. Kellogg, "Climatic Non-Limits to Growth" (1974; processed), p. 11.

3. *Inadvertent Climate Modification: Report of the Study of Man's Impact on Climate* (M.I.T. Press, 1971), p. 42, fig. 3.6.

4. Crude estimates are that carbon dioxide has been increasing at the rate of 0.7 percent each year and that a further increase of about 18 percent might cause a 0.5° increase in surface temperatures.

warmer the ocean, the less carbon dioxide it can absorb. Thus, activities that warm the oceans could increase the amount of carbon dioxide in the atmosphere, thereby causing still more warming—an example of positive feedback, or amplification of a change in the climatic system.

Smog and dust pollution may have a cooling effect, but current estimates that take account of the absorption of sunlight by man-made particles in the lower atmosphere indicate that over land (where most of the particles are released) they cause a net warming. Most concerned scientists believe that there is insufficient evidence that pollution caused either the warming trend before 1940 or the cooling trend thereafter. They observe that the earth's temperature fluctuated sharply in the past before mankind could have played a significant role.[5]

The frequency and amount of precipitation may also be affected by various human activities. Reid Bryson and others argue that bad farming practices, which produced great amounts of dust, turned Rajastan, in northwest India, from a fertile agricultural area into a desert.[6] Bryson sees a layer of dust coming from agricultural practices in semiarid areas of Africa, China, and India, gradually building up in the atmosphere. Some scientists theorize that the increasing turbidity in the United States could eventually inhibit rainfall in some places and produce more deserts on the North American continent.

Lead iodide, one of the favored agents for seeding clouds, is being built up in the atmosphere in amounts that might inadvertently affect rainfall patterns. The lead in polluted air comes almost solely from automobile exhaust. Lead iodide pollution has increased widely in industrialized countries, primarily as a result of the rise in the number of autos. Once lead iodide is in the air, it does not disappear until it is washed or rained out. Meanwhile, it may accumulate in the air locally or

5. From an analysis of a 1.3-kilometer core of ice drilled from the Greenland Icecap, the Danish scientist W. Dansgaard sketched a curve of natural temperature fluctuations for the past 100,000 years, from which he predicted a warming trend to 1950, followed by cooling for the next twenty years. See Louise Purrett, "Ice Cores: Clues to Past Climates," *Science News*, vol. 98 (November 1, 1970), p. 369.

6. James T. Peterson and Reid A. Bryson, "The Influence of Atmospheric Particulates on the Infrared Radiation Balance of Northwest India," paper delivered at the First National Conference on Weather Modification, Albany, New York, April 28–May 1, 1968; and Reid A. Bryson and Wayne M. Wendland, "Climatic Effects of Atmospheric Pollution," in S. F. Singer, ed., *Global Effects of Environmental Pollution* (Springer Verlag, 1970), pp. 130–38.

be carried downwind. These lead iodide particles may initiate misty rains and very light snows, such as those common in New York City.

Alternatively, smog particles and smoke could inhibit rainfall. However, if there is a large source of moisture nearby, such pollution may cause increases in precipitation from heavy storms over the polluted area or downwind from it.[7]

Despite a lack of consensus to date about the impact of pollutants upon weather and climate, there is widespread concern about the possibility of future impacts if quantities of emissions continue to rise. Vincent Schaefer has warned:

If pollution sources lead to increased dustiness from ill-used land, more cloud nuclei from burning trash and many more ice nuclei from the lead-permeated exhaust of internal combustion engines, not only will we lose the possible advantage we now have of extracting some additional water from our sky rivers, but we might even be confronted with a drastic change in our climatological patterns.[8]

Eventually, pollution from separate sources may affect more than neighboring areas, as a global concentration of pollution begins to build. Morris Neiburger observes that

the pollutions from neighboring source areas affect each other, but at large distances the dilution and removal processes bring the levels down to the original background. In particular, we think that each batch of air entering the country from the Pacific Ocean is as clean as the previous one. However, we can visualize that if the rate of emission of pollution continues to increase, we will reach the stage in which the dilution and removal processes do not completely bring concentration back to the same value after a circuit of the Earth. . . . At each later circuit the concentration starts from a higher background value and reaches higher peaks. In the course of time, even the concentration over the oceans will be higher than the highest values ever reached anywhere at present, and the values reached in metropolitan areas would be unbearable.[9]

The natural processes for removing these pollutants may also be exponential, however, making buildup less of a problem than is portrayed by Neiburger.

7. See Stanley A. Changnon, Jr., "The LaPorte Weather Anomaly—Fact or Fiction?" *Bulletin of the American Meteorological Society*, vol. 49 (January 1968), pp. 4–11.

8. Vincent J. Schaefer, "The Inadvertent Modification of the Atmosphere by Air Pollution," *Bulletin of the American Meteorological Society*, vol. 50 (April 1969), p. 205.

9. Morris Neiburger, "The Role of Meteorology in the Study and Control of Air Pollution," *Bulletin of the American Meteorological Society*, vol. 50 (December 1969), p. 964.

Deliberate Attempts to Change Weather and Climate

Over the last few decades, many experiments have been aimed at intentionally changing weather and climate. The efforts are directed at finding an instability in the weather or climate system, which, if given appropriate stimulation, could trigger the desired effect.

Most attempts to modify the weather involve seeding clouds or fog with various chemicals. Silver iodide crystals have been used when cloud temperatures are below zero (Celsius) in an attempt to clear fog, increase rainfall, reduce hail or lightning, or modify tornadoes or hurricanes. The seeding can be done by dropping the seeding agent from aircraft or by firing rockets from the ground.

Climate changes might be deliberately initiated through programs to influence the extent of ice in the Arctic and Antarctic, modify oceanic circulation, modify land and ocean surfaces and divert rivers, regulate cloudiness, introduce contaminants into the atmosphere, modify the ozone layer, and modify tropical and cyclonic storm systems.

A few of these programs have been undertaken, but none has been for the express purpose of attempting to modify weather or climate. Although much research still needs to be done to understand fully the effects of international large-scale modification programs, the World Meteorological Organization reported as early as 1963 that

it is not unrealistic to expect that mankind will eventually have the power to influence weather, and even climate, on a large scale. However, the complexity of the atmospheric processes is such that a change in the weather induced artificially in one part of the world will necessarily have repercussion elsewhere.[10]

Behind the various weather and climate modification experiments lies an emerging awareness that the weather and climate systems are a resource that may be capable of being altered deliberately for major economic gain. In some cases, an increase in rainfall is sought to increase agricultural output. In other cases, weather modification is eyed as a potentially cheaper method of reducing damage from tropical storms.

We must emphasize, however, that there is little consensus among meteorologists as to the state of the art for most techniques of weather

10. *Second Report on the Advancement of Atmospheric Sciences and Their Application in the Light of Developments in Outer Space* (Geneva: World Meteorological Organization, 1963).

modification. Statisticians in particular have often vigorously attacked the results of weather modification experiments as lacking statistical validity. The World Meteorological Organization has issued a Statement on Weather Modification, which concludes that "although some experiments have apparently yielded positive results, the possible practical benefits of weather modification can be realized only through an increased research effort."[11]

The Distribution of Weather Modification Capabilities

As with other technologies, the developed countries enjoy a technical leadership in research and experimentation about weather and climate modification, and can be expected to develop the most sophisticated techniques. Some types of weather modification technology, however, involve techniques accessible to the rest of the world. As the technology matures, many countries should be able to initiate changes in weather conditions. Today, the United States, Israel, and Australia probably have the most advanced programs in cloud seeding to induce precipitation. U.S. scientists have recently performed experiments in seeding multiple clouds to induce them to merge. Indian scientists have conducted promising experiments in seeding warm clouds. China has significant programs aimed at developing technology to induce rain. The USSR has the most advanced program in hail suppression. The United States began an intensive scientific program on hail suppression in the early 1970s. Switzerland, France, Argentina, and several countries in East Africa also have made notable experiments in hail suppression.

Managing Human Impact on the Weather and Climate

Interest in creating a regime to regulate alterations of the weather and climate is fairly recent, and it is not as widespread as interest in regimes for the ocean or for outer space. This is partly because of the ignorance of the intricacies of the weather and climate system, and partly because of the relatively early stage of human intervention in the system. For the time being, most international activity for managing the

11. World Meteorological Organization, "Present State of Knowledge and Possible Practical Benefits in Some Fields of Weather Modification," EC-XXXVI, Appendix, pp. 5–7.

weather and climate system is likely to be concerned less with specific uses of the meteorological system and more with guiding and promoting the increased knowledge that is needed. Even so, as the weather and climate system comes under increased scrutiny, various proposals are being advanced to deal internationally with various aspects of its use.

The Existing System: Limited International Accountability

The existing regime lacks the means effectively to control deliberate efforts to change the international weather and climate, or to regulate projects that may inadvertently affect meteorological conditions. Precedents that may affect the regime for weather modification, however, are beginning to emerge in the tort law concerned with international environmental problems. Further, a normative basis for deciding future conflicts of interests is being slowly built into various international declarations and conventions on the human environment.

The Trail Smelter Arbitration, which concerned the flow of polluting fumes from a Canadian company across the border into the state of Washington, was a step toward creating a principle forbidding environmental damage by one country to another. The arbitral tribunal held the Canadian smelter responsible for the damages caused when its fumes crossed the border into the state of Washington.[12] At the same time, it ordered comprehensive studies of the meteorological conditions in the Columbia River valley to determine under what conditions the fumes would produce unacceptable concentrations. As a result of the studies, the smelter was ordered to vary the amount of sulfur dioxide released into the air according to weather conditions, in order to prevent further damage from air pollution in the state of Washington.

Although the subject of weather modification per se has not been the subject of international treaty-making, the UN International Law Commission observed in 1949, "There has been general recognition of the rule that a state must not permit the use of its territory for purposes injurious to the interest of other states in a manner contrary to international law."[13]

The closest thing to an explicit international attitude toward weather modification is found in the declaration and recommendations of the 1972 United Nations Conference on the Human Environment. Principle 21 of the declaration provides that states "have the responsibility to

12. For a discussion of the case, see "Trail Smelter Arbitral Tribunal," *American Journal of International Law,* vol. 35 (October 1941), pp. 684–734.
13. *Survey of International Law,* vol. 34, UN Doc. N/CN/1/Rev. 1, 1949.

ensure that activities within their jurisdiction or control do not cause damage to the environment of other States or of areas beyond the limits of national jurisdiction." Principle 22 calls for extending the law of liability and compensation to cover environmental cases. Recommendation 70 of the Stockholm conference states that governments undertaking activities "in which there is an appreciable risk of effects on climate" should:

(a) Carefully evaluate the likelihood and magnitude of climate effects and disseminate their findings to the maximum extent feasible before embarking on such activities;
(b) Consult fully other interested States when activities carrying a risk of such effects are being contemplated or implemented.[14]

The recommendation appears to apply to activities that may incidentally affect climate as well as to those designed primarily to change climate.

The 1974 Nordic Environmental Protection Convention, agreed upon by Sweden, Norway, Finland, and Denmark, was a landmark effort to provide procedures for environmental protection at a regional level. The convention applies to activities on the land as well as the continental shelf areas of the signatory nations. It requires the operators of certain activities to obtain a permit before commencing and to provide notice of the permit to all affected contracting states. It also provides for enjoining injurious activities to prevent further injury and for offering relief to anyone who suffered injury by obtaining compensation through the national judicial systems.

Considerable progress has been made recently toward banning hostile modification of the weather and climate. In 1975, at the Geneva Disarmament Conference, the United States and the USSR tabled, in parallel, identical drafts of a convention to prohibit the "military or any other hostile use of environmental modification techniques having widespread, long-lasting or severe effects as the means of destruction, damage or injury. . . ."[15] The term "environmental modification techniques" as used in the draft convention refers to

any technique for changing—through the deliberate manipulation of natural processes—the dynamics, composition or structure of the Earth, including its

14. For the text of the declaration and recommendations, see *United Nations Conference on the Human Environment,* Report to the Senate by Senator Clairborne Pell and Senator Clifford Case, 92:2 (GPO, 1972), pp. 18 and 36.
15. Draft Convention on the Prohibition of Military or Any Other Hostile Use of Environmental Modification Techniques (August 21, 1975). Text in *Department of State Bulletin,* vol. 73, no. 1890 (September 15, 1975), p. 419.

biota, lithosphere, hydrosphere, and atmosphere, or of outer space, so as to cause such effects as earthquakes and tsunamis, an upset in the ecological balance of a region, or changes in weather patterns (clouds, precipitation, cyclones of various types and tornadic storms), in the state of the ozone layer or ionosphere, in climate patterns, or in ocean currents.[16]

(The final text does not define environmental modification techniques.) The conference sent a revised text of the convention to the UN General Assembly, which voted in December 1976 to open it for signature and ratification by states. The convention contains the controversial "troika" language, which limits its scope to those techniques having "widespread, long-lasting, or severe effects." It applies only among states that are party to the convention and will come into effect when twenty states have signed and ratified it.[17] The convention specifically exempts from its prohibition the use of environmental modification techniques for peaceful purposes.

Most international activity in the environmental field is still in the form of UN resolutions and declarations of principles. Countries are highly resistant to negotiating international limits on their experimental programs, especially in the field of peaceful weather and climate modification, which still is mistakenly regarded by most laymen and politicians as a matter only for future generations to worry about.

National Zones

Since weather is often identified with the visible clouds in the nearby atmosphere, a common presumption has been that states will react to problems arising from attempts to modify the weather by claiming sovereignty over the atmosphere. The dispute in the winter of 1976–77 between Idaho, Montana, Oregon, and Washington over cloud-seeding operations to relieve the drought portends increasing attempts by states to claim property rights to the water in the clouds directly above them.[18] Two international conventions governing air navigation initially developed the rule that states should have complete and exclusive sovereignty over their own airspace.[19] There is considerable disagreement

16. Ibid., pp. 419–20.

17. Convention on the Prohibition of Military or Any Other Hostile Use of Environmental Modification Techniques, UN Doc. A/C.1/31/L.5/Rev. 3, December 2, 1976.

18. Louisiana, Nebraska, North Dakota, South Dakota, New Mexico, and Colorado have asserted sovereignty over moisture in their atmosphere.

19. Convention Relating to the Regulation of Aerial Navigation, Paris, October 13, 1919, 11 L.N.T.S. 173 (1922); Convention on International Civil Aviation, 61 Stat. 1180, T.I.A.S. 1591.

about whether this rule was intended to apply only to navigation or whether it was to apply to all activities affecting airspace.

Some legal literature also has suggested that the regime of zones outlined by the Geneva Conventions of the late 1950s for the oceans might be taken to include weather.[20] Zones analogous to internal waters, territorial seas, contiguous zones, continental shelves, and the high seas would be created for the weather and climate system. There would be several zones at different heights, with progressively diminishing degrees of sovereignty associated with greater distances from the earth.

Such zones would have little validity, however, when applied to weather and climate. Certainly fog dispersal operations, which are conducted very close to the ground, are not likely to affect neighboring countries, unless the national border is near. And injection of contaminants high into the atmosphere is likely to affect more than one state. But almost all weather modification activities that involve interference directly in the atmosphere are conducted at levels in between. The size of the state, its location in relation to neighboring states, and its potential influence on atmospheric circulation patterns are the important variables, rather than how far above land the operation is conducted.

International Management

Some would argue that strengthened international accountability provides the only opportunity to avoid the international conflicts that would otherwise result from the proliferation of weather modification capabilities. Such an approach might involve negotiation of a universal treaty obligating countries to assume responsibility (including financial compensation), to other countries and to the international community at large, for any unilaterally induced changes in the weather or climate that might cause damage to the resources of other countries. It might also provide for universal international help to inadvertent victims of weather and climate changes, whether or not these were due to human or natural causes.

The treaty might include the obligation to participate in international consultation, monitoring, and dispute resolution before and during the conduct of projects likely to have transnational effects. The treaty could go so far as to prohibit large-scale experiments unless states that might be affected gave their prior consent.

The implementation of such a regime of international accountability

20. John Cobb Cooper, "Legal Problems of Upper Space," *Proceedings of the American Society of International Law* (1956), pp. 85–93.

would probably require a network of regional and global institutions to coordinate information and analysis of the weather and climate and to authorize weather and climate modification projects with transnational effects. Consultation services, scientific advisory panels, and dispute resolution machinery would probably be most appropriately lodged in a global institution because of the strongly interacting properties of local and global weather and climate systems.

CHAPTER SIXTEEN

Rainmaking and Typhoon Modification

Efforts to increase rain and modify hurricanes or typhoons,[1] unlike some weather modification schemes, have achieved legitimacy as experimental programs worthy of some public support. In at least fifty-five countries, there have been attempts to increase rainfall or snowpack, and the U.S. government has experimented actively with hurricane modification. Yet these programs raise important international issues, and the way they are handled will set a precedent for other programs in environmental modification.

Attempts to modify rainfall can generate international political conflict for several reasons: Communities 100 miles or more downwind of a target may find their precipitation affected. What helps one community may hinder another. Farmers may want more rainfall; resort owners less. Typhoon modification also poses inherently international problems, for the storms traverse international ocean areas, and usually continue landward across at least several countries.

Rainmaking and Snowpack Augmentation

Attempts to increase rainfall or snowpack in specific areas utilize cloud-seeding techniques. Particles (the substance differs, depending on the temperature of the clouds) are introduced into clouds in the hope of triggering precipitation. Seeding is accomplished either from airplanes or from generators on the ground. Governments, agricultural co-

1. The same type of storm is called a hurricane in the Atlantic, a typhoon in the Pacific, and a cyclone in the Indian Ocean.

operatives, and individual farmers have been willing to invest significant amounts of money in cloud-seeding programs in the hope of obtaining relief from drought, even though the technology is still far from scientifically reliable. With the new concern over food scarcities and the potential scarcity of water, communities may turn increasingly to cloud seeding to relieve droughts and bad weather conditions.

Cloud seeding may have effects other than stimulating rain in the target areas: it may suppress precipitation; it may affect the size and duration of clouds; and it may affect precipitation downwind. The downwind effects are of particular concern in the present study, since they raise the possibility of international disputes.

The downwind effects of cloud seeding are not entirely clear, but the evidence to date suggests there may be significant downwind effects from increased precipitation for 100 to 200 miles.[2] In cases where that area included foreign populations, it might produce conflict if bad weather conditions downwind were attributed to cloud-seeding programs rather than natural variations, or if downwind countries believed they were receiving proportionally too little of the additional water supplies. On the other hand, this type of program offers a unique opportunity for states to engage in common programs for coordinating the use of water resources.

To date, there have been three international scientific conferences concerned with cloud seeding: the first in Australia in 1971, which was sponsored jointly by the American Meteorological Society and the Australian Council of Scientific and Industrial Research Organizations; the second in Tashkent, USSR, in October 1973, and the third in Boulder, Colorado, in August 1976—the latter two sponsored by the World Meteorological Organization (WMO). The WMO also has a Working Group on Cloud Physics, which meets regularly to exchange data, assess the state of the art, and respond to requests from the WMO Secretariat.

The WMO Executive Committee Panel on Weather Modification recommended at its session in October and November 1974 that the WMO sponsor an international experiment on enhancing rain in a semi-

2. An evaluation of the effects on Jordan, Syria, and Lebanon of the Israeli seeding program from 1961 to 1967 indicated increases in precipitation at distances of 50–70 miles downwind. Glen W. Brier, Lewis O. Grant, and Paul W. Mielke, Jr., "The Evidence for Extra-Area Effects From Purposeful Weather Modification Projects," *Proceedings of the Fourth Conference on Weather Modification* (Boston: American Meteorological Society, 1974), pp. 510–15.

arid region.[3] This project would be designed to determine whether it is possible to increase precipitation under the given meteorological conditions in the chosen region. The results would be particularly useful to countries considering programs of their own or considering hiring commercial operators.[4]

3. "Report of the Third Session of the Executive Panel on Weather Modification Commission on Atmospheric Sciences Working Group on Cloud Physics and Weather Modification," World Meteorological Organization, Toronto, October 28–November 2, 1974 (processed).

4. When a commercial company seeded clouds in Niger in September 1973 to alleviate the effects of the Sahelian drought, there was little way either of knowing the effects of the cloud seeding or of calculating the economic benefits. During the period of seeding, rainfall was greater than it was in the period before the clouds were seeded, which led many people in the area to conclude that the cloud-seeding program had in fact helped the country. The operation was not designed to test scientifically whether the increase in rainfall was due to cloud seeding or to natural fluctuations.

In several scientifically conducted experiments attempts have been made to calculate the benefit–cost ratio of cloud seeding to increase precipitation. In a cloud-seeding program in Florida in the spring of 1971, the increase in water from seeding was estimated to be about 10^5 acre feet, and the cost about $165,000. This yielded a benefit–cost ratio of 32:1 if the water went for municipal purposes, and 68:1 if it went for agricultural crops. See W. L. Woodley and others, "Florida Cumulus Seeding Experiment for Drought Mitigation, April–May 1971," NOAA Technical Memorandum ERL OD-9 (November 1971), pp. 133–34. If the program had been designed as an operational one rather than as a scientifically designed experiment, estimates indicated that the benefit–cost ratio would have been considerably higher.

Often there are problems in calculating the ratio of benefits to costs. The experimental cloud-seeding program in Israel currently costs about $550,000 annually. It is estimated that an operational cloud-seeding program designed to add water to the Kinneret (Lake Tiberias) watershed would cost about $360,000. Those persons assessing the cost–benefit ratio of an operational program regard it as more difficult to evaluate the benefits. In part this is because of the difficulty in calculating the additional expenses of exploiting the precipitation increase, which varies with the distance of the area from the Kinneret. Best available calculations indicate that the benefit–cost ratio would vary between 70:40 for the Tel Aviv area and 70:60 to the South. In Israel, it is possible to evaluate alternative sources for acquiring more fresh water— reclaimed sewage and desalinization. Desalinization is still too costly, while reclaimed sewage is still being tested for use in agriculture, which does not require water as fresh as for drinking supplies. For details on the Israeli program, see A. Gagin and J. Neumann, "Rain Stimulation and Cloud Physics in Israel," in W. N. Hess, ed., Weather and Climate Modification (Wiley, 1974), pp. 454–94.

Typhoon (Hurricane) Modification

The objectives of typhoon modification might be to reduce the winds of a storm, to direct its path, or, perhaps for malevolent reasons, to increase the storm's intensity. There are two primary methods that researchers think might modify typhoons: seeding with ice nuclei; and modifying the rate at which heat is transferred from the ocean to the atmosphere (this might be done by spreading monomolecular films on the ocean surface to retard evaporation of the water, or by setting off an explosion to bring the deeper, cooler water to the surface). The theory behind seeding with ice nuclei is that this will make the eye wall of the typhoon expand outward, thereby spreading the storm's energy and lessening its intensity. In 1969, Hurricane Debbie was seeded with ice nuclei. A 30 percent decrease in winds was observed on the first day of seeding, and a 15 percent decrease on the second day. These results are impressive, but not yet conclusive, evidence that seeding modifies hurricanes.[5]

There are several potential side effects of typhoon modification: seeding a typhoon may possibly cause less precipitation over a wider area, because reducing the storm's winds may prevent the storm's precipitation from reaching as far inland as usual; diversion of a typhoon also could cause a locality to lose precipitation; and efforts at modifying a typhoon may inadvertently increase its intensity.

Typhoons are typically transnational phenomena, and some of the anticipated results of attempts to modify them could engender conflict between states. Even if a project actually reduces the intensity that a storm might have reached, if the overall intensity of the storm is observed to increase after seeding, it will be difficult to convince affected populations that modification has in fact been beneficial. In other cases, there may be fears that the seeding of a typhoon will lead to a modification in the amount of rainfall in one country or to a redistribution of rainfall between countries. Even at the present experimental stage, these concerns suggest that it is necessary for the state conducting typhoon modification to consult widely with countries in the area and to develop suitable arrangements for managing the experiments to ensure that it will not have adverse effects upon states in the area.

5. Details of the experiment appear in R. Cecil Gentry, "Hurricane Debbie Modification Experiments, August 1969," *Science*, vol. 168 (April 24, 1970), pp. 473–75.

Past experiments have not been characterized by such accountability. In its Atlantic hurricane program, the U.S. government operated under an informal executive rule that prohibited seeding of a storm anticipated to move within fifty miles of shore within an eighteen-hour period. The U.S. posture was that it did not regard itself as liable for any damage caused by the experiment. This may be consistent with the U.S. Federal Tort Claims Act, which exempts from liability to suit all cases except those in which an officer or an employee of the United States is negligent in the exercise of a nondiscretionary function and excludes recovery for damage that occurs in a foreign country. While it may be arguable whether federal weather modification projects can be classified as a discretionary function, it is probable that the act would exclude recovery for damage occurring in another country from U.S. hurricane modification programs.

When the United States planned to shift its typhoon modification experiments to the Pacific Ocean in 1977, it was pressured to develop guidelines and processes for conducting the program to avoid, or at least to minimize, conflict with other countries in the area. The WMO Technical Conference on Typhoon Modification held in Manila in October 1974 recommended that states in the region accept a "twenty-four-hour limit" as the guideline for seeding typhoons: that is, the seeding of typhoons would be permitted on an experimental basis, as long as they were not expected to reach land within twenty-four hours.[6] These plans have been dropped, but consideration is being given to other similar experiments.

Institutional Needs and Approaches

The international issues caused by rainmaking and typhoon modification seem inherently unsuitable for resolution by national means. At-

6. The proposed twenty-four-hour limit was noteworthy in that it would have eliminated any requirements as to distance from shore, but would have relied exclusively on the predicted forward speed of the typhoon. This means that facilities for forecasting typhoons would have to be sophisticated if they were to determine accurately the speed of the typhoon, and that most states that could be affected by the typhoon would essentially have had to rely on a postmortem in obtaining the data used to predict the speed of the typhoon. It would have been necessary to establish procedures for verifying when seeding of the typhoon begins in order to ensure against the possibility that the country conducting the experimental modification could circumvent the guideline by disguising the hour at which seeding was to begin.

tempts to extend national jurisdiction into the atmosphere cannot significantly deal with the problem of effects in one state from activities in the atmosphere of another state. The need, rather, is for procedures that permit all who may be affected to be included in the planning of projects. This argues for weather modification to be managed at least on a regional basis. At a minimum, procedures for voluntary accountability should be worked out among the countries within a region. The accountability procedures should provide for obligatory consultations with all the countries that might be affected by an activity intended to modify weather. This would include all countries within a 200–300-mile radius of any cloud-seeding activities, and all the countries that lie on the predicted path of a typhoon that is to be the subject of modification experiments.

More comprehensive accountability procedures would go beyond these very limited consultations. Because it is very difficult to delineate regions appropriate for all potential weather modification situations, it would be desirable to have an institution with universal membership under whose aegis regional arrangements would be put together on an ad hoc basis. Such an institution could also serve as the focus for all states that want to engage in modification experiments or to register their proposed programs. The international body could then notify all potentially affected states in order to ensure timely consultations about the proposed activities.

It would also be desirable for the international community to develop and agree upon guidelines for conducting operations whose effects would cross national borders. This would be an appropriate extension of Principle 21 of the Stockholm Declaration on the Human Environment, which makes states responsible for ensuring that their activities do not cause damage to the environment of other states or areas.

At a minimum, processes for advance consultation among concerned parties are important for working out mutually acceptable arrangements for conducting such programs. If states likely to be affected by cloud seeding have not been consulted, or are dissatisfied with the assessment provided by the modifying state, they should be able to ask the advice of experts on an international scientific advisory panel about the likely consequences of the program. The international scientific panels would need to be authorized to monitor cloud-seeding operations to assess direct effects and to identify second- and third-order consequences for ecology, trade patterns, and so on.

It may be appropriate to establish conciliation procedures to which concerned parties could turn before the program begins, to challenge the timing, coverage, and other aspects of the program. This may be particularly useful for programs from which it is anticipated that some states may benefit at the expense of others. A state that feared a proposed cloud-seeding program might harm its interests could approach a conciliation body and attempt to negotiate an arrangement that would be less harmful to its interests. For example, it might be possible to appease tomato or cherry growers downwind who fear more rain would damage their produce by delaying the operation by a few weeks or shifting its location slightly. Meteorological experts could be available as conciliators in such cases.[7]

Procedures are also needed for handling disputes that arise after cloud-seeding activities have taken place and for providing compensation for identifiable damage resulting from these activities. Principle 22 of the Stockholm Declaration on the Human Environment provides that "states shall co-operate to develop further the international law regarding liability and compensation for the victims of pollution and other environmental damage caused by activities within the jurisdiction or control of such states to areas beyond their jurisdiction."[8]

In sum, while some of these international accountability processes can be initiated on a bilateral or regional basis, managing the cumulative impacts of many discrete programs eventually may require larger-scale institutional means. The immediate physical effects of discrete cloud-seeding programs may be confined to a limited area, but in aggregate may create thermal anomalies sufficient to alter circulation and precipitation patterns on a large scale. Effects on ecology, the economy, social behavior, and political conflict may occur both within a single country and on a larger scale. There may be aggregate impacts on international trading patterns from cloud-seeding programs designed to raise agricultural productivity locally. Impacts on rural development, on unemployment, on commodity exchanges, and on similar other functions will also need to be taken into account.

7. For elaboration and detailed analysis of methods for resolving disputes, see Edith Brown Weiss, "Weather and Climate Modification Disputes," in R. E. Stein and A. Chayes, eds., *International Environmental Disputes* (American Society of International Law, forthcoming).

8. Text of the declaration, *United Nations Conference on the Human Environment*, Report to the Senate by Senator Claiborne Pell and Senator Clifford Case, 92:2 (GPO, 1972).

Much of what has been said of rainmaking also applies to typhoon modification experiments. Here, the requirements of international accountability suggest that those engaging in such experiments must notify countries in the area of their proposed plans for seeding, and of the time when the operation is scheduled to occur. It would be desirable, but politically difficult, to require the consent, either implicit or explicit, of countries that could be affected by a proposed experiment. This would require developing processes for extensive consultation between countries, for assessing internationally the likely effects of the program, and for monitoring the operations internationally.

The United States and other countries experimenting with typhoon modification might perhaps fulfill their obligations under Principle 21 of the Stockholm Declaration on the Human Environment by publicly, and in advance, assuming responsibility for the effects of planned modification projects; by agreeing to procedures for settlement of disputes, should an allegation of damage be made; and by considering measures such as posting a bond to cover compensation for any damage that may be inflicted upon other countries.

In any case, the United States should support international monitoring of the effects of such experiments and procedures for making this information available to all parties concerned.

If and when typhoon modification reaches an operational stage, there will be additional concerns. States with the technological capability for modifying typhoons might be blamed if they seed the storms, or if they elect not to seed the storms and they subsequently inflict considerable damage. This suggests the desirability of an international process to determine which storms to seed.

At a minimum, when typhoon modification becomes operational, parties should have access to an international scientific advisory panel for advice on the likely effects of the proposed program. When the assessment of this panel contradicts the claims of the state planning a project, the countries involved should be expected to engage in extensive consultation with a view to resolving the differences.

Stronger accountability would involve an international decision process mandated by treaty to authorize typhoon seeding only after experiments had demonstrated that a prospective project would not adversely affect the regional and worldwide climate. This would require continuous monitoring, open exchange of information, and regional and global assessments of the cumulative impact, both in time and in space, of typhoon modification programs.

As typhoon modification progresses, means should be made available to facilitate the transfer of knowledge gained in the experimental program to all regions of the globe where such storms occur. The knowledge gained in modifying typhoons in the Pacific should be made available to countries in the Indian Ocean to help in modifying cyclones. Again this suggests an international network for notifying others of such programs, for monitoring the modification efforts, and for disseminating the data on the program.

CHAPTER SEVENTEEN

Major Changes in the Weather and Climate

Too little is known about the sources of large-scale or even global changes in climate and weather to isolate natural changes from those that may be significantly induced by man's alteration of the natural environment. Consequently, international policies concerned with human-induced climate change may have to cover any climate change, even if it is caused naturally.

These gross changes are creating some of the most difficult moral and political problems for the human race. If weather and climate changes are naturally induced, does the entire international community bear some responsibility for helping those who might be most adversely affected? Where there are presumably many diverse human activities contributing to the gross changes, who is to be held responsible for the damages or for bearing the costs of restricting the activities?

The Threatening Trends

Large-scale changes in the earth's weather systems and climate may be the result of any of three kinds of phenomena: naturally caused changes resulting from long-term biospheric trends, variations in solar output, or unique events such as volcanic action; human activities undertaken for purposes other than weather change that might unintentionally induce large-scale changes in the weather or climate; and projects deliberately designed to modify the weather or climate.

Natural Biospheric Changes

During the last few years, there have been signs that the global climate pattern may be changing. Climatologists agree that there is no particular reason to expect a return in the near future to the generally favorable conditions of the last several decades, but they disagree about the direction any changes will take. Some climatologists believe a cooler, more variable climate lies ahead. This would mean that droughts and floods would not be abnormal occurrences, but would recur with much greater frequency and intensity.[1] Other experts point to events that suggest a global warming trend over the next fifty years.[2] Whichever view is correct, such large-scale climatic changes could have profound implications for world food production because of the resulting changes in the length of growing seasons and in the patterns and quantity of precipitation.

Human-Induced Inadvertent Change

Human activities may inadvertently affect climate and may trigger undesired changes. At least one climatologist argues that man's industrial and agricultural practices, which send pollutants and dust particles into the atmosphere, may be partially responsible for the severity of recent droughts and floods.[3] Special concern must be focused on human activities that could sufficiently alter temperature in climatically unstable regions to trigger long-lived changes in climate.[4]

1. Statement of the International Federation of Institutes for Advanced Study Workshop on the Impact of Climate Change on the Quality and Character of Human Life, as adopted by the IFIAS Board of Trustees, October 3, 1974.

2. See, for example, William W. Kellogg, "Climatic Non-Limits to Growth" (1974; processed). See also WMO Bulletin, July 1976 and January 1977.

3. See Reid A. Bryson, "Climatic Modification by Air Pollution II: The Sahelian Effect," Report 9 (Institute for Environmental Studies, University of Wisconsin–Madison, August 1973; processed). For an analysis of the sensitivity of climate to small changes, see Reid A. Bryson, "A Perspective on Climatic Change," Science, vol. 184 (May 17, 1974), pp. 753–60.

4. On a geological time scale, virtually anything either man or nature does that alters the climate is reversible, that is, the planet will recover. Man-made deserts will recover in time if we stop grazing on them or on their borders. Freon will eventually disappear (in a hundred years or so). Over time, extra carbon dioxide will be dissolved in the deep oceans or laid down in peat bogs. The closest thing to an irreversible change would be the removal of the Arctic Ocean ice pack, which *might* not come back for millions of years, if ever. Exploitation of the resources in the Arctic and Antarctic and navigation of the polar regions may collectively lower the albedo far enough to initiate melting of the ice caps. Once a critical threshold is crossed, the melting might become an irreversible process, and any melting of the ice caps of Greenland and the Antarctic would raise the mean sea level of the world. In other cases, specific

Projects to modify land or ocean surfaces over large areas may at the same time modify weather and climate by causing increases or decreases in the rate at which heat is transferred from land or ocean surfaces to the atmosphere. This in turn could affect patterns of atmospheric circulation.[5] There are at least two kinds of projects that could cause such changes: damming or diverting rivers to create large lakes or irrigation systems; and destroying land features such as forests or mountains.

The USSR's proposals to divert rivers that flow toward the Arctic Ocean, turning them instead toward the south, may be of particular concern in this regard. Diversion of this sort would mean that the fresh water that normally flows into the Arctic and freezes at a more rapid rate than salt water would no longer be available.[6] Some scientists calculate that diversion of these rivers on a sufficiently large scale could initiate melting of the Arctic Ocean ice pack.

The consequences of such projects are highly uncertain. But our knowledge of the physical interdependencies in the global climatic system suggests that they could initiate unstable meteorological conditions in many countries.

Techniques for Intentionally Inducing Change

Means that might be employed deliberately to initiate major changes in weather and climate include melting polar ice, diverting ocean currents, changing land and ocean surfaces, diverting rivers, controlling the

---

pollutants may directly alter the chemical balance of the atmosphere, as, for example, the ozone layer, with injurious effects to large communities. The cumulative impact of many sources of pollution may change the earth's temperature and thereby change atmospheric circulation patterns in such a way as to trigger more frequent droughts, floods, and other meteorological disasters. Such climatic changes would cause widespread economic disruption, alter the production of food, and affect industrial production. They would have consequences of second and third order on ecological patterns, vegetation, trade patterns, public health, social behavior, and political conflict.

5. J. S. Sawyer has estimated that if we have a heat anomaly of about 10 percent of the net solar energy of the sun available at the earth's surface, affecting several million square kilometers for at least one month, it would be sufficient to cause a change in climate. J. S. Sawyer, *WMO-IUGG Symposium on Research and Development, Aspects of Long-Range Forecasting*, WMO Technical Note no. 66 (Geneva: World Meteorological Organization, 1964).

6. A. Biryukov, "Rerouting Rivers," *New Times*, no. 6 (1971), pp. 26–27; "Water in Wrong Places," *Nature*, vol. 231 (May 21, 1971), p. 140; Theodore Shabad, "Soviet Rivers to Grain Land," *New York Times*, October 29, 1973.

degree of cloudiness (as in the Arctic), introducing pollutants into the atmosphere, depleting the ozone layer, and changing tropical and cyclonic storm systems. Most of these techniques have yet to be tried, and many of them are still beyond human capability, but their potential for causing widespread disturbance is great and merits critical attention from the international community before any country attempts to initiate them unilaterally.

International Community Responses

The international community has begun to react to some of these problems. The World Meteorological Organization established a panel of experts on climate change. The panel in 1976 issued a statement on the subject and a technical report elaborating on the statement.[7] The WMO has said it plans to convene an international conference on the implications of climate change for world food production and the human environment. Formal interest by the WMO in the topic dates to 1974, when the executive committee recommended that a panel of experts be established. The WMO and the International Council of Scientific Unions have been sponsoring studies on modeling climate. In July 1974 they studied the topic at an international conference, to which the UN Environment Program contributed. UNEP has indicated it is also concerned with problems of climate change. While such steps are useful, they fall short of the need for systematic and comprehensive attention to the weather and climate.

Recommendations

The first step in coping with any kind of climate change would be to strengthen greatly the existing cooperative programs among governments and scientists for information gathering and analysis. There are needs for a substantial expansion of facilities for observing and monitoring the significant climatological factors, for more sophisticated models of climate, and for ways to identify critical thresholds of climatic disasters.

One means of increasing the required international climatological cooperation would be to establish a scientific advisory panel to warn of

7. The text of the statement appears in *WMO Bulletin*, July 1976; the text of the technical report in *WMO Bulletin*, January 1977.

impending changes, to identify critical thresholds for climatic disasters in the most fragile parts of the climatic system—such as the Arctic and the Antarctic—and to assess the impact of man's activities on specific climatic changes. The panel could also evaluate projects and their likely consequences. Such a panel should be composed of experts in the appropriate atmospheric and oceanic fields, with consultants from related fields available as needed. The panel evaluating a discrete proposal probably should be appointed on an ad hoc basis, according to the nature of the problems raised. This would allow for flexibility, and should avoid excessive bureaucratization of the panel's operations. The panel could be established initially under existing international bodies such as the United Nations Environmental Program or the World Meteorological Organization, but most probably with a joint working arrangement between these two organizations and appropriate linkage to the International Council of Scientific Unions.

There is some precedent for this approach in the handling of programs for outer space. The Consultative Group on Potentially Harmful Effects of Space Experiments of the International Committee on Space Research, established in 1962 under the International Council of Scientific Unions, was mandated to determine whether proposed scientific experiments in outer space and on the other planets would have harmful effects. Members of the group were scientists. They could make recommendations, but they had no formal authority to act.

The proposed scientific panel for weather and climate modification would be essentially advisory for the time being. The panel's advice would not be formally binding. If the community interest in the global weather and climate is to be protected, however, states should attempt to reflect the advice of the panel in their decisions in this field. Initially, states could seek the panel's advice on a voluntary basis. As confidence in the panel developed, it might be possible to negotiate a mandatory procedure for seeking the panel's advice.

The U.S. National Environmental Policy Act (NEPA) requires federal agencies to prepare an environmental impact statement for all government actions that might have significant environmental effects, and to incorporate the findings into the governmental planning for specific projects.[8] This requirement applies both to actions undertaken di-

8. The annual reports of the Council on Environmental Policy spell out these requirements in some detail. See *Environmental Quality: The Fifth Annual Report of the Council on Environmental Quality* (GPO, December 1974), pp. 371–420, for elaboration of NEPA requirements.

rectly by the federal government and to private activities that require government approval (such as licenses for nuclear power plants). The government has already applied it to international activities, including international negotiations. It might also be applied to induce the United States to heed the advice of the proposed scientific panel, if and when it is formed. In 1974, a draft impact statement was prepared on the U.S. negotiating position for the Law of the Sea Conference. Senator Claiborne Pell introduced a bill in 1976 calling for international environmental impact statements, which would apply to modifications of weather and climate. There is evidence that other countries also are considering adoption of similar proceedings.[9]

It would be important to have many avenues through which proposed large-scale experiments might come to the panel's attention. States could bring experiments to the panel for consideration, and the UN Environmental Program and interested private groups should have access to the panel to alert them to potential projects.

A major area of the scientific panel's work would be concerned with the effects of large-scale projects. The report of the Study of Man's Impact on Climate in 1971 by a highly respected international group of scientists recommended that "an international agreement be sought to prevent large-scale . . . experimenting in persistent or long-term climate modification until the scientific community reaches a consensus on the consequences of the modification."[10] One of the panel's first tasks in this regard would be to define large-scale programs. There is now no consensus as to what constitutes large-scale. The SMIC report defines it as a program that directly affects more than one million square kilometers; other scientists define it in terms of a thermal anomaly in an area of several million square kilometers during one month or more in time. With reference to weather modification, some meteorologists view a large-scale program as one that encompasses an area with a circumference of at least five hundred kilometers.

In evaluating all potential cases of climate change, panel members would face difficult problems in establishing at what point they have sufficient knowledge to clearly discern the effects. Whatever the probabilities given for a specific effect, if human activities are deemed the cause, the decision whether to take the risk of triggering that effect will still be a political decision.

9. Ibid., pp. 400–01.
10. *Report of the Study of Man's Impact on Climate: Inadvertent Climate Modification* (M.I.T. Press, 1971), pp. 18–19.

When measures are in fact taken to ameliorate adverse climatic trends, provision will have to be made for monitoring and assessing the effectiveness of the measures. It will be important that this information be widely disseminated, carefully evaluated, and then fed into ongoing efforts to observe and understand climatic change. This argues for procedures that involve the scientific panel not only in prior assessments of proposed projects, but also in observation and monitoring of projects from start to finish (and even beyond, during the time over which feedback mechanisms may operate).

Consideration should also be given to establishing systems of compensation. For the next few decades at least, it is unlikely that scientists will be able to agree on the effects of a project, either before or after it is undertaken. For this reason, some scientists have argued for a form of no-fault climate insurance that would compensate all victims of adverse climate changes, regardless of cause.[11] Otherwise, the traditional legal standards for proving cause will be likely to prevent compensation until much more is known about the weather and climate system.

11. See, for example, W. W. Kellogg and S. H. Schneider, "Climate Stabilization: For Better or for Worse?" *Science*, vol. 186 (December 27, 1974), pp. 1163–72.

CHAPTER EIGHTEEN

Toward International Accountability in the Alteration of the Weather and Climate

The preceding review of the international problems in managing both specific weather modification projects and large-scale effects of human activity on the weather and climate systems points to the need for a comprehensive international regime for regulating alterations of the weather and climate.

Summary of Major Findings

The complexity of the weather and climate system and the mobility and interaction of its components make it indivisible into national jurisdictions. Regional weather and climate systems are also unlikely to conform to the boundaries of a particular set of countries.

Attempts to modify precipitation or storms in one locality are likely to affect the weather patterns of countries downwind. For situations in which downwind countries might be harmed by or object to anticipated effects, there should be some means for the countries that might be affected to register their concern in advance of a project; to bring international pressure on those planning a project to redesign, delay, or cancel the project; and to obtain compensation for damage.

Since the countries affected will vary with particular weather modification projects, multilateral regional procedures for consultation and coordination will be inappropriate unless their membership is flexible.

The weather and climate may be changed as a by-product of human activities pursued for other objectives. Countries may inadvertently inflict large economic costs on their neighbors and grossly destabilize

233

global climatic patterns. Many of these external effects are as yet poorly understood; some are rather well understood by the scientific community, but determining which particular activities are generating what effects often requires complicated monitoring and analyzing. With the expansion and dissemination of awareness of these side effects, grievances by negatively affected populations are bound to grow and to produce pressures for international machinery to make environmental impact assessments of a wide range of human activities, and eventually to require international regulation of potentially harmful projects.

In general, the existing regime lacks adequate rules and institutions for assuring that those who might change the weather and climate are accountable to those who would be affected. The UN resolutions on environmental responsibility lack teeth. The new convention banning hostile alterations of the environment bypasses completely the problem of the harmful effects of projects undertaken for peaceful purposes.

Recommended Comprehensive Regime

The starting point for adequate international management of the weather and climate would be an international consensus that the weather and climate are international resources, and that therefore no transnational alterations of the weather or climate are legitimate unless authorized (explicitly or implicitly) by the affected countries. In situations in which significant effects would be felt by only a limited number of countries, the involved countries could constitute themselves as a regional consulting and authorizing group for the pertinent environmental modification activities. In other cases, however, where there is substantial scientific expectation that the global biosphere may be affected, universal international forums would be the only legitimate authorizing bodies.

This concept implies a prohibition of all hostile international uses of environmental modification techniques. It also implies a ban on purportedly benign environmental projects opposed by countries that could demonstrably be harmed.

Implementation

When it comes to implementing such a broad concept of international accountability, the first need is a credible and respected process for assessing the sources and impacts of weather and climate modification. Without a determination of what and who is causing a particular perturbation and who is affected and to what extent, it will not be possible to decide the appropriate composition of the consulting and authorizing groups, let alone to award compensation to injured parties.

Fortunately, even though the science of meteorology is full of uncertainties and gaps in knowledge, there has been substantial international cooperation among meteorologists. The international institutional basis for gathering meteorological information and forecasting the weather is well developed and, if carefully built upon, could provide a foundation for the assessment capabilities required by the proposed regime.[1]

1. The formal record of cooperation in meteorology dates to the first International Meteorological Congress in Brussels in August 1853, which met to standardize meteorological observations from ships for maritime transport. Twenty years later, meteorological observations made from land were standardized.

After the Second World War, the expansion of jet aviation created new demands for meteorological data from high levels of the atmosphere for use in aviation weather forecasting, which led to further international cooperation in making high-level meteorological observations. The development of satellites and high-speed computers for transmitting data served as a catalyst for the present international network for predicting weather and understanding global atmospheric circulation—namely, the World Weather Watch and the Global Atmospheric Research Program.

The World Weather Watch (WWW), established in 1968 under the World Meteorological Organization, has three parts: (1) the Global Observing System, which produces data about the weather system for both the WWW and the Global Atmospheric Research Program; (2) the Global Data Processing System, which processes, stores, and retrieves data; and (3) the Global Telecommunications System, which collects, exchanges, and distributes observational and processed data among global, regional, and national meteorological centers.

The Observing System of the WWW includes observations by fixed ocean stations, buoys, ships, ground stations, balloons, aircraft, rocketsondes, orbital satellites, and geostationary satellites. The WWW now has two weather satellite systems: the U.S. ITOS satellite system; and the USSR Meteor system. In 1977, the WWW hopes to have two or three polar orbiting meteorological satellites in continuing operation and at least four geostationary satellites.

The data processing system of the WWW consists of 3 world meteorological centers (Washington, Moscow, Melbourne), 21 regional meteorological centers, and 147 national meteorological centers. The world meteorological centers concentrate on storing and retrieving data for planetary research and

There are some potentially negative trends, however. A few countries may be moving away from the WMO system in the direction of regionalizing or even nationalizing weather information. Western Europe, for example, has established a regional meteorological center, which will have a computerized operation capable of processing large amounts of meteorological data. The United States and the USSR are increasingly independent of other countries in gathering data on the weather.

For the United States, one of the issues is whether to merge military and civilian meteorological satellite programs under military management or to retain separate systems, since the amalgamation of the two programs would save money. The military meteorological information system is itself being centralized within the United States and becoming more independent of foreign bases. Military management of all U.S. meteorological satellites would endanger the WWW and the Global Atmospheric Research Program. It would cause countries to be anxious over how much of the data gathered about the weather system was being fed into the WWW and to fear that, for reasons of national security, the United States might at some point curtail the transmission of data from weather satellites, which others had come to depend upon.

Thus, the pattern of voluntary international cooperation that has been developed to gather and disseminate meteorological data shows signs of giving way to a more complex pattern in which the more technically sophisticated states begin nationalizing or regionalizing meteorological information. Rather than making meteorological information an international common good, these developments could transform advanced weather information into a national commodity or the preserve of blocs of nations.

This would be shortsighted, for, as indicated above, a respected international information collection and analysis system is the foundation for effective regulation of environmental modification. The rationale for a credible and influential international system was well put by Deputy Assistant Secretary of State Christian A. Herter, Jr. As yet, he argued,

scientific and governmental responses are "ad hoc", usually after a threat has surfaced . . . we need a framework of knowledge on the global situation against

---

applications, while the regional centers focus on storing and retrieving data for large-scale research and applications. National meteorological centers are responsible for retrieving only the data originating from their national observational facilities, and do not have central processing facilities unless their own national needs require them.

which the new and old threats can be judged. Above all, we need an international voice, not just a U.S. voice, that is so authoritative and so persuasive that decisionmakers in all countries cannot fail to respond.[2]

Institutional Recommendations

An international system for collecting and analyzing environmental information is the first step toward effective international management of weather and climate modification. This information system could be built on two legs: the ongoing cooperation between the World Meteorological Organization and the International Council of Scientific Unions (ICSU), and the EARTHWATCH program of the UN Environmental Program. The WMO and the ICSU have been conducting joint studies on the physical basis of climate and climate modeling, and the WMO executive committee, in June 1974, recommended that the WMO establish a panel of experts to serve as a focal point for assessing the implications of climatic change on the world environment and food production. EARTHWATCH already has under way an Information Referral System—a directory, on a global, computerized basis, of national inventories of environmental information—and the UN Environmental Program is engaged in a continuing discussion with other UN specialized agencies and national governments on the design of a global environmental monitoring system. The UN Environmental Program's goals for the global monitoring system include:
—an assessment of global atmospheric pollution and its impact on climate;
—an assessment of the state of ocean pollution;
—an assessment of the response of the terrestrial ecosystem to environmental pressures;
—an assessment of critical problems arising from agriculture and land use practices; and
—an improved international disaster warning system.[3]
We endorse such an integrated approach to environmental monitoring as the basis for effective international management of the weather

2. Christian A. Herter, Jr., address before the International Conference on Environmental Sensing and Assessment, Las Vegas, Nevada, September 17, 1975 (processed).
3. Ibid.

and climate system, for the weather and climate segments of the total environment cannot be understood in isolation from the larger pattern of interactions among land, sea, air, and outer space.

These integrated functions for collecting, monitoring, and analyzing information should probably be housed under one institutional roof. We are indifferent at this point as to whether this is the WMO or the UN Environmental Program.

The global organization should be able to call upon panels of scientific experts in the fields of meteorology and the environment generally, and to provide such experts on an ad hoc basis to regional groups. Parties considering projects that could significantly modify the weather or climate would be obliged to submit their plans to such panels for assessment. The panels would produce and publish environmental impact statements, but, at the onset of this system, it would remain for national governments to act or refrain from acting on the basis of these international scientific assessments.

At a later stage, once the monitoring system had achieved credibility, and a pattern of voluntary respect for its findings had been established, it might be possible to negotiate a procedure for compulsory compliance. This would obligate governments to proceed with or forgo projects, heeding the findings of the global organization's scientific panels.

The fully developed system would include adjudicatory services, with its own judicial personnel or perhaps specially empaneled tribunals of the International Court of Justice. This international adjudicatory system would rule over all cases involving violation of international environmental conventions and over disputes between countries. It would provide a range of services, including panels for mediation, arbitration, and fact-finding.

CHAPTER NINETEEN

Toward Effective International Management of the Ocean, Outer Space, and the Weather

The expansion of human activity in the ocean, outer space, and the weather has raised fundamental questions about international regimes. To what extent should these shared realms continue to be used under the traditional norms of open access and free use, or to what extent should they be more heavily regulated? Where there is need for heavier regulation, how should such regulation be organized and managed—primarily by national governments within clearly demarcated jurisdictions, or primarily by the international community through rules that limit national freedom of action?

The Pattern of Problems and Responses

The answers to the fundamental questions about regimes vary for each of the three realms of our study, and also for specific fields within each of the three realms. These varied answers flow from the detailed analyses of the particular uses presented in the preceding chapters. We will not in this chapter again restate the particular problems and recommendations presented in the body of the study, but will rather attempt to distill the larger pattern of problems and responses suggested by the more detailed analyses. This cumulative pattern can be described by a set of six general propositions.

The nonland realms are largely indivisible. It is theoretically possible to parcel out the seabed and ocean space, to extend national airspace indefinitely, and even to claim as national the weather currently in the atmosphere over a country. Such divisions, however, cannot give a country effective control over many of the resources of value in these realms. The waters of the ocean flow across any boundaries that might be drawn, and in the process carry nutrients, fish, and pollutants with them. Local wind and weather patterns eventually flow all around the globe; their sojourn in the airspace of any one country is only temporary. The current uses of outer space that are of potential economic significance require satellites in orbit—that is, the satellite must be able to move independently of the restrictions of national airspace.

The resources of the nonland realms are increasingly scarce. This growing scarcity is partly a function of improvements in technology that have made (or are expected to make) many of the resources exploitable (for example, minerals of the seabed, the geostationary orbit, and tropical storms), and partly a function of the increase in the number of users of shared resources (such as straits, the electromagnetic spectrum, and airspace).

Norms of open access and free use, the traditional approach to using the nonland commons areas, are incompatible with the resource scarcities and must give way to some form of allocative regime. Only for resources that are, for all practical purposes, inexhaustible can regimes of open access and free use be sustained. (The assumption of inexhaustibility used to prevail for the waters of the high seas and even for fish beyond narrow territorial seas; it also used to prevail for much of the airspace and all of outer space.) For resources that are scarce, allocations will take place either on the basis of unilateral appropriations, or by some agreed method of determining rights of access and use (the former is illustrated by assertions by coastal states of ownership of the petroleum resources on nearby continental shelves; the latter is illustrated by proposals for an international agency to auction off leases to sites in the deep seabed that are assumed to be rich in manganese nodules).

For most of the resources at issue, efforts by countries to unilaterally appropriate portions are bound to generate international conflict and are unlikely to be sustained without coercion. The forecast of conflict associated with unilateralism is based on the inherent physical indivisibility of many of the resources, and the locational overlapping of various resources. (Besides the examples of indivisibility given above, examples of locational overlapping are oil drilling sites that conflict with oceanographic information gathering areas that conflict with maritime navigation routes.)

Internationally negotiated assignments of jurisdiction are in many cases likely to prove unstable and require frequent renegotiation. This forecast, too, is based on nondivisibility and overlapping of many of the pertinent resources. It is also based on the expectation that the quality and distribution of technological capabilities, which make a particular allocation acceptable at one time, are likely to change in ways that dissatisfy some parties to an agreement. (Thus, some of the parties to a particular assignment of oil drilling areas may demand renegotiation after the discovery of a new oil pool that traverses existing jurisdictional lines, or when drilling on one side of a boundary begins to deplete the exploitable supply on the other side. Similar problems, arising from technological change, are likely to affect fisheries jurisdictions that overlap ecologies of interdependent species. Negotiated allocations of portions of the frequency spectrum to particular users may also become unsatisfactory to some of the parties because of technological changes that alter their requirements for use of the spectrum.)

The growing conflicts over rights to the resources of the ocean, outer space, and the weather and climate systems, plus the essential nondivisibility of these realms, and the volatility of the technologies affecting their use add up to a requirement for substantial international management. Where resources are abundant, the fact of their nondivisibility would be compatible with regimes of open access and free use. Where resources are scarce but easily and durably divisible among countries, regimes based on firm national jurisdictions would appear rational. But where resources are likely to be scarce in relation to international demand and simultaneously nondivisible among countries, neither regimes of open access and free use nor regimes based on national resource zones are likely to provide effective management.

The Characteristics of Effective International Management

The foregoing outline of problems and responses to the proliferation of uses of the nonland areas points to the requirement for substantial international management of these realms. It also suggests the characteristics of their effective international management.

Effective international management for the ocean, outer space, and the weather and climate system requires first and foremost that there be networks of political and legal accountability in each of these realms congruent with the interdependencies of user and resource. This requirement can be translated into four principles.

Parties directly and substantially involved in particular activities affecting the nonland realms should be members of the international consultative and authorizing groups for such activities. At a minimum, this principle indicates an obligation on the part of all users to consult with the most directly affected parties. A fuller implementation would accord parties decisionmaking weight corresponding to the degree to which they are involved (being involved includes being victimized by the externalities of the programs initiated by others, as well as incurring investment costs).

Those who affect the condition of the commonly used realms should be answerable for their actions to the international community. This principle is consistent with UN resolutions on the ocean and outer space that at least these realms are the "common heritage of mankind." It also points to some agency capable of holding users to account in the name of the world interest. (It could, for example, be the basis for requiring that users who deplete or degrade the resources or who displace other users pay rent to a global or regional agency.)

The international community should have the authority to define and apply the accountability obligations, which should be binding on all countries and special groups using the common resources. This would require an international panel of scientific experts to determine which activities are likely to directly and substantially affect particular populations and which activities are likely to affect the conditions of the resources and environments themselves.

National or regional jurisdiction over parts of the nonland areas should be only custodial. This would allow for temporary delegations of authority or title by the international community to particular states or institutions. These states or institutions would be obligated to act as trustees for the larger community and to abide by whatever rules or regulations are agreed to by the larger community.

Implementing International Management

Attaining effective international management in each of the three major realms of this study will require different policies and institutions; moreover, the recommended policies and institutions differ from sector to sector. In the oceans, with a central need to accommodate different kinds of users, the basic imperative is for a strategy to transform institutional pluralism into an integrated and heavily institutionalized process of comprehensive ocean management. In outer space, each special sector —remote sensing, direct broadcasting, maritime satellites—raises analogous issues of international accountability, efficiency versus equity, and conflict resolution, but their accommodation is achieved principally by specific policies and institutions unique to each sector. The only need for a multisector, integrated approach in space is where the various sectors use common resources: the electromagnetic spectrum and the geostationary orbit. We find a general agency for outer space projects desirable as a coordinating mechanism, but far from imperative. In weather and climate, a major need is for great flexibility in putting together institutions for consulting and for authorizing projects on an ad hoc basis, but under the aegis of a body that would oversee the weather and climate system as a whole.

Recognizing these differences, there is a general need, common to all these fields, for movement in the direction of greater international management based on the principles of accountability outlined above. While we have no illusions that nations will accept obligations to be bound by the principles and processes of accountability merely out of logic or idealism, there are opportunities to create incentives for users of the nonland realms to accept limits on their prerogatives in return for reciprocity from others. The challenge for statesmanship will be to single out early those areas of necessary and potential reciprocity, and to enlarge the incentives for cooperation. Meanwhile, diplomatic efforts must attempt to restrain more parochial interests from pressuring their governments into preemptive claims, and to build (through education and persuasion) public interest constituencies that will support mutual limitations on national sovereignty in favor of the larger world interest in peaceful and just management of the commonly used realms.

More specifically, such an implementation strategy would have four stages.

Progressive internationalization of capabilities for gathering and assessing information about the nonland realms, to provide the international community with more independent sources of information and analysis of the growing uses of these realms and their economic and political implications.

In ocean affairs, in earth applications of space technology, and in weather, reliable information is a key ingredient in the conservation and allocation of resources. Control over information is also a means of exerting economic advantage and political power. Accordingly, the availability of independent and international information sources has been recognized as essential for effective international management. The international importance of information has been reflected, for example, in the controversy over offshore oceanographic research, in the debate at the United Nations over the disposition of data on earth resources gathered by satellite, and in suggestions for international panels of experts to assess weather modification projects.

Although it is neither desirable nor possible to "denationalize" all or most information about the nonland realms, the international public interest is best served if multiple sources of information coexist and compete for attention. The process of ensuring mutual accountability will be better served if independent sources of information can be called upon directly by members of the international community who wish, for example, to demonstrate the reasons for restricting certain types of weather modification experiments, to generate corrective action for specific deteriorations of the environment, or to clarify whether data on earth resources is being misused.

Expansion of international consultative processes—involving those who use and those who are affected by activities in the ocean, outer space, and the weather and climate systems—aimed at clarifying conflicting interests and exposing the range of choices available to the international community.

The principal responsibility for assuring meaningful consultation falls on the countries with advanced scientific and technological capabilities. In general, their response to the efforts by the less advanced to bring their actions under international purview has been to admit only grudgingly and minimally that they should be accountable to those who might be affected. The behavior of both the United States and the USSR in the Law of the Sea debates, and the behavior of the U.S. government in response to demands for greater international cognizance of satellite-based direct broadcasting and remote sensing technologies fit this traditional pattern. The indispensability of greater international consultation, however, appears to have been recognized by the United States in its response in the fall of 1975 to developing country demands at the Seventh Special Session of the United Nations.[1]

1. Henry A. Kissinger, "Global Consensus and Economic Development," address before the UN General Assembly, September 1, 1975 (Department of State; processed). See also Kissinger's "International Law, World Order and Human Progress," address before the American Bar Association, August 11, 1975, Department of State Press Release 408.

Interests and actions in the global commons are shaping a material basis for new institutional links among communities. In their formative stages, most of these links are likely to be based on function and to concern small groups of countries. Over the long run, however, the emergent management problems will require an expansion of community decision authority and a widening of membership in these communities. Each area now has the possibility of defining a variety of different nuclei of countries, corporations, and other interest groups, which together could make up the core of a pragmatic, flexible, and steadily widening consultative process. These nuclei can be identified, for instance, among those who share the contours of an ocean basin, who depend upon a given satellite technology, who are tied to a specific ecological or weather system, who use the ocean for specific resource or nonresource purposes, and so on.

A consistent effort to limit extensions of exclusive national authority in the nonland areas during the buildup of the needed international accountability networks.

In certain policy areas, the scaffolding for the international accountability networks is already being established—for example, in the Intergovernmental Maritime Consultative Organization, the International Telecommunication Union, and the World Meteorological Organization —but pressures are meanwhile growing on national governments to extend their sovereign control while the nonland areas are still free for the grabbing. Current international agreements to arrest this creeping nationalism could include arrangements for making national action contingent on review and assessment by nonnational scientific sources, of the sort we have earlier suggested, and adversary processes (not necessarily judicial) in which others directly affected by prospective action can question or challenge it. Most of the burden, however, for holding the line against nationalistic preemption of fields of activity that should be internationalized will have to fall on forward-looking national leaders themselves. This points to the urgency of creating wider domestic public constituencies for supporting more enlightened policies by their governments.

A major campaign of worldwide public education in the nature of the stakes in the regimes that are adopted for commonly used international realms.

The connection between the alternative regimes considered in this study and the prospects for an increase or reduction of international conflict, particularly between the have and have-not nations, needs to be widely understood and disseminated, as do the consequences for health and welfare that might flow from mismanagement of these shared environments.

These fields have heretofore been the province of narrow specialists, and direct interest in legislative action and administrative decisions bearing on their management has been confined to special industry groups. The literature comprehensible to the layman is small, but growing. The required expansion of lay and media interest in the United States can perhaps best be stimulated by visible demonstrations of interest and concern at the topmost political levels of the government, and by members of Congress.

Policy Choices for the United States

The basic policy question raised by this study is to what extent the United States should help in the establishment of international machinery for managing the ocean, outer space, and the weather and climate system that will to some degree limit U.S. freedom of action in these environments. The answer to this question requires weighing both material and political costs and benefits.

Our general assessment of the material costs and benefits from the policies for international management that we are proposing is that, while most would involve net economic gains for the whole international community, some of them may involve net economic costs for the United States, at least in the short run.

In global terms, most of our recommendations should lead to more efficient use of the resources of the nonland realms. Thus, we have recommended that the shippers pay the environmental costs of their activities in the form of better safety equipment, navigational procedures, and licensing schemes; but we have argued against regulations formulated and imposed unilaterally by coastal states on international navigation, since this would make for higher costs of goods and services transported by sea than would be incurred if navigational rules were universally standardized. In the area of fisheries, changing the rule of open access to a system of limited access would help preserve fish stocks and species by lowering demand to a level that can sustain the stocks over the long run. Similar matching of demand to supply can be expected from our recommended system of bidding for scarce orbital and frequency resources. In these and other cases, moves to balance demand and supply should lead to an increase in the efficiency with which the resources are used by the world as a whole.

Increases in global efficiency should increase the total value of output from these resources. The United States, however, will not always receive any or all of that increase. Our proposals for more stringent international navigational standards to reduce the risks to ocean ecologies might mean that U.S. companies would pay more for ocean shipment of goods than they would under a more permissive regime (but less than under a regime of unilateral controls by coastal states). The effects would be most noticeable in the price of imported oil, but even so would most likely involve only small increases. Under our proposed fisheries arrangements, more of the fish close to U.S. shores would be available for domestic consumption, but the U.S. share of tuna and shrimp might fall slightly. Our proposals for international leasing of deep sea mining sites might mean somewhat less deep sea production by U.S. firms than under a free access regime; still, the economic impact of the recommended regime change would be slight since the capable mining companies are unlikely to want to significantly disrupt the international nickel market by rapidly increasing the total supply, no matter what the ocean regime. If an international revenue sharing scheme is adopted for oil and gas on the outer continental shelf, the result indeed might be a smaller return in taxes to the U.S. Treasury, but there need not be any decline in total output of U.S. firms. Some international management of ocean scientific research might reduce the total number of experiments, as each might cost a bit more because of the requirements of international coordination. U.S. predominance in this field should not change, however.

In outer space, most of our recommendations could slightly increase the costs of U.S. programs by requiring the U.S. government to devote more effort to international consultations. Some slight changes in the designs of satellite systems might result from the consultative processes, but this is not an effect we anticipate soon. More resources probably would be devoted to making the fruits of U.S. space activities available to less capable countries, but the U.S. government—not multilateral agencies—would still retain control over the amount of U.S. resources committed to the international programs. The most substantial multilateral institution we have proposed in the space field, an international maritime satellite organization, could result in fewer contracts for U.S.

firms than if major maritime satellite services were sold to the world directly by U.S. comunications entities. Charging for the use of frequency and orbital resources, as we recommend, could increase the costs of communications, but the amount and duration of the cost increases are uncertain, since the very act of charging for frequency and orbit use is likely to generate improvements in the technology and to stimulate development of cable systems, thereby lowering or leaving unchanged the unit costs of communication.

Our recommendations in the field of weather modification imply an increase in governmental resources devoted to the study of the weather and climate system, and to the coordination of activities with other governments. Additionally, our proposals for greater international accountability in experiments on large-scale environmental modification could increase costs (probably not greatly), particularly if experimental designs must be modified to respond to international concerns.

In sum, our recommendations might involve an overall decline in the U.S. share of the total benefits from use of the world's nonland realms relative to the share available to other countries. In only a few cases, however, would this decline in relative share mean a decline in absolute benefits. In most of the fields studied here, the decline in the relative U.S. share of world output would reflect only a lowered rate of growth of absolute benefits to the United States.

Our general assessment of the international political costs and benefits of our recommended international management policies, while highly conjectural and based on many uncertainties, suggests that such an approach would not only service the objectives of world order, but would also be advantageous to the United States over the longer term. This judgment is supported by a number of considerations.

The people of the United States have a vital stake in the condition of ecological systems essential to the healthy survival of the human species. Without a firm and internationally approved system of mutual restraints, other countries will be unlikely to limit their current assaults on the ocean and atmospheric ecological systems, especially as the larger and long-term effects of current action are very uncertain.

The United States has a high interest in orderly and moderate processes for resolving international conflict. The nonland realms especially, because of their indivisibility and the growing competition for their resources, are prone to conflict. The increasing disputes over jurisdiction and use of resources in these realms are likely to lead to coercive situations unless accountability processes and institutions are in place and utilized at least, by the major powers.

The United States has general but very basic interests in averting the polarization of international relations along a North-South, noncommunist industrial countries versus developing countries axis. Such a polarization would provide opportunities for Third World militants to mobilize a tight anti-Western coalition on issues of peripheral interest to some of its members, but of high interest to the United States, such as navigation through straits or international regulation of ocean pollution. The U.S. interest in avoiding such international populism can be served through a progressive response to the demands of countries that are technologically disadvantaged for distribution of benefits from exploitation of the resources of the ocean, outer space, and the weather, and also to their demands for a greater role in management of these realms.

The fundamental policy choice, therefore, is reduced to whether the United States should incur relatively small, near-term domestic economic costs in the service of global economic efficiencies and international political order, or whether the considerations of national (sometimes special interest) economic returns should dictate U.S. policy in light of the uncertainty of many of the international effects. We recommend that U.S. policy pursue the desirable end of greater international accountability in the use of the ocean, outer space, and the weather, recognizing the uncertainty of benefits, even though this might involve near-term material costs. We advocate this approach, not from abstract altruism or internationalist sentiment, but because it is central to basic U.S. interests.

Index